Advance Praise for

# Intersectionality & Higher Education: Theory, Research, & Praxis, Third Edition

"This book illuminates theoretical, methodological, and practical applications of intersectionality in relation to diverse identities, institutional contexts, and disciplines. It serves as an essential resource to any reader seeking to be a good intellectual steward of intersectionality in research and practice."

—Anne-Marie Núñez, Executive Director, Diana Natalicio Institute for Hispanic Student Success, The University of Texas, El Paso

"The most common question I hear from students and colleagues is how to use intersectionality in research and practice. These essays provide many answers, addressing the specific needs of diverse groups across the academy with wisdom and reflexivity. The book is a welcome resource for faculty, professional staff, and administrators."

—Elizabeth R. Cole, University Diversity and Social Transformation Professor of Women's Studies and Psychology, University of Michigan

# Intersectionality & Higher Education

# Intersectionality & Higher Education

## Theory, Research, & Praxis, Third Edition

Donald "DJ" Mitchell, Jr., Editor

with Jakia Marie and Patricia P. Carver, Associate Editors

Foreword by Jessica C. Harris

PETER LANG

New York · Berlin · Bruxelles · Chennai · Lausanne · Oxford

Library of Congress Cataloging-in-Publication Data

Names: Mitchell, Donald, Jr., editor. | Marie, Jakia, editor. |
Carver, Patricia P., editor.
Title: Intersectionality & higher education: theory, research, & praxis, third edition /
edited by Donald "DJ" Mitchell, Jr., Jakia Marie, Patricia P. Carver.
Other titles: Intersectionality and higher education
Description: Third edition. | New York: Peter Lang, [2024] | Second edition published
in 2019. | Includes bibliographical references.
Identifiers: LCCN 2024000931 (print) | LCCN 2024000932 (ebook) | ISBN
9781636678764 (paperback: alk. paper) | ISBN 9781636678771 (pdf) | ISBN
9781636678788 (epub)
Subjects: LCSH: Minorities—Education (Higher)—United States. | Education,
Higher—Social aspects—United States. | Multicultural education—United States. |
Identity (Psychology) | Racism in education—United States. |
Educational equalization—United States.
Classification: LCC LC3731. I566 2024 (print) | LCC LC3731 (ebook) | DDC 378.1/
9820973—dc23/eng/20240215
LC record available at https://lccn.loc.gov/2024000931
LC ebook record available at https://lccn.loc.gov/2024000932
DOI 10.3726/b21687


Bibliographic information published by the Deutsche Nationalbibliothek.
The German National Library lists this publication in the German
National Bibliography; detailed bibliographic data is available
on the Internet at http://dnb.d-nb.de.




Cover design by Peter Lang Group AG




ISBN 9781636678764 (paperback)
ISBN 9781636678771 (ebook)
ISBN 9781636678788 (epub)
DOI 10.3726/b21687


© 2024 Peter Lang Group AG, Lausanne
Published by Peter Lang Publishing Inc., New York, USA
info@peterlang.com - www.peterlang.com

# Contents

List of Figures and Tables                                                    ix

Acknowledgments                                                               xi

Foreword                                                                     xiii
  JESSICA C. HARRIS

Preface                                                                      xvii
  DONALD "DJ" MITCHELL, JR.

**Part I: Theory**                                                            1

1. *Intersectionality, Identity, and Systems of Power and Inequality*         3
   CHARMAINE L. WIJEYESINGHE AND SUSAN R. JONES

2. *Intersectionality: A Legacy from Critical Legal Studies and Critical*
   *Race Theory*                                                             17
   ALLISON DANIEL ANDERS AND JAMES M. DEVITA

3. *Intersectional Embodiments in Higher Education*                          33
   BRIANNA R. RAMIREZ

4. *Living Liminal: Conceptualizing Liminality for Undocumented*
   *Students of Color*                                                       47
   ROSE ANN E. GUTIERREZ

5. *Thinking Theoretically with and Beyond Intersectionality: Frameworks*
   *to Center Queer and Trans People of Color Experiences*                   59
   ANTONIO DURAN AND ROMEO JACKSON

**Part II: Research**                                                        71

  6. *Metaphorically Speaking: Being a Black Woman in the Academy is
     Like...*                                                                73
     CHRISTA J. PORTER

  7. *Queer Women and Femme Students of Color Seeking Help After
     Surviving Dating Violence in College*                                  87
     NADEEKA KARUNARATNE

  8. *Navigating Multiple Oppressions: The Intersectional Experiences of a
     Chinese American College Student with Dis/abilities*                  101
     YAN WANG AND BETH L. GOLDSTEIN

  9. *Latina/x Identities and Oppression in Higher Education: A Case in a
     Hispanic-Serving Institution*                                         121
     HILDA CECILIA CONTRERAS AGUIRRE

 10. *Liminality as a Necessary Companion to Intersectionality*            135
     LISA DELACRUZ COMBS AND RENEE L. BOWLING

 11. *Backward Thinking: Exploring the Relationship Among
     Intersectionality, Epistemology, and Research Design*                 149
     DANIEL TILLAPAUGH AND Z NICOLAZZO

**Part III: Praxis**                                                       163

 12. *The Unlikely Allies Conference: An Intersectional Approach to
     Diversity Training Between White and Black
     Women in Academia*                                                    165
     NICOLE M. WEST

 13. *Intersectionality as Praxis for Equity in Medicine: Developing the
     LMSA Premedical Program*                                              185
     KATHERINE ARIAS GARCIA AND MARIA ROSARIO G. ARANETA

 14. *From Kitchen Tables to Black Spaces: Where Black Women Graduate
     Students Work Against Intersectionality Crisis*                       197
     MARQUITA D. FOSTER, BELINDA COLEMAN, INDIA COOLEY, AMANI
     FRANCIS, JACQUELINE STEVENS, JANA BROWN, ANDREA PICKENS,
     ALYSIA HUNT WILLIAMS, AND SHANNIKA BACCHUS

 15. *No Longer Cast Aside: A Critical Approach to Serving Queer and
     Trans Students of Color in Higher Education*                          211
     MEG E. EVANS AND JASON K. WALLACE

# Contents

16. *Hitting the Books: Partnering for Intersectional Leadership Education* 221
    S. GAVIN WEISER, TASHAY DENNIE, AND MALLORY JALLAS

17. *Weaving In and Out of Ourselves: Syllabus Formation and Assignment*
    *Development Through the Centering of Intersectionality* 231
    RUBY OSORIA

*Editor Biographies* 241

*Author Biographies* 245

# List of Figures and Tables

**Figures**

Figure 4.1.  Conceiving a Frame of Liminality Interlaced in Racism, Nativism, and Xenophobia 52

Figure 9.1.  Representation of Latina Undergraduates and Graduate Students at HSIs and All Institutions–Latinas' Representation as Faculty 122

Figure 14.1. Intersecting Identities with an Emphasis on Black Women's Linguistic Authority 201

**Tables**

Table 9.1.  Participant Demographics 127

Table 10.1. Participant Identities and Characteristics 140

Table 12.1. Composition of UAC Dyads and Triads 176

Table 14.1. Observed Participants' Linguistic Repertoire 207

# Acknowledgments

We would like to thank those who made the publication of the third edition of *Intersectionality & Higher Education: Theory, Research, & Praxis* possible. First, we thank all the chapter authors who helped shape this volume through their contributions and blind peer reviews. Second, we thank Dr. Jessica C. Harris for contributing the Foreword. Third, we thank Allison Jefferson, Joshua Charles, and Charmitha Ashok—at Peter Lang—for all that they brought to the production of this volume. Finally, we thank a host of family, friends, and colleagues, whose love and support keep us going each day.

# Foreword

JESSICA C. HARRIS

I have immersed myself in intersectional scholarship and practice for some time now. And throughout the years, I have been consistently humbled and constantly reminded of how little I know about intersectionality. Recently, while working on a writing project grounded in intersectionality, I engaged with several contemporary scholarly articles, books, and YouTube videos that explored intersectionality.

One specific YouTube video stuck with me. In the video, Kimberlé Crenshaw delivered a 15-minute speech to participants of the 2020 MAKERS Conference. The MAKERS Conference "is a global leadership event that convenes the most powerful names in business, entertainment, tech and finance to explore ways to advance equality in the workplace" (Coburn & Forgione, 2020, para. 2). The 2020 Conference adopted the theme, "Not Done," to represent where we are in the women's movement—we exist in a world in which more work must be done to achieve gender equity.

With this theme in mind, Crenshaw opened her speech by exploring what intersectionality is and how it can help us understand why we are not yet done. She also explained how intersectionality might help us get this work done. She stated:

> What intersectionality is, is a prism, it's a framework. It's a template for seeing and telling different kinds of stories about what happens in our workplaces, what happens in society, and to whom it happens. Now, some part of why we're not done is predicated on what we haven't been able to see, what's not remembered, the stories that are not told. So, intersectionality is like training wheels to get us to where we need to go. It's glasses, high index glasses, to help us see the things we need to see. (MAKERS, 2020)

Crenshaw suggested that intersectional failure is the reason we are not yet done. Intersectional failure occurs when intersectionality is absent, denied, forgotten, or intentionally distorted within spaces and places where the effects of multiple systems of oppression are present (Crenshaw, 1989, 1991; Southbank Center, 2016). Intersectionality challenges intersectional failure by centering stories that have been silenced and forgotten. Intersectionality allows us to work toward intersectional repair, or what is right, inclusive, and more effective (Crenshaw, 1989, 1991; Southbank Center, 2016). Crenshaw closed out her 2020 MAKERS speech with the memorable statement that intersectionality "can inspire us to get shit done" (MAKERS, 2020).

Although Crenshaw referenced the women's movement in her speech, we can, and should, apply her message to higher education contexts. Intersectional failure has influenced our inability to substantively engage equity, inclusion, and radical social justice in postsecondary education. The chapters in this book demonstrate many of these intersectional failings. But the chapters also allow us to think about intersectional repair. Chapter authors explore these ruptures and repairs as it relates to methodology, everyday experiences of students, faculty, and staff, and praxis.

Methodologically, some chapter authors encourage us to engage with the intellectual genealogy of intersectionality prior to employing the framework in our research. This includes (re)reading foundational work on intersectionality, sitting with how intersectionality relates to one's epistemology and research design, and exploring other intersectional frameworks that might better serve the populations and issues at hand. Through these chapters, authors call out the intersectional failure that occurs when intersectionality is mis/used; when it is employed as a buzzword, as an additive framework, and/or is not grounded in the Black feminist knowledge from which it developed (Harris & Patton, 2019). The chapters also encourage intersectional repair, suggesting how we might move forward by substantively engaging with intersectionality in ways that further, rather than hinder, radical social justice and institutional transformations.

Through this book, we also explore the everyday experiences of Black women faculty at a historically White institution, Latinx students navigating a Hispanic-Serving Institution, Queer Women and Femme Students of Color survivors of dating violence, undocumented Students of Color, and a Chinese American college student with dis/abilities, to name a few. These chapters explore individual and community-level stories that are often silenced and invisibilized within and by postsecondary institutions. The stories contained in these chapters demonstrate not only the ways that multiple intersecting systems of oppression influence the everyday experiences of multiply minoritized individuals, but they also offer stories of resilience, survival, and meaning making.

Several of the final chapters in this book focus on intersectional repair through praxis. We learn how a premedical program for underrepresented medical students can take an intersectional approach to address systems of oppression students face in medical school. We also explore the Leadership for Liberation Pop-Up Library, a leadership education program aimed at engaging students in dialogue about intersectionality and liberation. These chapters, alongside others, show how intersectionality (theory) can be realized in action (practice) to work toward intersectional repair.

Through each book chapter authors use intersectionality as a "prism" to seek out and tell different kinds of stories. These stories, and the authors use of intersectionality, continue to inspire me to "get shit done" (MAKERS, 2020). My hope is that they also inspire you, your colleagues, your institutions, and beyond to work toward justice, equity, intersectional repair, and, to "get shit done" (MAKERS, 2020).

Jessica C. Harris
University of California, Los Angeles
Los Angeles, California

## *References*

Coburn, C., & Forgione, B. (2020). *MAKERS announces speakers for the 2020 MAKERS Conference, Feb 10-12 in Los Angeles.* Verizon. https://www.verizon.com/about/news/makers-announces-speakers-2020

Crenshaw, K. (1989). Demarginalizing the intersection of race and sex: A Black feminist critique of antidiscrimination doctrine, feminist theory, and antiracist politics. *University of Chicago Legal Forum, 1989*(8), 139–167.

Crenshaw, K. (1991). Mapping the margins: Intersectionality, identity politics, and violence against Women of Color. *Stanford Law Review, 43*(6), 1241–1299.

Harris, J. C., & Patton, L. D. (2019). Un/Doing intersectionality through higher education research. *Journal of Higher Education, 90*(3) 347–372.

MAKERS. (2020, February 14). *Kimberlé Crenshaw. The 2020 MAKERS Conference* [Video]. YouTube. https://www.youtube.com/watch?v=cSTf89pLcl0

Southbank Center. (2016, March 14). *Kimberlé Crenshaw—On Intersectionality—Keynote—WOW 2016* [Video]. YouTube. https://www.youtube.com/watch?v=-DW4HLgYPlA&t=245s

# *Preface*

Donald "DJ" Mitchell, Jr.

This is my third time writing the preface for an edition of *Intersectionality & Higher Education: Theory, Research, and Praxis*, but this time feels different. The first two times, I felt like I was helping advance the understanding of intersectionality within higher education contexts, but now, I am helping protect intersectionality. I do not mean this in a patriarchal or parental sense; I understand my positionality and my personal connection to a framework primarily advanced by Black women for decades, even centuries, so I hope my words are not misinterpreted. When I say "protect," I mean it literally, considering the recent attacks on intersectionality and critical race theory, particularly in higher education, over the past few years. I realize why we are here, but I question how we are here simultaneously. How could intersectionality—the recognition of interlocking systems of oppression and how the most marginalized are rendered invisible through single-axis analyses (e.g., exploring *just* racism or *just* homophobia; Crenshaw, 1989, 1991)—be under attack? As Crenshaw (2023) so powerfully articulated, *"Intersectionality is a uniting framework"* [emphasis added]. Crenshaw went on to note:

> People see common cause with each other. So, the reality is that Black people are not just straight; they're not just men; they're not just middle class. When we expand our understanding of Black reality to include the way that patriarchy, homophobia, [and] class shapes our reality, so we can better transform it. It means that we have connections with other movements and other people. And that is exactly why they're trying to force us to give up intersectionality.

Why are so many against the liberation and inclusion of all? Why are so many against justice? While society continues to wrestle with these questions,

I do know that intersectionality is a framework that propels us toward inclusion, liberation, and justice. As I have noted before (see Mitchell, 2019), I contend higher education is an ideal place to incubate the liberatory ideals countless individuals constantly strive for across the globe. This is why my colleagues and I persist in editing this critical text—we believe understanding intersectionality and acting based on this understanding help us realize these ideals.

*"Intersectionality is a uniting framework"* (Crenshaw, 2023)—a framework that has been primarily advanced by Black women and Women of Color for centuries. I pay homage to Frances Beal, Lisa Bowleg, Sumi Cho, The Combahee River Collective, Patricia Hill Collins, Elizabeth Cole, Anna Julia Cooper, Natasha Croom, Angela Davis, Lori Patton Davis, Bonnie Thorton Dill, Ange-Marie Hancock, Jessica Harris, bell hooks, Deborah King, Audre Lorde, Jennifer Nash, Anne-Marie Núñez, Christa Porter, Sojourner Truth, Alice Walker, Nicole West, Charmaine Wijeyesinghe, and Nira Yuval-Davis, among several others. I honor them for helping us understand intersectionality, and as Lila Watson has articulated, I realize my liberation is bound in theirs.

Like the first and second editions, this text is organized into three sections: theory, research, and praxis. While some of the pieces from the first two editions of the volume are included in the present edition, new chapters have been added articulating, applying, and advancing intersectionality within higher education settings. *"Intersectionality is a uniting framework"* (Crenshaw, 2023), and without it, we will never achieve the higher education students, faculty, staff, administrators, and community members deserve to inhabit; we will never see the world many of us hope to see. This time feels different, but what remains unwavering is my belief in the power of understanding intersectionality. Together with Dr. Marie, Dr. Carver, and the authors of this text, we present to you the third edition of *Intersectionality & Higher Education: Theory, Research, and Praxis.*

## References

Crenshaw, K. (1989). Demarginalizing the intersection of race and sex: A Black feminist critique of antidiscrimination doctrine, feminist theory, and antiracist politics. *University of Chicago Legal Forum, 1989*(8), 139–167.

Crenshaw, K. (1991). Mapping the margins: Intersectionality, identity politics, and violence against Women of Color. *Stanford Law Review, 43*(6), 1241–1299.

Crenshaw, K. [@sandylocks]. (2023, February 13). Intersectionality is a uniting framework...Black people are not just straight. They're not just men. They're not just

middle class. [Tweet] https://twitter.com/sandylocks/status/1625255118693101
600?s=20

Mitchell, D., Jr. (2019). Preface. In D. Mitchell, Jr., J. Marie, & T. Steele (Eds.),
*Intersectionality & higher education: Theory, research, and praxis* (2nd ed., pp. xv–
xix). Peter Lang.

# Part I: Theory

# 1. Intersectionality, Identity, and Systems of Power and Inequality

CHARMAINE L. WIJEYESINGHE AND SUSAN R. JONES

The concept of identity has received attention in many facets of higher education, including teaching (Goodman & Jackson, 2012; Jones & Wijeyesinghe 2011, Mohajeri et al., 2019), research (Museus & Griffin, 2011; Torres et al., 2009; Stewart, 2009, Sullivan & Cross, 2016) and student affairs practice (Abes, 2016; Jones & Abes, 2013; Jones & Stewart, 2016; Wijeyesinghe, 2017). Knefelkamp and colleagues (1978) noted that the developmental orientation of the college student personnel field, in particular, emphasized "the importance of responding to the whole person, attending to individual differences, and working with the student at his or her developmental level" (p. viii). Over the years, the ways in which the "whole person" has been conceptualized have shifted, with varying emphases on the parts and the whole (Torres et al., 2009), and although the social world and its contexts have always been considered in identity theories, exactly what constitutes context has evolved to also include larger structures of inequality (Duran & Jones, 2019).

In this chapter, we focus on two areas increasingly linked in theory, research, and practice in higher education: models of social identity development (the parts) and the framework of intersectionality (the whole). We begin by exploring how intersectionality addresses themes often seen in the study and representations of identity. Next, we focus more specifically on the implications of applying an intersectional lens to models grounded in individual identity narratives. We conclude the chapter by identifying several issues and questions, referred to as tension points, that have arisen in our work related to identity and intersectionality.

## *Intersectionality and Psychosocial Perspectives on Identity*

The question of "Who Am I?" has been the bedrock of identity research and models for decades. The study of identity in higher education emerged primarily from the psychological tradition of Erik Erikson (1959/1994), who described the psychosocial nature of identity development. From this perspective, identity evolves through a complex pattern of interaction between internal stages of growth and external social forces. Reflecting the sociocultural norms of his time, Erikson's conceptualization of these social forces or contexts led to very narrow views of individuals from nondominant groups. This realization led subsequent scholars in student development, racial identity development, and other fields to investigate social identities as significant contributors to understanding the whole person.

The term *social identity* has its roots in social psychology and the work of Tajfel (1982), who highlighted the role of intergroup dynamics and perceptions of group membership in understanding identity. Tajfel defined social identity as "that part of the individual's self-concept which derives from their knowledge of their membership in a social group (or groups) together with the value and emotional significance attached to that membership" (p. 2). Understanding identities as socially constructed means that "their significance stems not from some 'natural' state, but from what they have become as the result of social and historical processes" (Andersen & Collins, 2007, p. 62). Contemporary understandings of psychosocial identity, or how individuals see and understand their experiences in relation to various groups or roles they inhabit, incorporate specific attention to socially constructed groups that are tied to larger systems of power, privilege, and inequality (Abes et al., 2019). As Weber (2010) noted, "[A]t the individual level, race, class, gender, and sexuality are fundamental sources of identity for all of us: how we see ourselves, who we think we are. They are, in fact, so fundamental that to be without them would be like being without an identity at all" (p. 119).

Intersectionality is a meaningful and relevant framework for higher education scholars and practitioners because it acknowledges an individual's multiple social identities, thus creating a more complete portrayal of the whole person. While Dill and colleagues (2007) noted that "to a large extent, intersectional work is about identity" (p. 630), it is not *only* about identity (Collins & Bilge, 2016; Jones & Abes, 2013). Although Nash (2008) referred to "intersectionality's theoretical dominance as a way of conceptualizing identity" (p. 3), the framework does not seek to unveil how each person within a marginalized group or many groups develops their own sense of self under systems of oppression. It also does not foreground individual identity narratives (Collins, 2019). Instead, intersectionality highlights how people—as members of multiple groups of individuals—experience marginalization and inequality, even in movements designed to further social justice and institutional change (Dill et al., 2007; Wijeyesinghe, 2021). Clearly, individual voices inform the understanding and analysis of how inequality as well as privilege are experienced. Honoring the day-to-day experiences of *each person,* however, is not a core function of intersectionality.

Intersectionality attends to identity by placing it within a macrolevel analysis that ties individual experience to a person's membership in social groups, during a particular social and historical period, and within larger, interlocking systems of advantage and access. This complex view of identity more fully describes how individuals, as members of social groups constructed and affected by larger systems, experience their lives, interactions, and various contexts (Abes et al., 2019; Collins & Bilge, 2016; Dill & Zambrana, 2009). In describing her model of "simultaneity," Holvino (2012) indicated that such an orientation toward identity

> attends to the ways in which race, gender, class, sexuality, and nation are not just about a personal and individual identity, but about the social and institutional processes that determine opportunities, which also produce and reproduce racial, gender, class, and other social differences. (p. 172)

An intersectional perspective also forms a foundation for understanding the interconnections between systems of power and privilege in which personal narratives related to identity develop, evolve, and are understood. Therefore, not only are the experiences of social groups complex and mutually constituted, so are the systems of power and privilege, such as classism, ageism, Christian hegemony, and racism, that so strongly shape personal and group experience (Collins, 2019; Wijeyesinghe, 2021). Extending the perspective that identity at the individual level embodies multiple social locations that interact and influence each other to larger social systems allows us to see how forms of oppression interface, support, and reinforce each other, as well as the experience of individual people based on their respective identities (Collins & Bilge, 2016; Kendall & Wijeyesinghe, 2017; Wijeyesinghe, 2019). For example, Suzanne Pharr's (1988) classic book, *Homophobia: A Weapon of Sexism,* provides compelling analysis of how the interconnectedness of two systems of oppression, homophobia and sexism, combine with economic issues to create institutional heterosexism. In terms of interventions, Matsuda suggested a technique of "ask[ing] the other question. She wrote "When I see something that looks racist, I ask, 'where is the patriarchy in this?' When I see something that looks sexist, I ask, 'Where is the heterosexism in this?'"

(Matsuda, as cited in Nash, 2008, p. 12). This strategy forces an analysis of how these systems reinforce one another and connects privilege and oppression in more complex ways.

## Intersectionality and Models of Identity Development

Several insights are revealed when psychosocial approaches to identity development are examined in the context of intersectionality. First, psychosocial theories often focus on experiences and developmental tasks facing a person or the experience of a person based on one social axis, such as race. Intersectionality complicates identity (Collins & Bilge, 2016; Dill & Zambrana, 2009), because it highlights the intricacies of individuals' experiences when they embody multiple identities simultaneously. In addition, intersectionality acknowledges the diversity within social groups, often overlooked in earlier identity theories that described experiences based on a single social identity. Given this complexity and diversity, the question arises as to whether new identity models can legitimately attend to one "Black experience," or a single experience of being queer, since individuals who share one common social identity (such as race, or gender, or faith identity) may differ across several others. Those differences often include multiple locations of privilege and subordination (Collins, 1991; Weber, 2010) that must be acknowledged and integrated into interventions that promote equity and social justice (Kendall & Wijeyesinghe, 2017). For example, if a campus organization sponsors a program on the lives of Latinx students on campus, the event and the chosen speakers should address a range of experiences in addition to those attributed to race, ethnicity, and nationality.

Second, several identity models link an individual's multiple social group memberships and the salience that the individual attaches to each social identity at different life stages or in different contexts (Cross & Fhagen-Smith, 2001; Jones & Abes, 2013; Wijeyesinghe, 2012). While context and salience are reflected in how each person experiences identity in daily life, intersectionality does not directly and purposefully address the concept of salience at the level of each individual's experiences. As opposed to understanding social identities as discrete parts of an individual, each with its own level of personal significance, intersectionality encourages the consideration of multiple identities, notwithstanding the salience individuals attach to them personally. A core tenet of intersectionality addressing the unveiling of power, recognizing interconnected structures of inequality, and promoting social justice, may be helpful in expanding how we view the concept of salience. People may feel drawn to various movements for social change—such as women working to address sexism in the workplace—based on the salience they attach to their various social identities. If such actions do not also recognize the interconnection among race, class, and other social memberships, interventions may address the needs of only some of the people within that entire social group, such as White women in the aforementioned example.

Last, linking personal identity narratives to larger systems of domination helps individuals understand the connection between the social groups they inhabit and their day-to-day experiences within society, as well as concepts of privileged and marginalized positions. People working in social justice education often encounter individuals who deny that they receive any social benefit from being, for example, White, male, heterosexual, or economically advantaged. Intersectionality is useful as an awareness building tool, in that through it, peoples' experiences transcend the lens of individual and personal, to that of a socially constructed group, differentially influenced by access to power and privilege. Increased recognition of the connection between personal identities and social systems that either support or confront oppression is an essential component in engaging people in social justice work (Carastathis, 2013; Goodman, 2011). Understanding how these systems shape opportunity and experience at the individual level is a cornerstone of anti-oppression work and can serve to motivate individuals to engage in actions toward a more just and equitable society, another cornerstone of intersectionality (Adams et al., 2023; Goodman, 2011).

In light of the analysis thus far, one may begin to wonder: can models of psychosocial identity development capture core tenets of intersectionality, and are these models examples of intersectional practice? We believe that identity development models can integrate several themes drawn from intersectionality. Jones and Abes (2013) noted that "identity models *informed* [emphasis added] by intersectionality offer better ways of capturing the complexity of identity and portraying the full range of factors, contextual influences, social identities, lived experiences, and structures of power that contribute to a holistic interpretation of identity" (p. 154). Examples of such models include the Intersectional Model of Multiple Dimensions of Identity (Jones & Abes, 2013), the Intersectional Model of Multiracial Identity (Wijeyesinghe, 2012), and Simultaneity (Holvino 2012). To varying degrees, these models acknowledge the interplay among multiple social group memberships (such as race, gender, class, age, sexual orientation) and the fluid nature of identity. In addition, they all specifically reference the impact of larger social, political, institutional, and historical contexts on how individuals develop and experience their identities. Authors of new models exploring individual narratives from an intersectional framework should continue to investigate several areas: how various social group memberships and identities interface and mutually constitute others, how a more universal and omnipresent conception of salience can exist alongside a sense of personal connection to various identities, and how to represent the influence and confluence of all identities in models that primarily focus on one (such as gender, sexual orientation, or race).

## Tension Points: Issues and Questions Related to the Interplay Between Identity and Intersectionality

A number of questions emerged as we considered the relationship between identity and intersectionality, how each informs the other, and the issues that arise when we attend to individual narratives, identity, and larger structures of inequality. We use the term *tension points* to describe these questions and issues, and we explore some of the more pressing ones in this section of the chapter. Fundamentally, these tension points reflect, or are informed by such questions as the following: how can evolving conceptualization and application of intersectionality assist in understanding, mapping, researching, and teaching about social identity? Is intersectionality experienced at the individual as well as the social group level? And what, if anything, do psychosocial models that highlight the experiences of individuals offer intersectionality, and how can they inform the development of intersectional interventions in higher education practice?

### Identity

As we noted throughout the chapter, an intersectional perspective of identity requires the connecting of individual lived experience to larger structures of privilege and oppression. Therefore, there may be limits to the extent and the ways that intersectionality can be applied to the experience of individuals, even when psychosocial models of identity development include references to larger social systems, power, and privilege. As theorists and practitioners, we are faced with the following question: can identity truly be an individual experience when people embody social identities that carry meaning in society and result in differential access to resources and control of various domains that fundamentally influence a person's life, regardless of whether the person acknowledges the existence or influence of those identities?

Psychosocial identity models that incorporate intersectional themes, like those examples mentioned in the previous section, can enhance our understanding of key concepts such as social group memberships and social location, institutional power and privilege, and oppression and liberation. This knowledge lays the groundwork for discussions that move beyond individual experiences to how systems of power and privilege support and intersect and the need to create interventions that reflect multiple social locations and concerns.

Tensions between managing the individual experience of identity and further reaching aspects of intersectionality should be considered when planning and implementing actions for social change. Dill and colleagues (2007) noted that "in the discussion surrounding identity, it is the tension between intersectionality as a tool for illuminating group identities that are not essentialist, and individual identities that are not so fragmented as to be meaningless" (p. 631). Attending to the mutually constituting nature of forms of oppression is not the same as treating them as the same or as so intertwined that the ways in which they differ become unrecognizable or disappear. Therefore, theories and change efforts must acknowledge common aspects and interconnections, while also attending to areas where experiences of identity and forms of inequality differ. Intersectionality, with its emphasis on individual and social location within multiple groups, pushes researchers, faculty, and practitioners to acknowledge the diversity within socially constructed groups, while avoiding the obscuring of real differences between manifestations of oppression by applying intersectionality uniformly (Luft, 2009).

## Salience

In relation to identity, intersectionality illustrates how we embody all of our social identities and experience the world based on larger, interconnected systems that respond to these identities, at all times and in all circumstances (Wijeyesinghe, 2019). Weber (1998) pointed out the following:

> Race, class, gender, and sexuality simultaneously operate in every social situation. At the societal level, these systems of social hierarchies are connected to each other and are embedded in all social institutions. At the individual level, we each experience our lives and develop our identities based on our location along all dimensions, whether we are in dominant groups, subordinate groups, or both. (p. 24)

Tension may arise when individuals feel that their lived experience reflects one, or only some of their social identities, as when a queer, White man who is economically privileged feels that his identity is grounded primarily in his sexual orientation and resists considering how his race, economic position, and gender afford him social power and privilege. Intersectionality frames all identities as being mutually constituted, meaning that social identities are not discrete entities that are isolated from the influences of all others. Therefore, while the man described here may define himself and view the world primarily through the lens of sexual orientation, his class, race, emotional and physical ability, faith background, and other social groups also influence his particular experiences as a queer man. Thus, his experiences of being queer would be different if one or more of his other identities changed, for example, if he were Asian or economically disadvantaged. Scholars and practitioners may encounter challenges to operationalizing core tenets of intersectionality when there are the perceived gaps between the lived experience of identity salience by the individuals with whom they are working and the perspective that all identities are at play at all times.

Tension related to salience also occurs at the systems levels of analysis. At a broader social level, intersectionality highlights that it is not possible to grasp an understanding of the complex interplay of power, privilege, and social structures if we view forms of oppression as singular and separate units (like racism, ableism, sexism, classism), or if the focus is only on those forms of oppression that feel most salient to an individual, in a specific setting, or at a certain point in life. A more intersectional level of awareness recognizes

> that each of us simultaneously experiences all of these dimensions, even if one is foregrounded in a particular situation, and can help us see the often obscured ways in which we benefit from existing race, class, gender, sexuality social arrangements, as well as the ways which we're disadvantaged. Such an awareness can be key in working together across different groups to achieve a more equitable distribution of society's valued resources. (Weber, 1998, p. 25)

Decades after Lorde (1983) so aptly highlighted that there is no hierarchy of oppressions, individuals may still feel that there is, based on how they live and experience their range of social identities.

## Privileged and Oppressed Identities

Intersectionality centers the voices of people and groups previously overlooked or excluded, especially in the analysis of inequality and efforts to remedy specific social problems. An ongoing debate among intersectional scholars and observers of the popularity of the framework foregrounds the question of definition—what exactly is intersectionality and who is intersectional (Harris & Davis, 2019; Kendall & Wijeyesinghe, 2017; Nash, 2008; Warner & Shields, 2013)? Stated another way, is intersectionality a general theory of identities or a theory focused only on those people from multiple marginalized social groups? Nash (2008) argued, "In its emphasis on [B]lack women's experiences of subjectivity and oppression, intersectional theory has obscured the question of whether all identities are intersectional, or whether only multiply marginalized subjects have an intersectional identity" (p. 9). If intersectionality is applied as a general theory of identity, all people may locate themselves within its purview. However, if intersectionality is primarily grounded in the experiences of individuals with multiple marginalized identities, those people with privileged identities are outside of the framework. Of course, many individuals inhabit both privileged and oppressed identities, so these boundaries may not be so clearly drawn.

What seems critical to us is what Nash (2008) advocated for as "a nuanced conception of identity that recognizes the ways in which positions of dominance and subordination work in complex and intersecting ways to constitute subjects' experience of personhood" (p. 10). The question of whether intersectionality applies to everyone reinforces a point made earlier, that intersectionality is not simply about multiple identities, which we all have, but multiple identities connected to groups and structures of power, thus, paving the way for a "both/and" approach (Pope et al., 2021). Considering the application and relevance of intersectionality to people and groups who receive social advantages begins to draw some boundaries related to privileged and oppressed identities.

The purpose of intersectionality is not simply to locate individuals within a matrix of domination and privilege. Instead, intersectionality sheds light on the ways that some people within social groups receive benefit while others are disproportionately targeted and constrained by certain social-structural situations (this was Crenshaw's [1991] initial analysis of the inutility of a gender-only lens when investigating domestic violence against women). Yet, individuals who hold multiple privileged identities can use an intersectional analysis in ways that are productive and contribute to a more socially just society. The task then becomes less about locating oneself within an intersectional framework and more so about using intersectionality to understand the experiences of others and the social structures that perpetuate privilege and oppression.

From discussion, research, and application of intersectionality in various settings, we may develop a greater awareness of how intersectionality captures the lived experiences of people who hold multiple privileged identities or how experiences related to these identities are mediated by any targeted groups to which these individuals belong. Caution is advised, however, so that the core tenet of intersectionality related to foregrounding the experience of marginalized groups remains central to its understanding and application and to prevent it from becoming a lens that is co-opted to reinforce and re-center the experience of those people and groups with privileged identities.

## Conclusion

In closing this chapter, we reaffirm that identity and intersectionality are relevant to each other and can be used to explore questions and areas unanswered by foundational theories within the fields of student, racial, and social identity development. As authors of two models that are informed by intersectionality, we see psychosocial models that incorporate aspects of the framework as tools to enhance our understanding of the experiences of individuals and groups on campus. Yet, as new theories and approaches evolve, we also pay homage to the context, goals, and contributions of existing theories, especially those models that paved the way in the early years and formed the foundation for research and theory building related to identity.

Intersectionality is a powerful tool for understanding, constructing, and de-constructing: the experience of identity, the complex and mutually constituting nature of social identities, the relationships between identity and larger social systems, and the interwoven nature of manifestations of social oppression. While centering the interconnections inherent in intersectional analysis, we also must honor the unique aspects of various social identities, systems of inequality, and efforts to enact social justice. The journey of writing this chapter has led us to see that in relation to identity and intersectionality, the situation is not one of "either/or" when it comes to the exploration of individual narratives or narratives of larger group experiences influenced by social systems. Instead, we appreciate how these two levels of analysis inform each other, contribute to our understanding of identity, stretch our thinking, drive model building, and guide our work. Thus, our efforts as theorists, researchers, and practitioners becomes less about "capturing" intersectionality via models and more about using the complexity and connections in the framework to more fully understand the lived experience of individuals within the context of their social groups, oppression and inequality, and interventions for social change.

## References

Abes, E. A. (2016). Situating paradigms in student development theory. In E. A. Abes (Ed.), *Critical perspectives in student development theory* (New Directions for Student Services, No. 154, pp. 9–16). Jossey Bass.

Abes, E. A., Duran, A., Jones, S. R., & Stewart, D.-L. (2019). Rethinking student development. In E. S. Abes, S. R. Jones, & D.-L. Stewart (Eds.), *Rethinking college student development using critical frameworks* (pp. 239–252). Stylus.

Adams, M., Bell, L. A., Goodman, D., & Shlaskco, D. (Eds.). (2023). *Teaching for diversity and social justice* (4th ed.). Routledge.

Andersen, M. L., & Collins, P. H. (Eds.). (2007). *Race, class, & gender: An anthology* (7th ed., pp. 61–86). Thomson/Wadsworth.

Carastathis, A. (2013). Identity categories as potential coalitions. *Signs, 38*(4), 941–965.

Collins, P. H. (1991). *Black feminist thought: Knowledge, consciousness, and the politics of empowerment.* Routledge.

Collins, P. H. (2019). *Intersectionality as critical social theory.* Duke University Press.

Collins, P. H., & Bilge, S. (2016). *Intersectionality.* Polity.

Crenshaw, K. (1991). Mapping the margins: Intersectionality, identity politics, and violence against Women of Color. *Stanford Law Review, 43*(6), 1241–1299.

Cross, W. E., & Fhagen-Smith, P. (2001). Patterns of African-American identity development: A life span perspective. In C. L. Wijeyesinghe & B. W. Jackson (Eds.), *New perspectives on racial identity development: A theoretical and practical anthology* (pp. 243–270). New York University Press.

Dill, B. T., McLaughlin, A. E., & Nieves, A. D. (2007). Future directions of feminist research: Intersectionality. In S. N. Hesse-Biber (Ed.), *Handbook of feminist research* (pp. 629–637). SAGE.

Dill, B. T., & Zambrana, R. E. (2009). Critical thinking about inequality: An emerging lens. In B. T. Dill & R. E. Zambrana (Eds.), *Emerging intersections: Race, class, and gender in theory, policy, and practice* (pp. 1–21). Rutgers University Press.

Duran, A., & Jones, S. R. (2019). In E. S. Abes, S. R. Jones, & D.-L. Stewart (Eds.), *Rethinking college student development using critical frameworks* (pp. 171–186). Stylus.

Erikson, E. H. (1994). *Identity and the life cycle.* W. W. Norton. (Original work published 1959)

Goodman, D. J. (2011). *Promoting diversity and social justice: Educating people from privileged groups* (2nd ed.). Routledge.

Goodman, D. J., & Jackson III, B. W. (2012). Pedagogical approaches to teaching about racial identity from an intersectional perspective. In C. L. Wijeyesinghe & B. W. Jackson III (Eds.), *New perspectives on racial identity development* (2nd ed., pp. 216–239). New York University Press.

Harris, J. C., & Davis, L. P. (2019). Un/Doing intersectionality through higher education research, *The Journal of Higher Education, 90*(3), 347–372.

Holvino, E. (2012). The "simultaneity" of identities: Models and skills. In C. L. Wijeyesinghe & B. W. Jackson III (Eds.), *New perspectives on racial identity development* (2nd ed., pp. 161–191). New York University Press.

Jones, S. R., & Abes, E. S. (2013). *Identity development of college students.* Jossey-Bass.

Jones, S. R., & Stewart, D.-L. (2016). Evolution of student development theory. In E. A. Abes (Ed.), *Critical perspectives in student development theory* (New Directions for Student Services, No. 154, pp. 17–28). Jossey Bass.

Jones, S. R., & Wijeyesinghe, C. L. (2011). The promise and challenge of teaching from an intersectional perspective: Core components and applied strategies. In M. L. Ouellett (Ed.), *An integrative analysis approach to diversity in the college classroom* (New Directions for Teaching and Learning, No. 125, pp. 11–20). Jossey-Bass.

Kendall, F. E., & Wijeyesinghe, C. L. (2017). Advancing social justice work at the intersections of multiple privileged identities. In C. L. Wijeyesinghe (Ed.), *Enacting intersectionality in student affairs* (New Directions for Student Services, No. 157, pp. 91–100). Jossey-Bass.

Knefelkamp, L., Widick, C., & Parker, C. (Eds.). (1978). *Applying new developmental findings* (New Directions for Student Services, No. 4). Jossey-Bass.

Lorde, A. (1983). *There is no hierarchy of oppressions.* Council on Interracial Books for Children.

Luft, R. E. (2009). Intersectionality and the risk of flattening difference: Gender and race logics, and the strategic use of antiracist singularity. In M. T. Berger & K. Guidroz (Eds.), *The intersectional approach: Transforming the academy through race, class, & gender* (pp. 100–117). The University of North Carolina Press.

Mohajeri, O., Rodriguez, F., & Schneider, F. (2019). Pursuing intersectionality as a pedagogical tool in the higher education classroom. In W. C. Byrd, R. J. Brunn-Bevel, & S. M. Ovink (Eds.), *Intersectionality and higher education: Identity and inequality on college campuses* (pp. 166–178). Rutgers University Press.

Museus, S. D., & Griffin, K. A. (2011). Mapping the margins in higher education: On the promise of intersectionality frameworks in research and discourse. In K. A. Griffin & S. D. Museus (Eds.), *Using mixed methods approaches to study intersectionality in higher education* (New Directions for Institutional Research, No. 151, pp. 5–13). Jossey-Bass.

Nash, J. C. (2008). Re-thinking intersectionality. *Feminist Review, 89*(1), 1–15.

Pope, R. L., Reynolds, A. L., & Robinson, C. (2021). Embracing the complexities of race, racism, and social justice in changing times. In C. L. Wijeyesinghe (Ed.), *The complexities of race: Identity, power, and justice in an evolving America* (pp. 240–265). New York University Press.

Pharr, S. (1988). *Homophobia: A weapon of sexism.* Chardon.

Stewart, D. L. (2009). Perceptions of multiple identities among Black college students. *Journal of College Student Development, 50*(3), 253–270.

Sullivan, J. M. & Cross, W. E. Jr. (Eds.). (2016). *Meaning-making, internalized racism, and African-American Identity.* SUNY Press.

Tajfel, H. (Ed.). (1982). *Social identity and intergroup relations.* Cambridge University Press.

Torres, V., Jones, S. R., & Renn, K. A. (2009). Identity development theories in student affairs: Origins, current status, and new approaches. *Journal of College Student Development, 50*(6), 577–596.

Warner, L. R., & Shields, S. A. (2013). The intersections of sexuality, gender, and race: Identity research at the crossroads. *Sex Roles, 68*(11–12), 803–810.

Weber, L. (1998). A conceptual framework for understanding race, class, gender, and sexuality. *Psychology of Women Quarterly, 22*(1), 13–22.

Weber, L. (2010). *Understanding race, class, gender, and sexuality* (2nd ed.). Oxford University Press.

Wijeyesinghe, C. L. (2012). The intersectional model of multiracial identity: Integrating multiracial identity theories and intersectional perspectives on social identity. In C. L. Wijeyesinghe & B. W. Jackson III (Eds.), *New perspectives on racial identity development* (2nd ed., pp. 81–107). New York University Press.

Wijeyesinghe, C. L. (2017). Editor's notes. In C. L. Wijeyesinghe (Ed.), *Enacting intersectionality in student affairs* (New Directions for Student Services, No. 157, pp. 5–13). Jossey-Bass.

Wijeyesinghe, C. L. (2019). Intersectionality and student development: Centering power in the process. In E. S. Abes, S. R. Jones, & D.-L. Stewart (Eds.), *Rethinking college student development using critical frameworks* (pp. 26–34). Stylus.

Wijeyesinghe, C. L. (2021). Understanding and responding to resistance when intersectionality is used to address race, racism, and racial justice work. In C. L. Wijeyesinghe (Ed.), *The complexities of race: Identity, power, and justice in an evolving America* (pp. 216–239). New York University Press.

# 2. Intersectionality: A Legacy from Critical Legal Studies and Critical Race Theory

Allison Daniel Anders and James M. DeVita

Activists, scholars, and researchers in education studies (Bettie, 2003; Patel, 2013), higher education (Abes et al., 2007; Mitchell & Means, 2014; Strayhorn et al., 2008, 2010), human rights (Raj et al., 2002), political science (Berger, 2004), and women's studies (Collins, 2008; Davis, 1983; Lorde, 1984) have long studied intersectional experiences and the subordinated locations of targeted intersectional identities. They have argued for understandings and practices that acknowledge, support, and affirm people who experience targeting and they have offered ways to challenge and disrupt the subordinated locations that structures of discourse and institutions produce. Among these scholars is Kimberlé Crenshaw, an African American woman, legal scholar, critical race theorist, and activist who first coined the term *intersectionality* (1991a). Studying the ways structures produce and reproduce subordinated locations at the intersection of race, gender and other targeted identities, Crenshaw advanced not only specific analytics to examine such discrimination but also promoted intersectional coalition building as one form of response. In this chapter, we address intersectionality from the histories of critical legal studies and critical race theory[1] (CRT) in Crenshaw's work.

Specifically, Crenshaw (1991a) analyzed the relationship of the law, its production and reproduction of subordinated locations and the experiences of Black women and Women of Color[2]. She studied the ways structures, through institutions and through discourse, produce subordinated locations and position intersecting identities in particular ways. Her work included analyses of the intersections of culture, documentation, economic status, and language as well as race and gender. Crenshaw (1991b) also addressed and advocated for potential coalition building specifically across anti-racist work and feminist work. Addressing systemic inequities inside and outside the legal system Crenshaw invites activists and scholars to interrupt "intersectional disempowerment" (p. 1245). Crenshaw's conceptions of intersectionality deepen opportunities for activists, scholars, and researchers in higher education, who are committed to racial and social justice, to study relationships across structures and the experiences of Black women, Women of Color, and other individuals and groups who face targeting at the intersection of multiple identities, and to strategize against systemic inequities.

We trace intersectionality to its first use by Crenshaw and her applications because often her conceptualization of intersectionality has been applied as only identarian, and because White scholars have extracted salient points from the work of Scholars of Color without engaging deeply with the analytical tools she offers. Our aims are to situate the relevancy of intersectionality historically, and to encourage all activists, scholars, and researchers interested in ideas produced by Scholars of Color to study the context of such work before applying it to their own. When Crenshaw's ideas are reduced to only identarian work, we miss opportunities to address structures that produce subordinated locations. Crenshaw herself has noted the different ways scholars have engaged her work. While some read her work through CRT, others engage the idea of intersectional identities without the context of CRT or its histories.

> It always strikes me, and I always have a sense of people who have encountered intersectionality without having gone first through critical race theory, because they see it simply as identarian. They don't see the structure in it. And they don't see that contradiction is what I am actually trying to interrogate (Crenshaw, 2021-present).

Thompson (2003) warned that, "taking the work of [P]eople of [C]olor seriously requires studying their projects, not just quoting the occasional point that coincides with what we were going to say anyway" (p. 13). For us, engaging with Crenshaw's ideas also means studying the body of her work, and representing the historical and political context of her work, which includes the resistance to intersectionality and critical race theory that she and her colleagues endured and confronted first as law students and later as law professors amongst predominantly White, male colleagues at predominantly White law schools, conferences, and meetings, and in predominantly White, conventional legal scholarship (Crenshaw, 2002).

We begin with introductions to the context of critical legal studies (CLS) and address some of the historical tensions amongst CLS scholars and Crenshaw's leadership in helping to establish critical race theory. Tracing some of her earliest analyses of antidiscrimination law we include Crenshaw's critique of neoconservative influence on antidiscrimination law and the ways her critique informed her ideas about intersectionality. We follow these sections with Crenshaw's (1991b) work on structural, political, and representational intersectionality. Lastly, we offer as an example an application of Crenshaw's ideas to DeVita's (2010) study of Black, gay men in higher education. Ultimately, we argue that the application of Crenshaw's concept of intersectionality requires historical and political context and offers activists, scholars, and researchers ways to critique and disrupt the reproduction of subordinated locations (Anders et al., 2012; DeVita et al., 2014). In doing so, we invite readers to discern between Crenshaw's specific conceptions of intersectionality and other scholarship that emphasizes intersectional experience and/or intersections of identity.

The privilege that Whiteness provides in "white supremacist capitalist patriarchy" (hooks, 1992, p. 22), precludes any claim we (Anders & DeVita) might make about intersectionality and our own identities. Although Crenshaw did not exclude the possible application of intersectionality to analyze intersections of targeted and privileged identities together (for example, higher education experiences of White women or of White gay men), her emphasis on subordinated locations means that for us, as White researchers, we choose other language to refer to our experiences. For example, "intersections of identity" avoids misappropriating or co-opting Crenshaw's theoretical conceptions. Certainly, we do not occupy a subordinated location in what became the United States. Using intersectionality to theorize about our own lives would mean altering Crenshaw's arguments to fit our own needs. Our approach, however, is not prescriptive. We believe each individual must face the burden of application (DeVita & Anders, 2014). For us, keeping prominent and centered Crenshaw's emphasis on structure and subordinated locations at the intersections of targeted identities is what is important[3].

## Critical Legal Studies

In the 1970s civil rights lawyers faced "attacks on the limited victories they had only just achieved in the prior decade, particularly with respect to affirmative action and legal requirements for the kinds of evidence required to prove illicit discrimination" (Crenshaw et al., 1995, p. xvii). During the same time, in law schools across the United States, groups of predominantly White, male scholars with critical commitments organized in a critical legal studies (CLS) movement. They argued that neither the law nor legal education was neutral or apolitical, underscoring that the knowledge production in law schools produced discourse and practice that conferred particular forms and logics of legitimacy which in turn reinforced existing social power in the U.S. (Crenshaw, 1988; Crenshaw et al., 1995). For many CLS scholars, Antonio Gramsci's (1992) work on hegemony, often associated with critical theory, informed their theorizing about the enduring power of the law, the limits of rights-based approaches, and the role of dominant and hegemonic ideologies of the economy and the state. CLS scholars critiqued the role of the legal system in reproducing inequities (Crenshaw, 1995; Kairys, 1998) and "mainstream legal ideology for its tendency to portray American society as basically fair, and thereby legitimate[ing] the oppressive policies that have been directed toward racial minorities" (Crenshaw, 1988, p. 1356). Specifically, CLS scholars analyzed legal doctrine "to reveal both its internal inconsistencies (generally by exposing the incoherence of legal arguments) and its external consistencies (often by laying bare the inherently paradoxical and political worldviews embedded within legal doctrine)" (Crenshaw, 1988, p. 1350). They explicated the ideology and politics of court decisions and through their analyses provided opportunities for scholars to identify ways that the practice of law creates, legitimates, and reproduces "an unjust social order" (Crenshaw et al., 1995, p. xviii). A few legal Scholars of Color engaged with CLS in the late 1970s[4], and by the early 1980s the number of students and Professors of Color interested in critical legal studies increased. Crenshaw, first as a law student at Harvard Law School and later as a faculty member at the University of Wisconsin, was among them (Crenshaw, 2002).

### Critical Race Theory

Although CLS scholars disrupted conventional thought and teaching in many law schools through analyses of hegemony in legal doctrine, questions of racial power were not part of the work of CLS. Their critiques of dominance did not include white supremacy (Crenshaw et al., 1995; Delgado & Stefancic, 2001). In the 1970s and early 1980s, "race crits" began discussing racial dynamics within CLS and the group's dismissal of rights-based arguments (Dalton, 1995; Crenshaw, 1988). Although race crits agreed that rights discourse was indeterminate, many believed that a "rights discourse held a social and transformative value in the context of racial subordination that transcended the narrower question of whether reliance on rights could alone bring about any determinate results" (Crenshaw et al., 1995, p. xxiii). Law students, which included Crenshaw, and Faculty of Color involved both with CLS and the Alternative Course at Harvard Law School, caucused at

CLS conferences in the 1980s in order to develop critical analyses of race in substantive legal topics (Crenshaw, 2002).

In her analyses of equal process and equality of opportunity arguments, Crenshaw (1988) demonstrated the significance of race in critical legal scholarship. Then and now, neoconservative agendas tout equal process and equality of opportunity arguments. Neoconservatives and many neoliberals argue that equal process, or access to equal protection under the law, addresses the axis of economic and racial inequity in the U.S. They maintain that equal process is a sufficient doctrine; moreover, they contend that, "equal process is completely unrelated to equal results" (Crenshaw, 1885, p. 1343). Decoupling equal process from equal process outcomes allows neoconservatives to ignore evidence of disparity along economic and racial axes, to reproduce the myth of "color-blindness"[5], and to de-legitimate claims of discrimination based on race. In contrast, Crenshaw (1988) argued that if "color-blind" policies were "the only legitimate and effective means of ensuring a racially equitable society, one would have to assume not only that there is only one 'proper role' for law but also that such a racially equitable society already exists" (p. 1344). As the United States fails to reflect such histories, Crenshaw critiqued the separation of equal process from equal process outcomes and the myth of "color-blindness":

> Society's adoption of the ambivalent rhetoric of equal opportunity law has made it that much more difficult for black people to name their reality. There is no longer a perpetrator, a clearly identifiable discriminator. Company Z can be an equal opportunity employer even though Company Z has no blacks or any other minorities in its employ. Practically speaking, all companies can now be equal opportunity employers by proclamation alone. Society has embraced the rhetoric of equal opportunity without fulfilling its promise. (p. 1347)

According to Crenshaw (1988) "only in such a society, where all other social functions operate in a nondiscriminatory way, would equality of process constitute equality of opportunity" (p. 1345). In a society where groups of people have been treated differently, as is the case of the United States, advocates for the idea of "color-blindness" deny the histories of exploitation, oppression, and disenfranchisement and their effects. Moreover, they silence interpretations of society that center the relationship of ontology to epistemology. That is to say, the ways one is located and positioned in the world and the ways one is positioned (classed, gendered, and raced and so on) affect one's way of experiencing and knowing the world (Butler, 1999; Crenshaw, 1991b; Collins, 2008; Freire, 2000; hooks, 1992). Crenshaw (1988) signified Black experience as a meaningful and tactical response to neoconservative strategies designed to disrupt advocacy for economic and racial justice:

> The lasting harm must be measured by the extent to which limited gains hamper efforts of African-Americans to name their reality and to remain capable of engaging in collective action in the future... If the civil rights constituency allows its own political consciousness to be completely replaced by the ambiguous discourse of antidiscrimination law, it will be difficult for this constituency to defend its genuine interests against those whose interests are supported by opposing visions that also employ the same discourse. The struggle, it seems, is to maintain a contextualized, specified worldview that reflects the experience of blacks. (p. 1349)

Crenshaw urged African Americans to name their own realities in order to engage in collective action. Her critiques of neoconservative influence on interpretations of antidiscrimination law and her advocacy for the centrality of Black experiences historicize her work on intersectionality.

By the end of the 1980s, critical race theory had been named as a way to create a space for critical work where race was foregrounded in legal analyses. There is no unified school of thought. Rather, there were and are dozens of theoretical concepts and analytics. Crenshaw (2002) noted that the intellectual leadership and academic insurgency of African American law professor, Derrick Bell, "lit the path toward Critical Race Theory" (p. 1344). One shared aim across his work and activists and scholars in the movement was

> to understand how a regime of white supremacy and its subordination of [P]eople of [C]olor have been created and maintained in America, and, in particular, to examine the relationship between that social structure and the professed ideals such as "the rule of law" and "equal protection." (Crenshaw et al., 1995, p. xiii)

They sought not merely to "understand the vexed bond between law and racial power but to *change* it" (Crenshaw et al., 1995, p. xiii). In contrast to positions of incrementalism in the civil rights movement, critical race theorists questioned "the very foundations of the liberal order, including equality theory, legal reasoning, Enlightenment rationalism, and neutral principles of constitutional law" (Delgado & Stefancic, 2001, p. 3). CRT scholars argue that racism is endemic in the U.S. and that the histories of White supremacy and White dominance created a racial hierarchy that serve the social and material purposes of dominant Whites. While there is agreement among CRT scholars that racism is endemic in the U.S., some scholars argue racism is permanent and others do not (Bell, 1992). Some CRT scholars study the reproduction of legal precedent, others the diversity and at times conflict of Black interests in civil rights cases. Other scholars study the relationship between court decisions and the maintenance of the racial hierarchy in the status quo. Many CRT scholars critique liberalism, because neoconservative and neoliberal agendas that perpetuate the rhetoric of "color-blindness" limit redress, and therefore, allow condemnation of only the most "egregious racial harms" (Delgado & Stefancic, 2001, p. 22). CRT scholars also examine the ways rights-based tactics failed to produce substantive change. Others study the way "society invents, manipulates, or retires when convenient" (Delgado & Stefancic, 2001, p. 7) particular constructions of race. Many CRT scholars study ways race is socially constructed and deployed and differential racialization, or the ways "dominant society racializes different minority groups at different times in response to shifting needs such as the labor market" (Delgado & Stefancic, 2001, p. 8).

Crenshaw's (1991b) commitment to strategies for collective action underscores the importance of intersectional work in the movement. And analyses of subordinated locations of targeted intersectional identities informs larger projects including the represention of counter narratives against a majoritarian history of the United States (Lawrence, 1992). CRT scholars, many of whom are racial realists, reexamine "America's historical record," in order to confront and replace "comforting majoritarian interpretations of events with ones that square more accurately with minorities' experiences" (Delgado & Stefancic, 2001, p. 30). Celebrating and encouraging ontological and epistemological understandings of race and racism from the perspectives of people experiencing discrimination and subordinated locations, many CRT scholars pursue the production of counternarratives and legal storytelling. Analyzing the ways dominant groups position groups of people racially, culturally, and economically for their own purposes allows targeted individuals and groups to build collective action and deploy tactics against oppression in the prevailing economic and social order.

## Intersectionality

Crenshaw (1991a, 1991b) used intersectionality to conceptualize the intersections of race, gender and other subordinated locations in her analyses of antidiscrimination in legal cases, for example, cases where Black women and non-English-speaking immigrant Women of Color were plaintiffs. She criticized the courts for forcing Black women and Women of Color to articulate discrimination along only one category of identity. She argued that "the intersectional experience is greater than the sum of racism and sexism" and that "any analysis that does not take intersectionality into account cannot sufficiently address the particular manner in which Black women are subordinated" (p. 58). The experience of racism and sexism is neither discrete nor summative for Women of Color. Women of Color do not experience racism in the same ways that Men of Color do, nor do they experience sexism in the same ways that White women do. Procedurally, the courts denied claims of discrimination at the intersection of race and gender, and in doing so failed to account for the experiences of Women of Color, thus, reproducing systems of discrimination.

Crenshaw (1991b) conceptualized structural intersectionality, political intersectionality, and representational intersectionality as a set of analytics for legal studies and movement work. Structural intersectionality signifies the ways that the locations and subordination of Black women and Women of Color at the intersection of race and gender and other targeted identities creates experiences and outcomes that are qualitatively different from Black men and white women. To illustrate structural intersectionality, Crenshaw analyzed the issues of gender and race at the intersections of employment and housing, access to court advocates, and English as the language of the court in domestic violence cases. She examined the qualitative differences across women who have racial, economic, and linguistic privilege, and those who do not.

Crenshaw's (1991b) work on political intersectionality assessed the ways identity politics affect experiences of and participation by Women of Color in collective action. Crenshaw demonstrated political intersectionality by analyzing the ways dominant political agendas and social movements separate the politics of Women of Color into two (minimally) different subordinated groups: People of Color in pursuit of racial equity and women in pursuit of gender equity. In contrast, she advanced collective action across antiracist and feminist work where antiracist work amplifies gendered perspectives and feminist work amplifies raced perspectives from Black women and Women of Color.

Representational intersectionality is an analytical frame that addresses racist-misogynistic-sexist cultural constructions of Black women and Women of Color and the marginalization of the perspectives of Black women and Women of Color in racial justice work and feminist work (Crenshaw, 1991b). Representational intersectionality offers a way to analyze discriminatory representations at the intersections of multiple targeted identities and to amplify the voices of those who experience and speak back against them.

### Structural Intersectionality and LGBTQ+ Populations in Higher Education

Crenshaw's (1991b) structural intersectionality emphasized the ways policies, and practices benefit women with intersectional privilege (e.g., White, native English speaker, middle class, U.S. citizen). In higher education, ideally LGBTQ+ (lesbian, gay, bisexual, transgender, and queer) Individuals of Color will encounter systems of support that celebrate their identities. However, too often these institutions fail to support students holistically. For example, while many college campuses develop cultural centers to provide support for targeted students, typically, these centers reflect only one axis of identity (e.g., Black cultural centers and LGBTQ+ centers; Strayhorn et al., 2008, 2010). Even on campuses where collaboration is encouraged, supported, and realized, these centers represent the ways campuses have been structured to recognize the issues faced by students from specific targeted groups at the expense of individuals who must navigate subordinated locations of targeted intersectional identities. The resources, though needed and important, often are inadequate when students who embody and enact multiple targeted identities must negotiate everyday campus politics and potential intersectional discrimination.

Indeed, research on the experiences of Black gay males at predominantly White institutions (PWI) found that Black gay males seldom felt comfortable in either of the spaces established to support their identity affiliations (i.e., a Black cultural center and a LGBTQ+ center; Strayhorn et al., 2008, 2010). Black gay male undergraduates at PWIs frequently experienced homophobia in the Black cultural center and racism in the LGBTQ+ center. Experiences with discrimination in both places forced them to choose the least oppressive space. The development of separate resource centers is directly linked to tensions associated with a lack of systemic support for a particular group (i.e., Black or LGBTQ+), thus it should not be surprising that the distance established between physical spaces produced equally disparate social and political climates (Bentley Historical Society, 2007). Within institutional structures meant to serve them, individuals who identify as Students of Color and LGBTQ+ are forced to prepare for potential targeting of their identities in ways individuals who identify as White and LGBTQ+ do not.

On many campuses, it is not feasible to alter the physical spaces (e.g., distinct cultural centers) that have been established. Thus, programming and other initiatives are productive ways to provide support to address structural intersectionality. Educational programming focused on LGBTQ+ topics (e.g., safe zones, safe spaces) should be inclusive of discussions that examine the intersections of LGBTQ+ identities with other targeted identities (e.g., race/ethnicity, socioeconomic status). The failure to include other axes of identity reifies the whitewashing of LGBTQ+ identities and further marginalizes racial identities.

Additionally, a common feature of educational programs is the issuance of a card or sign, which indicates that the individual has completed the training and is a "safe resource" for LGBTQ+ people (Consortium, 2013). This sign becomes a public proclamation that an individual is an LGBTQ+ ally, presumably with the ability to support all LGBTQ+ individuals, including those with intersecting targeted identities. However, for example, any programs that reflect the neoconservative myth of "color-blindness" ignore the explicit experiences and needs of LGBTQ+ Individuals of Color and affirms a White normative view of LGBTQ+ experience. Such programs re-center White privilege and limit the potential support for LGBTQ+ Individuals of Color.

## Political Intersectionality and LGBTQ+ Populations in Higher Education

Paying close attention to political intersectionality may improve communication and resources in higher education and open new spaces for collective action. For example, the policies and initiatives supported by LGBTQ+ groups often lack of attention to the experiences and needs of LGBTQ+ Individuals of Color (Teunis, 2007; Ward, 2008). Ward's (2008) research on an LGBTQ+ community center revealed numerous practices that aligned with White normative culture; for example, the center "was sustained by its mainstream and corporate approach to diversity" (p. 582). Similarly, Teunis (2007) characterized various LGBTQ+ organizations' foci on marriage equality and military service as political agenda items that primarily privileged White, gay individuals. Teunis described the absence of attention to the intersections of identity in the pursuit of marriage equality this way:

> In the struggle for marriage equality, spokespersons are very generally white women and men who display little or no concern for critical political issues that face gays and lesbians of colour. That these struggles promote whiteness is not due to the inherent nature of the issues, but rather due to the manner in which they are promoted and in which they usurp all other concerns that drive the community. (p. 268)

Similar tensions face LGBTQ+ cultural centers on college campuses. First, although centers now exist on over 250 campuses across the United States and Canada (Postsecondary National Policy Institute, 2022), Historically Black Colleges and Universities (HBCUs) housed only five centers in 2023 (Campus Pride, 2023)—an increase of just two in the last decade (Human Rights Campaign, 2013). The prevalence of centers at PWIs suggests that services and support for LGBTQ+ individuals, educational programming for non-LGBTQ+ identifying individuals, and LGBTQ+-inclusive programs for all student are more likely present at PWIs. While the resources and community building from such centers are needed, on predominately white campuses, they also are more likely to reflect policies and practices generated in and reproduced by White normative culture.

While a meaningful campus resource, the creation of a center based along a single axis of identity at a PWI likely primes White potential L, G, B, T, or Q+ identified-students for leadership roles. As Teunis' (2007) and Ward's (2008) findings suggest, White LGBTQ+ leadership must actively center experiences of LGBTQ+ Students of Color in order to produce an inclusive platform in agenda setting. Institutional inclusion and inclusive organizing are paramount. An intersectional approach to support individuals with intersectional targeted identities would include an examination of the ways different identity groups could align resources and energies to benefit from a common goal.

In our own research (DeVita & Anders, 2018) participants taught us that "alliance means action." In an interview study with LGTQ-identified faculty, staff, and students in higher education, participants discerned between "straight" individuals who only identified as an "ally" through the posting of a safe zone or safe space placard and those who actively engaged in activities, events, and policy changes that support LGBTQ+ communities and other civil rights and justice work. One participant, a White male faculty member who identified as gay, discussed his frustration with passive "allies." He explained: "We need to join in what is called ideology politics. Joining with people of like minds, of like visions of the world, from different identity groups." Participants discussed the need for commitments to multiple issues in equity and civil rights work that included support for LGBTQ+ individuals. Many identified partner benefits, gender neutral bathrooms, and inclusive policies and practices across academic and student affairs in higher education.

Broader equity work includes anti-racist work and one such initiative is the development of an "anti-racism" working group as part of the Consortium of Higher Education LGBT Resource Professionals (Consortium, 2013). The inclusion of an "anti-racism" working group centered issues of antiracism within the consortium and is one example of how individuals and professional entities can begin to acknowledge subordinated locations and intersectional targeted identities on college campuses and work to diversify political agendas and collective action.

## Representational Intersectionality and LGBTQ+ Populations in Higher Education

Often in higher education, faculty and staff fraction into separate spaces acknowledgements of LGBTQ+ students and Students of Color. Consider the following examples: (a) end of year recognition ceremonies that honor LGBTQ+ students (e.g., Lavender graduation) and ceremonies that honor Students of Color (e.g., Black graduation ceremony); (b) separate commissions or committees for LGBTQ+ faculty, staff, and students, and for Faculty, Staff, and Students of Color; and (c) educational programming and events (e.g., film series, speaker series) that invite individuals to discuss issues of LGBTQ+ topics or race/ethnicity and that may or may not be co-sponsored by multiple offices or student organizations. In each of these examples, the representation of a single axis of identity is emphasized. Institutional structure, campus organization, and professional practice reinforce monolithic conceptions of identity. Often targeted individuals are supported partially but never holistically. We need not abandon programs students find meaningful, however, we all can reinvest in the ways programming is conceptualized so that the complexity of intersectionality is represented on our campuses.

Lastly, consider the example of center hiring practices and the diverse populations of individuals that center directors and staff must represent. At LGBTQ+ centers, student affairs professionals and students often assume that the leadership must identify as lesbian, gay, bisexual, transgender, or queer+. Often the LGBTQ+ center leadership then becomes *the* people who represent all LGBTQ+ issues for the campus. Similarly, student affairs professionals and students assume that the leadership at a Black cultural center must identify as Black or African American. The Black leadership becomes, too, *the* people who represent all Black issues for the campus. Certainly, targeted group experiences inform practice in campus centers. We are not arguing that the recruitment and retention of LGBTQ+-identified staff and Staff Members of Color is not important; it is important. Rather, we are inviting the complexity of intersectionality that Crenshaw emphasized into our visions for leadership– a leadership that expands intersectional awareness, where potential leaders demonstrate commitments to intersectional educational programming and intersectional coalition building across co-curricular and extra-curricular engagements. Administrators and student affairs professionals need to work against monolithic representations of targeted groups, complicate understandings of how multiple systems of oppression affect students, faculty, and staff, and affirm in more holistic ways the students they serve. Examining and then choosing to incorporate specific identifiable forms of intersectionality is a place to start. Crenshaw's structural, political, and representational intersectionality are productive forms to consider. Regardless of the form that is adopted, we believe that the clearer the definitions of intersectionality are, the more likely one will find traction in its everyday applicability.

## Concluding Thoughts on Crenshaw's Intersectionality

In this chapter, we introduced brief histories of critical legal studies and critical race theory. Crenshaw's (1991a, 1991b) intersectionality stemmed from critical theory and the law, oppositional debate between neoconservatives and critical legal scholars on antidiscrimination law and equal process, the subsequent weaponization of "color-blindness" by neoconservatives as a political tool, and the CLS critique of it as a myth. Centering structures and subordinated locations as well as onto-epistemological experiences of and among Black women and Women of Color, Crenshaw reminds us to theorize carefully and tactically when we engage in racial and social justice work. Applying her concept of intersectionality means working with not only the legacies of CLS and CRT and the theoretical sophistication of political, structural, and representational intersectionality but also with the lived experiences Crenshaw and her colleagues endured as they confronted predominantly White law schools, White colleagues, and White, conventional legal scholarship. We invite readers to work with memory and care as they apply Crenshaw's work to their own.

## Notes

1 For a different interpretation of Crenshaw's emphasis on the lived experiences of women living at the intersection of multiple targeted identities see McCall (2005) and Nash (2008). For a conceptual critique of the binary position between post-structuralism and essentialism, as represented in McCall (2005) and Nash (2008), see Moi (1999).

2 In "Mapping the Margins: Intersectionality, Identity Politics, and Violence Against Women of Color," Crenshaw (1991) used "Black women and women of color" in her arguments. To maintain alignment with her original work, we do same. Although more cumbersome in some places, we have chosen to use "women" instead of "female" wherever possible to avoid a connotation that there is an essentialized construction of the body linked to hegemonic binary frames of biology and an assignment at birth.

3 We do not suggest that researchers count the number of targeted identities to evaluate the applicability of Crenshaw's work. Instead, we encourage researchers to clarify the ways that structure, through discourse and institutions, positions and targets the intersections of particular identities and to emphasize that relationship in analyses.

4 The first Critical Legal Studies Conference was held in 1977 (Crenshaw, 2002).

5  In contemporary CRT and Dis/ability CRT work, "color evasiveness" has been used as a more inclusive term. As such, we place "color-blindness" in quotations to refer to its historic deployment as a strategy by right wing, neoconservative think tanks in the 1970s (see Crenshaw, 1988).

# *References*

Abes, E. S., Jones, S. R., & McEwen, M. K. (2007). Reconceptualizing the model of multiple dimensions of identity: The role of meaning-making capacity in the construction of multiple identities. *Journal of College Student Development, 48*, 1–22.

Anders, A. D., DeVita, J. M., & Oliver, S. T. (2012). Southern predominantly White institutions, targeted students, and the intersectionality of identity: Two case studies. In C. Clark, K. J. Fasching-Varner, & M. Brimhall-Vargas (Eds.), *Occupying the academy: Just how important is diversity work in higher education?* (pp. 71–82). Lanham, MD: Rowman & Littlefield.

Bell, D. (1992). *Faces at the bottom of the well: The permanence of racism.* Basic.

Bentley Historical Library, University of Michigan. (2007, October 17). *Gay, lesbian, bisexual, and transgender collections.* http://bentley.umich.edu/research/guides/gaylesbian/

Bettie, J. (2003). *Women without class: Girls, race, and identity.* University of California Press.

Berger, M. (2004). *Workable sisterhood: The political journey of stigmatized women with HIV/AIDS.* Princeton University Press.

Butler, J. (1999). *Gender trouble: Feminism and the subversion of identity.* Routledge.

Campus Pride. (2023). *HBCU clearinghouse for LGBTQ inclusion.* https://www.campuspride.org/HBCU/

Collins, P. H. (2008). *Black feminist thought: Knowledge, consciousness, and the politics of empowerment.* Routledge.

Consortium of Higher Education LGBT Resource Professionals. (2013). http://www.lgbtcampus.org

Crenshaw, K. (1991a). De-marginalizing the intersection of race and sex: A Black feminist critique of antidiscrimination doctrine, feminist theory, and antiracist politics. In K. Bartlett & R. Kennedy (Eds.), *Feminist legal theory: Readings in law and gender* (pp. 57–80). Westview.

Crenshaw, K. (1991b). Mapping the margins: Intersectionality, identity politics, and violence against Women of Color. *Stanford Law Review, 43*, 1241–1299.

Crenshaw, K. (1988). Race, reform, and retrenchment: Transformation, and legitimation in anti-discrimination law. *Harvard Law Review, 101*(7), 1331–1387.

Crenshaw, K., Gotanda, N., Peller, G., & Thomas, K. (1995). Introduction. In K. Crenshaw, N. Gotanda, G. Peller, & K. Thomas (Eds.), *Critical race theory: The key writings that formed the movement* (pp. xiii–xxxii). The New Press.

Crenshaw, K. (2002). The first decade: Critical reflections, or foot in the closing door. *UCLA Law Review, 49*(5), 1343–1373.

Crenshaw, K. (2021, September 2). Looking back to move forward: the insurgent origins of critical race theory. (No. 39) [Audio podcast episode]. In *Intersectionality Matters with Kimberlé Crenshaw*. African American Policy Forum. https://podca sts.apple.com/us/podcast/39-the-insurgent-origins-of-critical-race-theory/id144 1348908?i=1000534153352

Dalton, H. L. (1995). The clouded prism: Minority critique of the Critical Legal Studies Movement. In K. Crenshaw, N. Gotanda, G. Peller, & K. Thomas (Eds.), *Critical race theory: The key writings that formed the movement* (pp. 80–84). The New Press.

Davis, A. Y. (1983). *Women, race and class*. Vintage Books.

Delgado, R., & Stefancic, J. (2001). *Critical race theory: An introduction*. New York University Press.

DeVita, J. M. (2010). *Gay male identity in the context of college: Implications for development, support, and campus climate* (Unpublished doctoral dissertation). University of Tennessee, Knoxville.

DeVita, J. M., & Anders, A. D. (2018). LGTQ faculty and professionals in higher education: Defining allies, identifying support. *College Student Affairs Journal, 36*(2), 63–80.

DeVita, J. M., & Anders, A. D. (2014). Intersectionality and the performances of identities: Experiences of Black gay male undergraduates at predominantly White institutions. In E. Meyer & D. Carlson (Eds.), *Gender and sexuality in education: A reader* (pp. 464–478). Peter Lang.

Freire, P. (2000). *Pedagogy of the oppressed*. Bloomsbury.

Gramsci, A. (1992). *Prison notebooks*. Columbia University Press.

hooks, b. (1992). *Black looks: Race and representation*. South End.

Human Rights Campaign Staff. (2013, October 3). Fayetteville State University becomes third Historically Black College to open LGBT resource center. *HRC Blog*. http://www.hrc.org/blog/entry/fayetteville-state-university-becomes-third-historically-black-college-to-o

Kairys, D. (1998). Introduction. In D. Kairys (3rd ed.). *The politics of law: A progressive critique* (pp. 1–20). Basic.

Lawrence, C. R. III. (1992). The word and the river: Pedagogy as scholarship as struggle. *California Law Review, 65*, 2231–2298.

Lorde, A. (1984). *Sister outsider: Essays and speeches by Audre Lorde*. The Crossing Press.

McCall, L. (2005). The complexity of intersectionality. *Signs, 30*, 1771–1800.

Mitchell, D., Jr., & Means, D. R. (2014). "Quadruple consciousness": A literature review and new theoretical consideration for understanding the experiences of Black gay and bisexual college men at predominantly White institutions. *Journal of African American Males in Education, 5*, 1–13.

Moi, T. (1999). *What is a woman? And other essays*. Oxford University Press.

Nash, J. C. (2008). Re-thinking intersectionality. *Feminist Review, 89*, 1–15.

Patel, L. (2013). *Youth held at the border: Immigration, education, and the politics of inclusion.* Teachers College Press.

Postsecondary National Policy Institute. (2022, November). *LGBTQ+ students in higher education.* https://pnpi.org/wp-content/uploads/2023/06/LGBTQStudentsFactSheet-Nov-2022.pdf

Raj, R., Bunch, C., & Nazombe, E. (2002). *Women at the intersection: Indivisible rights, identities, and oppressions.* Rutgers, the State University of New Jersey, Center for Women's Global Leadership.

Strayhorn, T. L., Blakewood, A. M., & DeVita, J. M. (2008). Factors affecting the college choice of African American gay male undergraduates: Implications for retention. *NASAP Journal, 11,* 88–108.

Strayhorn, T. L., Blakewood, A. M., & DeVita, J. M. (2010). Triple threat: Challenges and supports of Black gay men at predominantly White campuses. In T. L. Strayhorn & M. C. Terrell (Eds.), *The experiences of black college students: Enduring challenges, necessary supports* (pp. 111–134). Stylus.

Teunis, N. (2007). Sexual objectification and the construction of whiteness in the gay male community. *Culture, Health, & Sexuality, 9,* 263–275.

Thompson, A. (2003). Tiffany, friend of People of Color: White investments in anti-racism. *Qualitative Studies in Education, 16,* 7–29.

Ward, J. (2008). White normativity: The cultural dimensions of whiteness in a racially diverse LGBT organization. *Sociological Perspectives, 51,* 563–586.

# 3. *Intersectional Embodiments in Higher Education*

BRIANNA R. RAMIREZ

Situated within Women of Color feminist traditions, this chapter re-centers the racialized *body* (Cruz, 2001; Dillard, 2000; Moraga & Anzaldúa, 1983) in intersectionality (Crenshaw, 1991) to advance an intersectional embodiments perspective in higher education. This theoretical consideration draws from the experiences and narratives of Chicana/Latina undergraduates who are first-generation college students from mixed-status immigrant families navigating a predominately White higher education context. The purpose of this chapter is to consider how intersecting systems of marginality construct and target the bodies of Chicana/Latinas within higher education, a U.S. institution that is rooted and continues to uphold histories and contemporaries of colonialism, White supremacy, and heteropatriarchy (Wilder, 2013). This chapter aims to center the body within intersectionality (Crenshaw, 1991) to consider how a theory of the flesh epistemological approach (Moraga & Anzaldúa, 1983) can advance an embodied intersectionality framework that makes visible how the body is the material site and target of intersecting oppressive ideologies and systems.

## *Intersectionality*

The Combahee River Collective (1983) argued the importance of recognizing the "interlocking" and "simultaneous" oppressions that Black women experience in U.S. society (p. 20). With the intent of challenging the "single-axis framework" (Crenshaw, 1989, p. 140) within anti-racist and feminist scholarship that distorts and erases Black women's experiences, Black feminist scholar and critical race legal scholar, Kimberlé Crenshaw (1989), coined intersectionality to argue the importance of drawing from a framework that understands how racism and sexism, converging systems of oppression, shape and underlie the lives of Black women in the United States (U.S.). Crenshaw (1989) argues how intersectionality attends to the "complexities of compoundness" (p. 167) of marginality in the lives of Black women and Women of Color (Crenshaw, 1991). Application of Crenshaw's theorization of intersectionality supports attending to the structural and institutionalized violence against Black women and Women of Color in the U.S.

## Centering the Body in Intersectionality

To expand Crenshaw's theorization of intersectionality that attends to how racism and systems of marginality underlie the lives of Women of Color, we should consider how the *body* is central to experiences of marginalization. Women of Color feminist scholars have centered the body as a site through which one experiences marginality, as systems of marginality act upon and against particular bodies (Cruz, 2001; Dillard, 2000; Moraga & Anzaldúa, 1983). Scholars agree that categories used to classify people are socially constructed, such that race is a socially constructed category and racism is the denial and allocation of power to socially constructed racial groups (Omi & Winant, 1994; Haney-Lopez, 2000; Solórzano & Yosso, 2002). The construction of bodies within particular categories is therefore one way in which systems of marginality act upon bodies as they function to assign, categorize, and mark people by socially designed labels and identities. The social construction of identity and how one understands and reconstructs the *self* is inherently fluid and contextual (Urrieta, 2007). Though socially constructed, race and racism and other systems of marginality shapes the everyday lives of people, as dominance, privilege, and hierarchy of power are tied and upheld by these systems.

Chicana/Latina feminist scholars offer theory of the flesh (Moraga & Anzaldúa, 1983), as an epistemological perspective that is intended to support the centering of the body as the site through which one is constructed and marked by ideologies and systems of oppression. Moraga & Anzaldúa (1983) situate a theory in the flesh:

> where the *physical realities of our lives*—our skin color, the land or concrete we grew up on, our sexual longings—*all fuse* to create a *politic born out of necessity.* Here, we attempt to bridge the contradictions in our experience:
> We are the colored in a white feminist movement.
> We are the feminists among the people of our culture.
> We are often the lesbians among the straight

We do this bridging by naming ourselves and by telling our stories in our own words [emphasis added]. (p. 19)

Theory in the flesh is situated where the realities of the lives of Women of Color *all fuse*, at the intersection of their experiences within systems of marginality they navigate everyday (Pitts et al., 2020). Theory of the flesh centers the body as the "material site" on which Women of Color experience intersecting marginalities they navigate and negotiate every day (Cervantes-Soon, 2014, p. 98). Centering the body as the site of marginalization considers how the body is treated in society because of the systems of oppression that delineate power and privilege to how particular bodies are constructed. Theory of the flesh locates the body as the site through which intersectionality is produced and experienced, where systems of marginality, *all fuse*, to produce "a politic born out of necessity" (Moraga & Anzaldúa, 1983, p. 19).

In considering the body as the site of marginalization through socially constructed systems and categorizations, also situates the body as the site of knowledge production, agency and resistance. Dillard's (2000) endarkened epistemologies considers the knowledge production and resistance of African American women that exists at the intersection and overlap of socially constructed identities and systems of oppressions. In that, the site of knowledge construction and resistance is through the bodies of African American women that are constructed as inferior by multiple systems of marginality in U.S. society. Similarly, Cruz (2001) argues that the Brown body is a site of agency that is central in creating new knowledge from the multiple and contradictory intersectional identities and locations. Acknowledging the Brown body as the site of knowledge construction, recognizes the power and legitimacy of the lived experiences, histories, and futurities of Women of Color (Cruz, 2001). Chicana/Latina feminists have theorized about the fragmentation that occurs to the bodymindspirit of Chicana/Latinas (Moraga & Anzaldúa, 1983) in higher education and U.S. society (Delgado Bernal et al., 2006), as Chicana/Latinas navigate intersectional forms of structural violence. Theorizing the connection of the body to the mind and spirit, and fragmentation as a form of structural and spiritual violence, recognizes that the attack on the body also causes harm to the mind and spirit, which are connected and one (Anzaldúa, 2002). By considering theory of the flesh, this chapter re-centers the body within intersectionality, to understand that it is how bodies are understood, constructed, and marked by intersectional systems of oppression that shape how particular bodies are treated, harmed, and experience and navigate intersectional forms of marginalization in higher education contexts.

## Chicana/Latina Undergraduates in Higher Education

Latinx students are a rapidly growing population in U.S. colleges and universities. In California, where 40% of residents and more than half of K-12 students are Latinx, 4 in 10 undergraduate students are Latinx. Chicana/Latinas specifically make up more than half of all Latinx undergraduate students (Campaign for College Opportunity, 2021). As a historically underrepresented population in U.S. higher education, Chicana/Latina s face various challenges to complete their college education and have some of the lowest college completion rates of all women (Gandara, 2015). In the past decade, there has been an increase in college enrollment rates for Latinx students, yet Latinx college students continue to face inequitable access to Research 1 (R1) institutions (Campaign for College Opportunity, 2021) and continue to experience the racist, colonial, heteropatriarchal roots and contemporaries of the university (Wilder, 2013).

The college experiences of Chicana/Latina undergraduates are underlined by larger systems of marginality that are present in U.S. society and institutions of higher education. These include racist and sexist microaggressions (McCabe, 2009), discriminatory financial aid policies and practices (Muñoz, 2013), perpetual lack of belonging and outsider status (Muñoz & Maldonado, 2012), and the pathologization of the Latina immigrant bodies (Pérez Huber, 2010). Marginality is experienced by Chicana/Latina students across the university spaces and contexts such as academic affairs, academic advising, student engagement, residence halls, and lecture halls (McCabe, 2009). Studies have found that Chicana/Latina s navigate higher education with multiple and sometimes conflicting roles and responsibilities as college students and members of their families (Sy & Romero, 2008; Espinoza, 2010). Often, Chicana/Latinas navigate cultural clashes between their ways of knowing and navigating and the whiteness of the institution (Delgado Bernal, 2002).

## Theorizing through Chicana/Latina Undergraduate Embodiments

To advance an understanding of how intersectionality is embodied through the everyday experiences of Chicana/Latina students in higher education, this chapter centers and attends to how the bodies of Chicana/Latina undergraduates are understood, marked, and treated within institutions of higher education that uphold histories and contemporaries of colonialism, white supremacy, and heteropatriarchy (Wilder, 2013). Cruz (2001) argues that understanding the regulation of the Brown body within educational contexts and systems is necessary for radical transformation and liberation. Within this spirit of intersectional liberation and justice, this chapter centers the body to advance an embodied intersectionality theorization of Chicana/Latina undergraduate experience at a predominately White institution. The theoretical offering in this chapter is co-constructed through and from the bodies of Chicana/Latina undergraduates and possible because of previous production of knowledge that began in the bodies of Black women and Women of Color.

The theoretical offering in this chapter is rooted in a larger study that centers the embodied experience and navigation of 15 Chicana/Latina undergraduates at a predominately White institution in southern California. Their higher education experiences were captured through Chicana/Latina feminista pláticas methodology (Fierros & Delgado Bernal, 2016) rooted in Chicana/Latina feminist epistemologies (Delgado Bernal, 1998). A *plática* is an everyday, fluid conversation between at least two people that "grew up pláticando" (Delgado Bernal, 1998, p. 98) and are marked by race, culture, language, class, and intersecting socially constructed identities and systems. Pláticas provide space for a fluid discussion, welcoming collaborators to bring their whole selves, histories, and experiences to data collection (Fierros & Delgado Bernal, 2016). Rooted in Chicana/Latina feminist epistemologies, this methodology recognizes and is intentional about centering the embodied everyday experience as site of knowledge construction. As a research methodology, pláticas is intended to challenge the Eurocentric perspective that research must be neutral and unbiased (Delgado Bernal & Villalpando, 2002).

Chicana/Latina undergraduates engaged in this study on a voluntary basis. The purposeful sampling (Creswell, 2012) of Chicana/Latina students at an R1 in California supported the selection of people with similar characteristics or identities that can best help to understand a phenomenon (Creswell, 2012). Students who agreed to participate engaged in three individual pláticas and two group pláticas. The pláticas were intended to explore how Chicana/Latina undergraduates experience their transition to a PWI context. The pláticas attended to how intersectional marginalized identities and structures underlie their experience.

The pláticantes are first-generation college students who emigrated to the United States as children or are daughters of immigrants, and who grew up in low-income and under resourced schooling contexts and communities. Five students identified as queer and two are undocumented. Students ranged in their majors, with five in the natural sciences, seven in the social sciences, and three in the applied sciences. The pláticas were analyzed through open-ended and thematic coding (Saldaña, 2014) to identify key patterns that emerged within and across student experience. As a Chicana researcher engaging in this theorization through the embodied knowledge of Chicana/Latina undergraduates, I recognize how my own body shapes this chapter and my research. As the oldest daughter of Mexican immigrants, my experiences and navigation of U.S. society and those of my family, are central to shaping how my body, and those of my family and community, has been and continue to be treated and marked as outsiders within U.S. society and institutions. These embodied and intersectional experiences of marginality in K-12 and higher education have led me to question the function of educational institutions and systems, recognizing how power continues to be exerted against my body in these spaces, and the bodies of Black, Indigenous, Students of Color historically and in the contemporary. Delgado Bernal (1998) argues that a Chicana researcher's cultural intuition, that is personal experience, existing literature, professional experience, and analytical research process shape how Chicana researchers engage in knowledge construction. I engage in this research with the intent of centering the embodiments and experiences of Chicanas/Latinas and Women of Color who are historically marginalized and excluded within higher education contexts and U.S. society. As Cruz (2001) argues that through scholarship, Chicana education researchers can engage in a "project of reclamation" (p. 622) that involves reclaiming, recovering and recentering the historical and contemporary narratives that are derived from exposing how systems of oppression function and invalidate the narratives and experiences of folks who are marginalized.

## *Intersectional Embodiments of Chicana/Latina Undergraduates*

This section advances the argument for centering the body in intersectional analysis through considering the experiences of Chicana/Latina undergraduates in a research-intensive PWI. Centering the body in intersectionality supports an understanding of how Chicana/Latina bodies are constructed as intersectional outsiders, or atravesadas (Anzaldúa, 1987), within higher education. It is the physical bodies of Chicana/Latina undergraduates, that are othered or marked as deviant because of how intersecting forms of marginality are upheld within these institutions. In the pláticas, students highlighted how their racialized, gendered, sexualized physical bodies were perpetually constructed in contradiction and contestation to the norm at their institution.

Jacqueline shared how she experiences higher education through how her body is perceived and understood within spaces on campus:

Once school started, my roommates in my first year, one was Latina, her name was Miriam, she was like tall, pale skin, blondish hair, greenish eyes. And the other roommate, Amina, also had pale skin, she's Asian. My other roommate was from South Africa, she was White. And so, in my head, I was like, I don't even know what to expect living with these people. So often I was in my room by myself and them (her roommates) were like, laughing it up and stuff like that. And I was in my room crying. I was like, Oh, my God, like, this just *feels so weird*. Because even the week we were moving in and like, I would see, like, all these different kids, and they're like, they're all White or Asian. And *I'm not*. I'm like, *chubby. I get really tan in summer, like a lot more tan than my usual color*. So I was there with my little *Brown* arms, and *I look nothing like these people*. I'm also 5'1" or maybe 5' 2" on a good day, so I *was just feeling like I'm just the short queer Brown women here* [emphasis added].

Jaqueline experiences and understands her dorming, housing, and overall experience in higher education through her body. She says, "I look nothing like these people" as she reflects on how her physical body is *different* from the bodies of the majority of students at her institution. Jacqueline names how her body is constructed by skin color, height, size, gender, and sexual identity within society and higher education. She does not see her body reflected among the bodies of students around her, who are White and Asian, and who make up the majority of the student enrollment at her institution. In considering how systems of marginality produce and uphold socially constructed identities and withhold power to people with marginalized identities, Jacqueline points to her body as the site through which she is racialized, gendered, and constructed as different from the norm within these institutions. She also makes visible that shared identities with her roommate, Miriam, who is also a Latina woman, does not mean their experience will be the same in higher education as Jacqueline is also constructed as brown, short, and queer in this U.S. society and in this institution. Centering the body in intersectional analysis supports making evident these nuances, differences, and contradictions among and between Chicana/Latina students.

It is through the body that we can also make visible how the construction and experience of difference are underlined and produced by intersecting systems of marginality that construct and marginalize the *short queer Brown women* body in U.S. society. We see through Jacqueline's experience that the *short queer Brown women* body is constructed as deviant within higher education through the lack of representation and connection to other bodies around her within these institutions. Intersectional difference is therefore produced and upheld in higher education institutions through how student bodies are constructed.

Jacqueline supports us in understanding how construction of bodies as different is underlined by intersectional systems of marginality. Centering the body in intersectional analysis elicits an understanding of how the body that is constructed as different from the norm in higher education, is also othered and acted against within these spaces. Women of Color argue that the body is the material site through which one experiences intersectional systems of marginality (Moraga & Anzaldúa, 1983). The Chicana/Latina undergraduates shared how they are presumed and treated as incompetent because of their racialized, gendered, and sexualized bodies.

Maria described her experience within a biological science major and courses:

> I feel like I always have imposter syndrome going into my classes, like *I'm not meant to be here*, especially STEM or bio courses. I want to be a doctor so I'm taking many bio courses and mostly other students in my classes also want to be doctors. I was in a class where the first day the professor tells us to look to our right and our left and see who is next to us because it's probably going to happen that about half of us won't make it through this class. The professor actually said that. And I thought to myself, *people here probably assume that because I'm Latina or because I have an accent, I'm gonna be one of the students who doesn't make it*. And I know this because whenever we have to do group work or check our answers with a partner in class, the professor will tell us to ask our neighbor or whatever, you know, *no one ever wants to work with me*. I have to ask first. Now I don't even know if I should ask because I swear, I've had people act like they didn't hear me when they are really ignoring me. So that feeling is always with me. And the people in my study group now are not mostly Latino because there are not many of us in those classes.

Maria's body is marked by racism, sexism, and nativism, as she is constructed as a Latina immigrant woman, and therefore outsider, within higher education and U.S. society. Maria's experience importantly highlights how her body is read and understood through these intersecting systems makes visible how power functions against her in heightened ways in particular hypercompetitive spaces on campus and in classes and programs where Latinx students and Women of Color are underrepresented. Maria mentions how her accent as a Mexican immigrant to the U.S. also shapes how she is constructed as one of the students who is presumed to not have the capacity to succeed in the course. Furthermore, considering the body in intersectionality uncovers how it is through the body that intersectional systems of oppression are upheld and reproduced since it is through the body that multiple marginalities are simultaneously experienced and result in the creation of a "new politic born out of necessity" (Moraga & Anzaldúa, 1983, p. 19). In this case, Maria's speech, accent, and ways of communicating, are used to further construct her as a foreigner or outsider in the U.S. and higher education through racist nativist assumptions (Pérez Huber et al., 2008). Centering the body can facilitate the uncovering and functioning of compounding and multiple oppressions that underlie the lives of Chicana/Latina undergraduates, which produce new forms of marginality at these intersections (Crenshaw, 1989).

Stemming from how bodies are constructed and treated in U.S. society and in higher education, impacts not just the bodies, but also the minds and spirits of students. As these experiences shape how students see and understand themselves within these contexts. We saw how Jacqueline described feeling "weird" as her physical body marked by race, ethnicity, gender, height, and body size in the university constructed her body as deviant from normative bodies in the institution. Maria also names experiencing "imposter syndrome" as she describes feeling that she does not belong and is presumed incompetent in biological sciences and STEM courses. In the pláticas, the Chicana/Latina undergraduates also shared feeling "crazy" and "weird" in the university. These feelings were tied to the intersecting systems that shaped how they experienced the university.

In the series of individual pláticas, Alex shared about experiencing higher education as the daughter of Mexican immigrants from a low-income community. Alex described:

> People know you are poor, you know? They assume all Mexicans are poor, and in my case, they are right. But they think they can just tell or assume *by looking at you*, what you wear, the shoes you have on, even my laptop isn't a Mac like everyone else here because I couldn't afford to get one. So when I walk into my classes and everyone has the newest clothes on, or carrying around the newest piece of tech, *I know that I am different, and I know they know that I'm different too.*

Alex recognizes how her body is marked as "poor" in a PWI context because she is Mexican and because of how her body shows up in this context, including the types of clothes she wears and the technology she carries with her in these spaces. Alex supports us in understanding how her body is marked by racism and classism within her navigation of higher education. She importantly points out how particular material items, such as clothes or technology, are in proximity with her body and used to uphold stereotypes and normative constructions of who is assumed to be low-income and what a low-income person physically looks like. In the pláticas, Alex continued in sharing how her conception of self is shaped by these experiences:

> I feel like I've noticed that it's so easy to feel like you're alone basically, like there's so many things that we kind of think about in our heads and I don't

know why it's so easy to think that you're the only one that's ever like going through what you're going through. Like *it makes you feel like you are crazy.* But here we see and learn that there are people like you, going through similar things, and it's a good reminder like you are doing fine, you are not alone, we learn that *there are people like you here and these people are going through similar things as you.*

Alex describes the feeling of isolation that she experiences in higher education and the toll this isolation takes on her mental, emotional, and social wellbeing, to the point that "you feel like you are crazy." This state of "feeling crazy" was described by many students and reflects the disruption, confusion, and complete disidentification students experience within the university. Alex is attending a university with students who are predominately White, cis male, middle-upper class income. She is surrounded by bodies that do not look or present like hers, and the feeling of being "the only one" impacts how she experiences, understands, and feels in these contexts. The White, colonial, heteropatriarchal ideologies within the university context often led students to situate the source of their experiences with marginality within the mujeres' own minds and bodies, leading students to feel that they were the problem, or it was them misinterpreting how they felt and experienced the university.

In considering intersectionality and the body, supports us in understanding how students' conception of self and wellbeing are harmed by how their bodies are constructed and treated in higher education. Centering the body within intersectional analysis makes visible that the harm to students who are racialized and marginalized in higher education, stems from how their bodies are constructed and treated as outsiders in the university. Centering the body is not intended to fragment or disassociate the body from the mind and spirit. Instead, centering the body in intersectionality can support locating the experiences, harm, and fragmentation of the bodymindspirit (Anzaldúa, 2002) in higher education to how particular bodies are constructed, marked, and treated by intersecting systems of marginality in these contexts. Therefore, the minds and spirits of particular bodies are harmed, attacked, and threatened by ideologies and systems of marginality because of how systems of marginality construct and deny power to bodies marked as outsiders, deviant, and imposter.

## *Towards Embodied Intersectionality Approach*

Through a theory of the flesh epistemological approach within intersectional analysis, this chapter argues how centering the body within intersectionality supports identifying *how* intersecting systems of marginality function against

Chicana/Latina undergraduates in higher education. This chapter advances the importance of centering the body within intersectional analysis to make visible how multiple systems of marginality act upon and against Chicana/Latina undergraduates. An embodied intersectionality approach centers how the systemic, structural, and ideological produce, uphold, and underlie student experience within higher education. This approach demonstrates how systems of marginality mark, assign, and situate student bodies within hierarchies of power that are upheld, reproduced, and constructed in particular ways within institutions of higher education. This supports an uncovering of intersectionality, in that the body does not experience marginality through multiple yet single-categorical axis (Crenshaw, 1989), but instead as a convergence of axes of marginality within, through, and against the body, that results in the emergence of new forms of marginality at the intersection of existing systems and in particular contexts.

Embodied intersectionality argues that institutions of higher education do not just uphold and reproduce systems of marginality in U.S. society, they also produce and create how these systems act upon and against racialized students through student bodies in these contexts. This approach to intersectionality also recognizes how the minds and spirits of particular bodies are harmed, attacked, and threatened by ideologies and systems of marginality because of how systems of marginality construct and deny power to bodies marked as outsiders, deviant, and imposter. Understanding how particular bodies experience higher education contexts through an embodied intersectionality lens is supportive of recognizing how power is exerted against and on students' bodies in these institutions and how institutions uphold and produce marginality. This theorization can facilitate higher education policy, infrastructures, and programming that are student intersectional embodiments centered, and consider an anti-racist, intersectional, embodied approach to serving students, including their bodies, minds, and spirits within higher education.

## References

Anzaldúa, G. (1987). *Borderlands/La Frontera*. Aunt Lute Books.

Anzaldúa, G. (2002). Now let us shift... the path of conocimiento... inner work, public acts. In G. E. Anzaldúa & A. Keating (Eds.), *This bridge we call home: Radical visions for transformation* (pp. 540–579). Routledge.

Cervantes-Soon, C. (2014). The US-Mexico border-crossing Chicana researcher: Theory in the flesh and the politics of identity in critical ethnography. *Journal of Latino/Latin American Studies, 6*(2), 97–112.

Combahee River Collective. (1983). The Combahee River Collective statement. In B. Smith (Ed.), *Home girls: A Black feminist anthology* (pp. 264–274). Kitchen Table: Women of Color Press.

Crenshaw, K. (1989). Demarginalizing the intersection of race and sex: A Black feminist critique of antidiscrimination doctrine, feminist theory, and antiracist politics. *University of Chicago Legal Forum, 1989*(8), 139–167.

Crenshaw, K. (1991). Mapping the margins: Intersectionality, identity politics, and violence against Women of Color. *Stanford Law Review, 43*(6), 1241–1299.

Creswell, J. W. (2012). *Educational research: planning, conducting, and evaluating.* Pearson.

Cruz, C. (2001). Toward an epistemology of a Brown body. *International Journal of Qualitative Studies in Education, 14*(5), 657–669.

Delgado Bernal, D. (1998). Using a Chicana feminist epistemology in educational research. *Harvard Educational Review, 68*(4), 555–583.

Delgado Bernal, D. (2002). Learning and living pedagogies of the home: The mestiza consciousness of Chicana students. *International Journal of Qualitative Studies in Education, 14*(5), 623–639.

Delgado Bernal, D., Elenes, C. A., Godinez, F. E., & Villenas, S. (Eds.). (2006). *Chicana/Latina education in everyday life: Feminista perspectives on pedagogy and epistemology.* State University of New York Press.

Delgado Bernal, D., & Villalpando, O. (2002). An apartheid of knowledge in academia: The struggle over the "legitimate" knowledge of Faculty of Color. *Equity & Excellence in Education, 35*(2), 169–180.

Dillard, C. B. (2000). The substance of things hoped for, the evidence of things not seen: Examining an endarkened feminist epistemology in educational research and leadership. *International Journal of Qualitative Studies in Education, 13*(6), 661–681.

Fierros, C. O., & Delgado Bernal, D. (2016). Vamos a platicar: The contours of pláticas as Chicana/Latina feminist methodology. *Chicana/Latina Studies,* 98–121.

Gándara, P. (2015). *Fulfilling America's future: Latinas in the U.S., 2015.* The Civil Rights Project and The White House Initiative on Educational Excellence for Hispanics.

Haney-López, I. F. (2000). Institutional racism: Judicial conduct and a new theory of racial discrimination. *Yale Law Journal, 109*(8), 1717–1884.

McCabe, J. (2009). Racial and gender microaggressions on a predominantly White campus: Experiences of Black, Latina/o, and White undergraduates. *Race, Gender & Class,* 133–151.

Moraga, C., & Anzaldúa, G. (Eds.). (1983). *This bridge called my back: Writings by radical Women of Color.* State University of New York Press.

Muñoz, S. M. (2013). "I just can't stand being like this anymore": Dilemmas, stressors, and motivators for undocumented Mexican women in higher education. *Journal of Student Affairs Research and Practice, 50*(3), 233–249.

Muñoz, S. M., & Maldonado, M. M. (2012). Counterstories of college persistence by undocumented Mexicana students: Navigating race, class, gender, and legal status. *International Journal of Qualitative Studies in Education, 25*(3), 293–315.

Omi, M., & Winant, H. (1994). *Racial formation in the United States: From the 1960s to the 1990s* (2nd ed.). Routledge.

Pérez Huber, L. (2010). Using Latina/o critical race theory (LatCrit) and racist nativism to explore intersectionality in the educational experiences of undocumented Chicana college students. *Educational Foundations, 24,* 77–96.

Pérez Huber, L., Lopez, C. B., Malagón, M. C., Velez, V., & Solórzano, D. G. (2008). Getting beyond the 'symptom,' acknowledging the 'disease': Theorizing racist nativism. *Contemporary Justice Review, 11*(1), 39–51.

Pitts, A. J., Ortega, M., & Medina, J. (Eds.). (2020). *Theories of the flesh: Latinx and Latin American feminisms, transformation, and resistance.* Oxford University Press.

Saldaña, J. (2014). Coding and analysis strategies. In P. Leavy (Ed.), *The Oxford handbook of qualitative research* (pp. 581–598). Oxford University Press.

Solórzano, D. G., & Yosso, T. J. (2002). Critical race methodology: Counter-storytelling as an analytical framework for education research. *Qualitative Inquiry, 8*(1), 23–44.

Sy, S. R., & Romero, J. (2008). Family responsibilities among Latina college students from immigrant families. *Journal of Hispanic Higher Education, 7*(3), 212–227.

Urrieta, L. (2007). Figured worlds and education: An introduction to the special issue. *The Urban Review, 39,* 107–116.

Wilder, C. S. (2013). *Ebony and ivy: Race, slavery, and the troubled history of America's universities.* Bloomsbury.

# 4. *Living Liminal: Conceptualizing Liminality for Undocumented Students of Color*

Rose Ann E. Gutierrez

Theoretical frameworks and conceptual models provide a frame to view, understand, and interpret the world. Frames, however, are filtered realities based on exposure to varying social and cultural contexts (Goffman, 1974). As such, frames are social constructs that influence how people communicate their perceived or imagined realities. What if society does not have a frame to understand—better yet, *recognize* a fundamental reality—that exists regarding a specific student population within higher education institutions? This has been the case for undocumented students in higher education who have been living in the shadows until former President Barack Obama passed Deferred Action for Childhood Arrivals (DACA) in 2012 that provided a renewable two-year period of deferred action from deportation while also being able to apply for a work permit in the United States (Suárez-Orozco et al., 2011; Teranishi et al., 2015). Prior to DACA, the United States did not have a policy for undocumented individuals that made them feel unapologetic and unafraid to come out of the shadows. Policies such as DACA influenced a set of emerging research on the educational experiences of undocumented students beyond high school. Society, however, still possesses limited frames in understanding the nuanced experiences compounded by the layers of oppression that manifest in the daily realities for undocumented students in higher education.

Intersectionality, presented by Kimberlé Crenshaw (2016), acknowledges, examines, and dissects the intersecting layers of oppression that Black women face that have "slipped through [our societal] consciousness because there are no frames for us to see them." Crenshaw posits intersectionality to be used as a frame "[acknowledging] the ways multiple social realities, structured by the dominant norms and values of institutions, converge to produce distinct, overlapping moments and experiences of disadvantages that are often rendered invisible by the majority" (as cited in Nguyen & Nguyen, 2018, p. 150). This chapter uses intersectionality as an analytical tool to conceive the overlapping and intersecting layers of oppression, subordination, and subjugation of undocumented Students of Color in higher education. I intentionally capitalize Students of Color, Immigrants of Color, and People of Color to challenge and reject conventional grammatical norms and reclaim this population's sense of identity, knowledge, and agency. Within overlapping systems of oppression, I explore and conceptualize liminality and its positive, unintended consequences for these students.

This chapter focuses on how racism, nativism, and xenophobia manifest in the daily realities of undocumented Students of Color. I recognize that undocumented students who may not racially identify as White but phenotypically pass off as White—thus receiving advantages of whiteness (Harris, 1993)—have challenges as well due to their undocumented status. My focus, however, is on Students of Color due to the layer of racism and racist nativism these students experience because of the historical social construction of race (Omi & Winant, 2015) in the United States. Immigrants of Color experience heightened anti-immigrant sentiments as immigrants and systemic racism as People of Color. These racist, nativist, and xenophobic attitudes are covertly expressed in practices and policies. Moreover, this chapter contributes to a sociocultural frame—offering an additional lens to conceptualize liminality—that expands an understanding of a population rendered invisible and oppressed by social structures. Overall, this conceptual model can untangle a complex social phenomenon like immigration, so researchers better understand educational trajectories and outcomes of undocumented youth.

This chapter is organized into four sections: (1) defining intersectionality and adapting its methodological approach within the context of developing this conceptual model; (2) providing an overview of the literature on liminality in social sciences and educational research; (3) introducing a conceptual model in examining race, nativism, and xenophobia in the liminal status of undocumented Students of Color and; (4) discussing implications for future research in higher education.

## Defining and Adapting Intersectionality

Intersectionality has foundational roots in Black feminist thought and pedagogy (Collins, 2009; Crenshaw, 1989). The concept provides a reference frame to examine overlapping forms of oppression and marginalization that is not captured from a single-axis analysis. Although I discuss the identities of undocumented Students of Color regarding their race, ethnicity, immigrant identity, and citizenship status, intersectionality is not to be a "totalizing theory of identity" (Crenshaw, 1993, p. 1244). In other words, the theory is not about adding identities and comprehensively naming it intersectionality but rather dissecting the overlaps and intersections of social categories that shape the life experiences of individuals (Núñez, 2014). Nguyen and Nguyen (2018) clarify how a single category conceals "institutional structure and culture" and these "[byproducts] of multiple social dominance" (p. 159). I adapt intersectionality to be used as an analytical tool to examine "the intersection of salient socially constructed identities and the extent to which individuals or groups are oppressed or marginalized as a result of interlocking, socially constructed systems of oppression associated with those identities" (Mitchell, 2014, para. 2).

I use Mitchell (2014), Núñez (2014), and Nguyen and Nguyen's (2018) analytical application of intersectionality in research to examine racism, nativism, and xenophobia for undocumented Students of Color as they experience liminal status. Intersectionality becomes a frame to acknowledge multiple social realities and overlapping, interlocking systems of oppression (Nguyen & Nguyen, 2018; Núñez, 2014) constructed by "dominant norms and values of institutions" (Nguyen & Nguyen, 2018, p. 150) to reproduce racial and social hierarchies. While enduring a state of liminality, this conceptual model argues for an asset-based reconceptualization of an ambiguous transitional and perpetual state of being solely negative. Although interlocking systems of oppression in combination with socially constructed categories have real and imagined consequences for undocumented Students of Color, these students, in their liminal status, develop ways of surviving and thriving in the midst of heightened anti-immigrant sentiments and public discourse (Muñoz & Espino, 2017; Muñoz & Maldonado, 2012).

## Liminality in Literature

Victor Turner (1969) initially conceptualized a *liminal space* as "neither here nor there; [people] are betwixt and between the positions assigned and arrayed by law, custom, convention, and ceremony" (p. 95). As such, liminality is a state of being in between worlds, spaces, and experiences which are often ambiguously defined. Ybema et al. (2011) expanded on Turner's premise by operationalizing liminality in two social contexts: (1) transitional liminality and (2) perpetual liminality. *Transitional liminality* refers to a transformational change from one identity to another. *Perpetual liminality* refers to an individual experiencing in-between occupying two identities for a prolonged time.

Due to *Plyler v. Doe* in 1982, the U.S. Supreme Court decided that K-12 public education cannot deny students access to education based on their immigration status. The court's decision has consequentially socialized undocumented students to be included socially, culturally, political, and legally. Essentially, undocumented students are U.S. citizens in heart and mind (Pérez, 2012). Students' legal inclusion, however, changes when students transition into adulthood at 18 years old (*transitional liminality*) and decide to pursue higher education. Policies and practices, specifically financial aid regulations contribute to inaccessibility and limited opportunities in higher education for undocumented students. Undocumented young adults reconcile with (social and cultural) inclusion and (political and legal) exclusion (Gonzales, 2016). As a result, they experience *perpetual liminality* in a continuous flux of belonging and not belonging (Menjívar, 2006). This proposed conceptual model aims to explore the liminal space—an in-between (Beech, 2011; Menjívar, 2006; Turner, 1969), ambiguous space where the intersection of salient socially constructed identities collides and how interlocking oppressive structures result in further marginalization of these groups (Mitchell, 2014).

Educational researchers have used the term liminality or liminal status to refer to an ambiguous transitional state for undocumented students (e.g., see Gonzales, 2016; Gonzales & Burciaga, 2018; Pérez, 2012; Suárez-Orozco et al., 2011; Teranishi et al., 2015; Torres & Wicks-Asbun, 2014). For undocumented students enrolled in higher education, liminality shows up in two ways: (1) educational institutions serving as a liminal, transitory state until they graduate and (2) their status as an undocumented student due to the ambiguity of their liminal identity. Liminality cannot be limited to solely referencing social identities and processes of transition. For undocumented Students of Color, liminality exposes interlocking systems of oppression they experience in higher education institutions that shape their life trajectory.

## Discovering Light within Dark, Compounded Forms of Oppression through Liminality

Undocumented Students of Color are at the epicenter of this discussion due to their distinct ways in experiencing overlapping layers of oppression through racialization, criminalization, and dehumanization in public discourse. Intersectionality (Crenshaw, 1989, 1991) provides a tool to analyze their intersections that can unveil hidden mechanisms operating in the reproduction of inequities in society. An intersectional lens clarifies what has intentionally been obscured by those in power who want to stay in power. This proposed model recognizes the interlocking systems of oppression based on nativist, racist, and xenophobic ideologies which have material consequences that insidiously discriminate through institutional policies and practices. I draw on Pérez Huber and colleagues' (2008) theoretical framework on racist nativism, Kim and Sundstrom's (2014) conceptual analysis on xenophobia and racism, and Higham's (1955) work in nativism in conjunction with Sundstrom's (2013) philosophical analysis of xenophobia. While important to distinguish the differences between racism, nativism, and xenophobia, they cannot be understood in isolation (Kim & Sundstrom, 2014). At the intersection of their work is a frame to examine how xenophobia is rooted in racist nativist sentiments and disguises racism, anti-Black discourse, and Islamophobia through nationalism. Race is entangled and at the epicenter of this tripartite overlap due to its social construction in the United States.

Higham (1955) defines nativism as an "intense opposition to an internal minority on the grounds of its foreign connection" and "influence originating abroad threaten[s] the very life of the nation from within" (p. 4). Golash-Boza (2015) defines racism as having two parts: an ideology and its practices. Entrenched in the ideology is that "races are populations of people whose physical differences are linked to significant cultural and social differences and that these innate hierarchical differences can be measured and judged" (Golash-Boza, 2015, p. 131), and practices consist of micro- and macro-level "[subordination] of races believed to be inferior" (Golash-Boza, 2015, p. 131). Xenophobia derives from Greek origins; xenos meaning "stranger" or "foreigner," and phobos meaning "fear." Kim and Sundstrom (2014) expand upon this definition of fearing strangers or foreigners and define xenophobia as civic ostracism, an "idea associated with a distinct set of attitudes, beliefs, and affects that are about national inclusion and exclusion" (p. 30). All definitions encompass an ideology separating groups based on presumed inferiority, foreignness, and nativity in a society to justify practices that exclude, ostracize, and subordinate. When used separately or in pairs, these ideologies can hide one form of oppression. For example, Islamophobia is a form of xenophobia but has been justified through nationalism (i.e., protecting a national identity). Therefore, prejudice against immigrants can be disguised as patriotism, so if discrimination happens to Immigrants of Color who also identify as Arab, Muslim, or Sikh, ostracization through nativism and xenophobic reasoning are justified but conceals racism. Scholars have produced literature connecting concepts in pairs and analyzing their ideological weight and meaning, yet a conceptual model identifying the overlap and intersections between the three concepts remain nonexistent.

For undocumented Students of Color, intersectionality acts as a reference frame to acknowledge their multiple social realities reproduced by socially constructed categories and unveil overlapping systems of oppression regarding racism, nativism, and xenophobia (see Figure 4.1). Their undocumented status adds a complicated layer in their reality within a liminal state of being.

The concept of liminality requires reframing since it has been traditionally defined in literature as an ambiguous, in-between state and often perceived negatively due to an association with fear and uncertainty. However, the state of being liminal for undocumented Students of Color can also function as a source of growth, sustenance, and building block for strategic daily practices. Occupying and living in multiple worlds where an undefined, ambiguous space exists cultivates divergent thinking (Anzaldúa, 1999) to maneuver through and around systemic and systematic barriers in this liminal space. In experiencing liminality, undocumented Students of Color tap into a new consciousness (Anzaldúa, 1999) that enriches their creativity, nurtures their sustenance, and builds their strength. For example, undocumented students

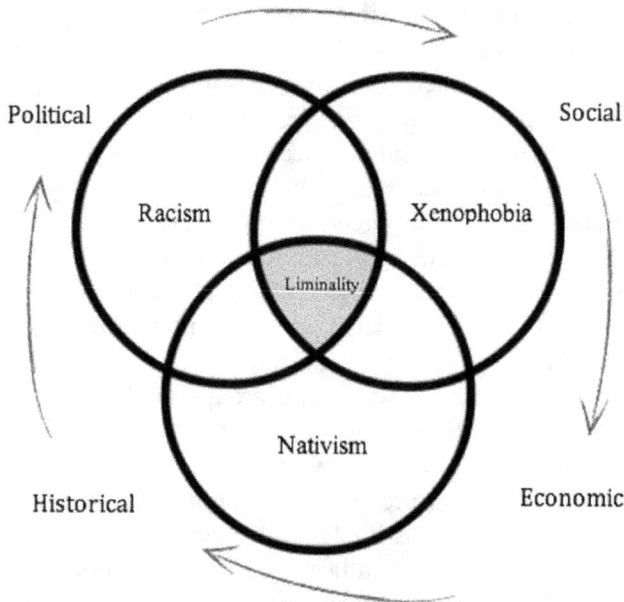

**Figure 4.1.** Conceiving a Frame of Liminality Interlaced in Racism, Nativism, and Xenophobia

Note. Author's image.

can also be in mixed-status families where they develop and prepare a contingency plan if government authorities imprison or deport family members. This type of pedagogical strategy of survival is a part of parental racial-ethnic socialization of families with members with undocumented statuses (Suárez-Orozco, 2015). In terms of educational institutions, a study by Pérez (2012) of undocumented Latino students in higher education revealed that educational institutions serve as a means of hope and reason for them to survive despite barriers. Muñoz and Maldonano (2012) found that undocumented Mexicana students develop positive self-identities fueling their persistence through college despite oppressive discourses of race, gender, and class in the classroom and contemporary United States. According to Suárez-Orozco (2015), undocumented youth "actively attempt to construct an identity that empowers them to believe in their self-worth" (p. 26) rather than be confined and defined by their undocumented and liminal status. Liminality forces undocumented Students of Color to develop strategies of survival within oppressive structures, like higher education institutions, where their networks share resources with one another, sharpen their ability to assess people and situation (i.e., who to trust and disclose information), and learn ways to cope with stigma, frustration, fear, and anxiety (Suárez-Orozco, 2015).

In addition to experiencing race and racism due to phenotypical characteristics associated with racialized groups, immigrants can be characterized by accent, generation status, and citizenship status. Through an intersectional lens, these characteristics offer a way for researchers to critically examine how Immigrants of Color continue to be racialized, criminalized, and dehumanized layered with being undocumented.

## Implications

Researchers need an analytical nexus to explicitly draw connections between racism, immigration, and higher education. Historically, the literature on these topics exists in separate vacuums. Immigration literature has focused on assimilation theories and perspectives based on the experiences of White Europeans which neglect the racialized impact for Immigrants of Color in the United States (Sáenz & Douglas, 2015). Moreover, immigration studies have traditionally focused on demographic aspects of immigration and has not incorporated social processes into analysis (e.g., social construction of race and citizenship; Sanchez & Romero, 2010). The exclusion of race in immigration literature becomes problematic as Immigrants of Color experience overlapping layers of oppression through their racialized and criminalized experiences in the United States. As such, they become targets in

institutionalized forms of violence (e.g., raids, midnight searches, city ordi-
nances, and changes to social services legislation; Sanchez & Romero, 2010).

Institutionalized forms of discrimination are embedded within policies
and practices in social institutions and act as hidden mechanisms that maintain racial and social hierarchies. Johnson (2009) recommends scrutinizing
immigration law and connecting it to race and immigration scholarship—as
it has not been done enough—because historically, immigration law has been
designed and continues to operate to prevent poor and Noncitizens of Color
from immigrating to and from the United States. There is a necessity in explicitly connecting racism, nativism, and xenophobia in educational research to
illuminate the ways undocumented Students of Color experience systemic
and systematic oppression in education institutions (Fan, 1997; Garcia, 1995;
Gordon & Lenhardt, 2007; Johnson, 2000, 2009, 2011; Martínez, 2012;
Romero, 2006, 2008; Sáenz & Douglas, 2015; Sanchez & Romero, 2010).
As the immigrant population in the United States continue increase to be
non-Europeans and are primarily Immigrants of Color, intersectionality
provides a promising reference frame to explore, analyze, and identify how
historically racialized immigrant communities continue to be oppressed in
institutional structures like higher education.

Future research should include exploring the experiences of Black immigrants, who continue to be an increasing population in the United States in
recent years. Primarily, immigration research and discourse has focused on
the experiences of Latiné and Asian populations, and these conversations
need to expand to immigrants from African, Caribbean, and Middle Eastern
countries. While the experiential knowledge of Immigrants of Color includes
pedagogies of migration (Benavides Lopez, 2016), this research comes from
Chicana/o/x and Latiné immigrants. More research needs to be conducted
to understand the nuanced ways undocumented Students of Color, particularly Asian, Black, and Pacific Islander undocumented students, know and
learn pedagogical strategies to survive and thrive in hostile sociopolitical contexts where they are racialized, criminalized, and dehumanized in addition
to navigating higher educational spaces. This conceptual model leads back
to the theoretical realm of research where researchers can continue to ask
questions that have not yet been asked to shed light on the unique, nuanced
experiences of undocumented Students of Color to provide them the necessary support in all facets of life.

When using intersectionality to examine the interlocking systems of
oppression for undocumented Students of Color and having a frame to
conceive their liminal space, researchers can begin to untangle complex
social phenomenon to understand educational trajectories and outcomes of

immigrant youth situated within a continuum of historical, political, economic, and social contexts. Furthermore, frames can uncover what has been rendered invisible. Reframing concepts illuminate connections where frames intersect and align (Snow & Benford, 1988) to transform society and reimagine future possibilities. Researchers need to continue to theorize—even in the absence of information—by retooling traditional methodologies and reconceptualizing concepts in research to expand frames of reference. Given the anti-immigrant climate in the United States, research needs to acknowledge historical and social connections—bounded by a common thread that sustains white supremacist ideology and practices. This chapter uses intersectionality to analyze interlocking systems of oppression for undocumented Students of Color that can unveil hidden mechanisms operating in the reproduction of inequities. In doing so, society can continue to untangle complex social phenomenon and contribute to an understanding of issues like immigration and globalization. As such, society can transcend thinking beyond disciplinary boundaries to transform future research, policy, and practice in higher education for *all* students.

## References

Anzaldúa, G. (1999). *Borderlands: La frontera* (2nd ed.). San Francisco, CA: Aunt Lute.

Beech, N. (2011). Liminality and the practices of identity construction. *Human Relations, 64*(2), 285–302.

Benavides Lopez, C. (2016). Lessons from the educational borderlands: Documenting the pedagogies of migration of Chicana/o, Latina/o undocumented immigrant students and households. *Association of Mexican American Educators Journal, 10*(1), 80–106.

Crenshaw, K. (1989). Demarginalizing the intersection of race and sex: A black feminist critique of antidiscrimination doctrine, feminist theory and antiracist politics. *University of Chicago Legal Forum, 1989*(8), 139–167.

Crenshaw, K. (1991). Mapping the margins: Intersectionality, identity politics, and violence against Women of Color. *Stanford Law Review, 43*(6), 1241–1299.

Crenshaw, K. (2016, October). *The urgency of intersectionality* [video file]. https://www.ted.com/talks/kimberle_crenshaw_the_urgency_of_intersectionality

Collins, P. H. (2009). *Black feminist thought: Knowledge, consciousness, and the politics of empowerment.* Routledge.

Dao, L. T. (2017). Out and Asian: How Undocu/DACAmented Asian Americans and Pacific Islander youth navigate dual liminality in the immigrant rights movement. *Societies, 7*(17), 1–15.

Fan, S. S.-W. (1997). Immigration law and the promise of critical race theory: Opening the academy to the voices of aliens and immigrants. *Columbia Law Review, 97*(4), 1202–1240.

Garcia, R. J. (1995). Critical race theory and proposition 187: The racial politics of immigration law. *Chicano-Latino Law Review, 17*(118), 118–154.

Goffman, E. (1974). *Frame analysis: An essay on the organization of experience.* Harper Torchbooks Year.

Golash-Boza, T. (2016). A critical ad comprehensive sociological theory of race and racism. *Sociology of Race and Ethnicity, 2*(2), 129–141.

Gonzales, R. G. (2016). *Lives in limbo: Undocumented and coming of age in America.* University of California Press.

Gonzales, R. G., & Burciaga, E. M. (2018). Segmented pathways of illegality: Reconciling the coexistence of master and auxiliary statuses in the experiences of 1.5-generation undocumented young adults. *Ethnicities, 18*(2), 178–191.

Gordon, J., & Lenhardt, R. A. (2007). Citizenship talk: Bridging the gap between immigration and the race perspectives. *Fordham Law Review, 75*(5), 2493–2519.

Harris, C. I. (1993). Whiteness as property. *Harvard Law Review, 106*(8), 1707–1791.

Higham, J. (1955). *Strangers in the land: Patterns of American nativism 1860–1925.* New Brunswick, NJ: Rutgers University Press.

Johnson, K. R. (2000). Race matters: Immigration law and policy scholarship, law in the ivory tower, and the legal indifference of the race critique. *University of Illinois Law Review, 2000*(2), 525–558.

Johnson, K. R. (2009). The intersection of race and class in U.S. immigration law and enforcement. *Law and Contemporary Problems, 72*(1), 1–35.

Johnson, K. R. (2011). Race and the immigration laws: The need for critical inquiry. In F. Valdes, J. M. Culp, & A. P. Harris. (Eds.), *Crossroads, directions, and a new critical race theory* (pp. 187–198). Temple University Press.

Kim, D. H., & Sundstrom, R. R. (2014). Xenophobia and racism. *Critical Philosophy of Race, 2*(1), 20–45.

Martínez, G. A. (2012). Arizona, immigration, and Latinos: The epistemology of Whiteness, the geography of race, interest convergence, and the view from the perspective of critical theory. *Arizona State Law Journal, 44*(175), 175–211.

Menjívar, C. (2006). Liminal legality: Salvadoran and Guatemalan immigrants' lives in the United States. *American Journal of Sociology, 111*(4), 999–1037.

Mitchell, D., Jr. (2014, November 21). Intersectionality to social justice = theory to practice [Web log post]. https://www.naspa.org/constituent-groups/posts/projectintersections-post-1

Muñoz, S. M., & Espino, M. M. (2017). The freedom to learn: The voices and experiences of undocumented students at Freedom University. *The Review of Higher Education, 40*(4), 533–555.

Muñoz, S. M., & Maldonado, M. M. (2012). Counterstories of college persistence for undocumented Mexicana students: Navigating race, class, gender and legal status. *International Journal of Qualitative Studies in Education, 25*(3), 293–315.

Nguyen, T-H., & Nguyen, B. M. D. (2018). Is the "first-generation student" term useful for understanding inequality? The role of intersectionality in illuminating the implications of an accepted—yet unchallenged—term. *Review of Research in Education, 42*(7), 146–176.

Nuñez, A. M. (2014). Employing multilevel intersectionality in educational research Latino identities, contexts, and college access. *Educational Researcher, 43*(2), 85–92.

Omi, M., & Winant, H. (2015). *Racial formation in the United States* (3rd ed.). Routledge.

Pérez, W. (2012). *Americans by heart: Undocumented Latino students and the promise of higher education.* Teachers College Press.

Pérez Huber, L., Benavides Lopez, C., Malagon, M. C., Velez, V., & Solórzano, D. G. (2008). Getting beyond the 'symptom,' acknowledging the 'disease': Theorizing racist nativism. *Contemporary Justice Review, 11*(1), 39–51.

Romero, M. (2006). Racial profiling and immigration law enforcement: Rounding up of usual suspects in the Latino community. *Critical Sociology, 32*(2–3), 447–473.

Romero, M. (2008). Crossing the immigration and race border: A critical race theory approach to immigration studies. *Contemporary Justice Review, 11*(1), 23–37.

Sáenz, R., & Douglas, K. M. (2015). A call for the racialization of immigration studies: On the transition of ethnic immigrants to racialized immigrants. *Sociology of Race and Ethnicity, 1*(1), 166–180.

Sanchez, G., & Romero, M. (2010). Critical race theory in the US sociology of immigration. *Sociology Compass, 4*(9), 779–788.

Snow, D. A., & Benford, R. D. (1988). Ideology, frame resonance, and participant mobilization. *International Social Movement Research, 1*(1), 197–217.

Suárez-Orozco, C., Abo-Zena, M. M., & Marks, A. K. (Eds.). (2015). *Transitions: The development of children of immigrants.* New York University Press.

Suárez-Orozco, C., Yoshikawa, H., Teranishi, R. T., & Suárez-Orozco, M. M. (2011). Growing up in the shadows: The developmental implications of unauthorized status. *Harvard Educational Review, 81*(3), 438–472.

Sundstrom, R. R. (2013). Sheltering xenophobia. *Critical Philosophy of Race, 1*(1), 68–85.

Teranishi, R. T., Suárez-Orozco, C., & Suárez-Orozco, M. (2015). *In the shadows of the ivory tower: Undocumented undergraduates and the liminal state of immigration reform.* The Institute for Immigration, Globalization, and Education.

Torres, R. M., & Wicks-Asbun, M. (2014). Undocumented students' narratives of liminal citizenship: High aspirations, exclusion, and "in-between" identities. *The Professional Geographer, 66*(2), 195–204.

Turner, V. (1967). *The forest of symbols.* Cornell University Press.

Ybema, S., Beech, N., & Ellis, N. (2011). Transitional and perpetual liminality: An identity practice perspective. *Anthropology Southern Africa, 23*(1–2), 21–29.

# 5. Thinking Theoretically with and Beyond Intersectionality: Frameworks to Center Queer and Trans People of Color Experiences

ANTONIO DURAN AND ROMEO JACKSON

The misuse of intersectionality (Crenshaw, 1989, 1991) remains a key site for a critical intervention within the epistemological landscape of higher education. That is, the intellectual labor of Black women continues to be erased through the lack of intentionality to, what Ahmed (2017) might call, a citation policy. In other words, higher education scholars have failed to trace a genealogy of intersectionality to its roots within a radical Black feminist tradition. Though the framework has traveled across a number of disciplines (Cho et al., 2013; Collins, 2015; Crenshaw, 2011; Hancock, 2007a, 2007b, 2016; McCall, 2005; Nash, 2008), intersectionality has both activist and scholarly historical origins that must be recognized. As intersectionality has gained prominence in the field of higher education, the questions become: how do we call attention to its history in Black feminist scholarship and activism? (Davis, 2016); moreover, when is it appropriate to employ other frameworks that accomplish complementary, yet different aims? As scholars who study the lives of Queer and Trans People of Color (QTPOC) on college campuses, we focus this chapter on the complexity that exists when choosing to utilize intersectionality *or* other frameworks to center QTPOC.

This chapter invites readers to envision a future of intersectional research that honors the contribution of Black feminist work while also critically pondering the usefulness of intersectionality to study the experiences of Queer and Trans People of Color. For the purposes of this chapter, we utilize the term *intersectional* to refer to analyses that examine how overlapping structures of power and oppression affect individuals and groups with multiple marginalized identities. In particular, numerous modes of analysis other than intersectionality exist that articulate the specific experiences of Queer and Trans Communities of Color, including Queer of Color critique (QOCC; Ferguson, 2004) and two spirit critique (TSC; Driskill, 2016). Intersectionality is not useless in understanding Queer and Trans People of Color experiences in higher education, but this chapter explores how QOCC and TSC may be more useful for researchers and practitioners working with QTPOC on college campuses. To provide scholars the tools to choose between these three frameworks, this chapter is organized in three sections: (1) a brief overview of QTPOC research in higher education, (2) the historical origins of intersectionality and its applicability to QTPOC, and (3) the unique features of QOCC and TSC that can inform QTPOC studies, including the similarities/differences to intersectionality. Ultimately, this theoretical exploration of frameworks that center QTPOC challenges higher education professionals to critically engage their use of intersectionality, thinking theoretically within its genealogy and possibly thinking beyond it.

## Overview of QTPOC Research in Higher Education

To situate this chapter within the broader higher education landscape, we offer a brief overview of research that studies the experiences of Queer and Trans Collegians of Color. In his systematic literature review on QTPOC research in higher education, Duran (2019) noted that despite the increase in research on queer students broadly, a lack of scholarship on Queer and Trans Students of Color still exists. Of the existing research, Duran (2019) identified sixty-eight scholarly texts (books, peer-reviewed articles, book/monograph chapters, and dissertations) that specifically focus on Queer Collegians of Color, in addition to noting two existing pieces that center Transgender Students of Color (i.e., Jourian, 2017; Nicolazzo, 2016).

Duran (2019) found that the following themes emerge in the extant literature on QTPOC in higher education: "coming out and finding sources of support, campus climate and navigating singular identity spaces, acknowledging the complex individuality of QPOC students, and the lack of resources/representation for these collegians" (p. 5). This scholarship, for example, has underscored how QTPOC make different decisions in living out their sexuality and gender compared to their White queer and trans peers (e.g., Eaton & Rios, 2017; Garvey et al., 2019; Goode-Cross & Good, 2008; Narui, 2014; Nicolazzo, 2016; Patton, 2011; Patton & Simmons, 2008); additionally, Queer and Trans Students of Color must contend with racism, heterosexism, genderism, and other oppressive systems within their collegiate environments (Blockett, 2017; Harris, 2003; Jourian, 2016; Mitchell & Means, 2014).

After the publishing of Duran's (2019) systematic literature review, scholars continued to shine light on Trans Communities of Color (Jourian & McCloud, 2020), including Indigenous trans people in higher education (Gutzwa, 2022). Moreover, other scholars attended to different institutional types, such as the experiences that QTPOC have at historically Black colleges and universities (Patton et al., 2020), as well as at Hispanic-Serving Institutions (Vega et al., 2022). Because Queer and Trans Students of Color experience their time at colleges and universities differently from their White queer and trans peers or heterosexual and cisgender Peers of Color, it is integral to comprehend and center their lives within higher education research. To understand the multiple axes of oppression that Queer and Trans Students of Color encounter, scholars have opted to utilize intersectional frameworks in their research, such as the ones discussed below.

## Paying Homage to the Genealogy of Intersectionality

Theories come with rich intellectual and activist histories that scholars must engage with in order to appropriately apply them to their work. As such, at the center of this section on intersectionality, we place Sojourner Truth's iconic speech "Ain't I a Woman," the Combahee River Collective Statement (1983), and, of course, the texts of Kimberlé Crenshaw (1989, 1991) who coined the term intersectionality within the academy and critical legal scholarship. By engaging the work above, we attempt to counter the epistemological erasure that furthers an anti-Black project within higher education scholarship. Importantly, this expunction typically targets Black women's work, rendering it to an epistemological death. For example, we argue the erasure of Kimberlé Crenshaw's texts when referencing intersectionality is a form of gendered anti-Blackness that, in turn, institutionalizes a Black feminist home theory (Nash, 2011). In the following section, we counter this institutionalization by highlighting the origins of intersectionality within Black women's work. Though not intended to be an intensive genealogy (see Hancock, 2016 for a more extensive historical exploration), we use two examples of Black women's intellectual production that laid the groundwork for Crenshaw's (1989, 1991) coining of intersectionality.

Though Crenshaw (1989, 1991) is often cited as the originator of the framework within the academy, intersectional arguments have existed as a tradition within Black feminist thought and Women of Color feminism far before Crenshaw's pathbreaking work (Cho et al., 2013; Collins, 2015;

Hancock, 2007a, 2016; Nash, 2008). Theorists have referenced examples of abolitionists such as Maria Stewart (Hancock, 2016) and Sojourner Truth (Crenshaw, 1989) to demonstrate the origins of intersectional thought outside of the academy. Of note, Sojourner Truth's (1851) "Aint I a Woman?" speech famously exposed how race and racism mediates access to womanhood, pointing to the hypocrisy of White femininity by stating, "Nobody ever helps me into carriages, or over mud-puddles, or gives me any best place! And ain't I a woman?" (para. 2). In calling attention to the category of women, Truth laid bare to the ways in which anti-Black racism and chattel slavery does not give Black women the "protection" of womanhood. That is, White women and Black women experience social oppression differently. Future movements echoed Truth's words as seen in the example of the Combahee River Collective (1983), a Black feminist lesbian organization, that wrote "it [is] difficult to separate race from class from sex oppression because in our lives they are most often experienced simultaneously" (p. 267). In this period of Black feminist mobilizing, the Combahee River Collective once again emphasized how White feminism obscured the lives of Black women. The Combahee River Collective Statement and "Aint I a Woman?" are two of the many ways that activists have engaged intersectional theorizing in the past, leading to the coining of the term by Crenshaw.

In her formative work, Kimberlé Crenshaw (1989, 1991) mapped the systemic and legal barriers that renders Black women invisible to anti-discrimination laws, drawing attention to the fact that Black women were experiencing the effects of gender and race discrimination simultaneously. Crenshaw (1989) made visible the experiences of Black women in legal contexts, and in her later essay, the ways in which anti-racist and feminist movements render Black women invisible (Crenshaw, 1991). Previously, those enforcing anti-discrimination policies framed racial and gender marginalization separately, which overlooked the unique forms of oppression lived by Black women. Crenshaw gave activists and academics language to name intersectional erasures that fail to approach social justice beyond a single axis of analysis. That is, intersectionality is not about individual identity (e.g., race, sex, and class); it is a mode of systemic and structural analysis of multiple forms of oppression (e.g., racism, sexism, and classism; Collins, 2000/2009; Crenshaw, 1989, 1991).

Intersectionality thus allows scholars and practitioners in higher education to understand how intersecting systems of racism, genderism, classism, and heterosexism affect Queer and Transgender Students of Color. For example, this framework illuminates how structures of domination can lead to heightened discrimination of QTPOC on college campuses and also contributes to their marginalization in spaces that only center one oppressed identity (e.g., those that focus on race *or* sexuality). Still, though some higher education researchers studying QTPOC have utilized intersectionality (e.g., see Blockett, 2017; Cisneros, 2015; Hughes, 2015; Miller & Vaccaro, 2016; Russell, 2012; Tillman-Kelly, 2015), other scholars have opted for different theoretical frameworks, such as quare theory (e.g., see Johnson, 2001) or Queer of Color critique (e.g., see Ferguson, 2004). Important to note, the work of Black (queer) feminists (e.g., Beal, 1970; Davis, 1981; hooks, 1981; Hull et al., 1982; Lorde, 1984) is foundational to any intersectional analysis that reaches far beyond the term intersectionality. As we demonstrate in the ensuing section, Queer of Color critique and two-spirit critique are indebted to Women of Color, Black, and Native feminist theories for laying the groundwork to address the specificity of oppression for Queer and Trans People of Color.

## Additional Potential Frameworks to Center QTPOC Experiences

Although intersectionality remains a key theoretical insight into the study of oppressive systems that impact individuals with multiple marginalized identities, other intersectional frameworks exist that may better serve higher education researchers when exploring the experiences of QTPOC. For example, Queer of Color critique (Ferguson, 2004) and two spirit critique (Driskill, 2016) both identify different discourses that lend themselves to study Queer and Trans Students of Color. Therefore, this section will detail the various histories and potentials for application that these frameworks have for QTPOC individuals, including their focus on colonial histories or materialist systems. Though these theories align with intersectionality in some notable ways, it is their departures that warrant attention from scholars and practitioners alike.

### Queer of Color Critique

Queer of Color critique is one framework that has started to emerge in QTPOC studies in higher education. Similar to intersectionality, Queer of Color critique stems from a history of Women of Color feminism and seeks to analyze the intersections of gender, race, sexuality, and nationhood. Notably, Roderick Ferguson (2004) is often credited for Queer of Color critique, advancing this lens in order to refute the whiteness and heteronormativity that undergirded the discipline of sociology. As Ferguson contends, canonical sociology "becomes an epistemological counterpart to the state's enforcement of universality as the state suppresses nonheternormative racial difference" (p. 21). In challenging canonical sociology, Queer of Color critique deconstructs and opposes the ways that the nation-state has regulated Queer of Color bodies and realities. To this point, Ferguson argued that social and cultural structures, in what is currently referred to as the United States, disproportionately disenfranchise Queer Communities of Color through social policy and economic discrimination. Differing from intersectionality's origins in critical legal studies, Ferguson constructed an argument rooted in materialism, interrogating how the nation-state's system of liberal capitalism reinforces the normalization of heterosexuality and exclusion of racial groups. The way that the nation-state utilizes capital, in Ferguson's perspective, results in policies that regulate Queer of Color communities, and specifically Black queer individuals. For example, though People of Color are frequently utilized for their labor in what is currently known as the United States, they are systematically denied access to social and material resources. In an attempt to navigate the larger capitalist system, Communities of Color are forced to align themselves with normalized modes of expressing gender and sexuality (e.g., through respectability politics) that then marginalizes Queers of Color.

Though Queer of Color critique began as a sociological project, scholars have started to imagine its potential for educational research. Describing the ways that researchers can deploy Queer of Color critique in education, Brockenbrough (2013) observed that "institutional policies, classroom cultures, identity politics, and interpersonal practices that produce the marginalized racial, gender, and sexual subjectivities of queer [Y]outh of [C]olor" (pp. 429–430) are rich topics for exploration. Queer of Color critique is an intersectional mode of analysis that interrogates the ways that policies and structures of educational institutions oppress Queer and Trans Collegians of Color. In particular, this theoretical tradition's focus on materialist systems creates the possibility for scholars to critically interrogate how Queer and Trans Collegians of Color experience differential fiscal and political realities on campus. For example, how does the distribution of identity center funds towards certain programming further marginalize Queer and Transgender Students of Color, causing a campus culture that obscures QTPOC realities? Higher education researchers, such as Means and Jaeger (2013), have noted the analytical power that Queer of Color critique can provide to QTPOC studies but have not fully elaborated on its potential. Scholars outside of education and sociology like cultural studies scholar, Andrea Smith (2010), have also extended Queer of Color critique, interrogating the ways that settler colonialism shapes identities. This leads us to highlight another theoretical framework that takes up a similar aim of identifying and resisting settler colonialism, which may consequently lend itself to QTPOC studies in higher education.

## *Two Spirit Critique*

Drawing on and expanding Native feminist theories, Qwo-Li Driskill (2016) offered a two-spirit critique (TSC) in the hopes of building a coalition between Native and queer studies. TSC makes the relationship between the regulation of gender, sexuality and settler colonialism central to understanding trans, queer, gender, and Native oppression. Intersectionality and TSC both seek to understand overlapping systems of oppression. However, TSC centers two-spirit people's resistance to colonialism, a depart from intersectionality's concern and theoretical origins with the experiences of Black women.

TSC asserts the need for an ongoing analysis of the relationship between settler colonialism and heteropatriarchy. The need for such an analysis expands outside of research on Indigenous peoples, for oppression happens "on occupied Indigenous lands and both over and through Indigenous bodies and peoples" (Driskill, 2016, p. 22). TSC is useful in understanding non-native QTPOC oppression within higher education because QTPOC oppression is not removed from settler colonialism. TSC resists the settler revisionist history of what is currently called the United States which suggests Native genocide and removal was predestined (Dunbar-Ortiz, 2014). Higher education scholars and practitioners can more accurately address contemporary issues facing QTPOC by understanding this truer history.

Making clear that there is no one TSC, Driskill (2016) suggested that there are seven practices of a TSC. For the purposes of this chapter, we highlight two practices as they may be the most helpful for higher education research. TSC: (1) sees two-spirit people and traditions as both integral to and a challenge to nationalist and decolonial struggles, and, (2) is woven into Native feminisms by seeing sexism, homophobia and transphobia as colonial tools.

These practices can inform research in three ways. First, Driskill (2016) saw TSC as an intervention into Queer of Color research that centers two-spirit memory. TSC allows scholars to understand the colonial tools at play that limit the possibilities of Queer and Trans People of Color. For example, two-spirit memory shows fluid gender identity and expression was common and integrated into Native nations with no need for formal documentation (Driskill, 2016). The need for formal documentation for students to change their name and gender markers thus functions as a colonial tool of gender at work within higher education. In remembering two-spirit people, we then know of a time before administrative processes regulated gender, opening possibilities for a future where gender identity is not regulated by the state nor universities and colleges.

Secondly, by centering two-spirit resistance, researchers who seek to study Queer and Trans Students of Color can be in solidarity with a decolonial project by gleaning lessons from two-spirit art and activism that furthers liberation for all QTPOC. Being aligned with a decolonial project starts with evoking Native feminist theories as a valued starting and ending place for theorizing race, gender, and nation (see Arvin, Tuck, & Morrill, 2013). Native theories also require engaging the material cost of decolonization (Tuck & Yang, 2012). Lastly, as Wilder (2013) showed, higher education continues to be deeply invested in a settler colonial and anti-Black project of what is currently called the United States.

Every researcher and practitioner should be interested in naming, understanding, and dismantling settler logics within higher education because it is only by dismantling settler logics that we can truly begin to honor the theoretical contributions of Black feminist thinking and start to imagine new liberatory possibilities for Queer and Trans People of Color in higher education. TSC offers researchers an entry point to understand how current epistemological and ontological norms further settler colonialism and Native oppression. At the time of this writing, TSC has not been used in higher education research, reflecting the ongoing erasure of Nativeness within educational research (Waterman & Lindley, 2013) beyond deficit models (Tuck, 2009).

## Conclusion

Ultimately, this chapter encourages scholars and practitioners to reflect on their use of intersectionality and other theoretical frameworks when studying QTPOC in college. Though intersectionality can serve as a powerful tool to illuminate systems of oppression that are embedded within university environments, individuals in higher education and student affairs have frequently misused and misappropriated this theory, obscuring its origins in Black feminist activism (Lange, 2017; Núñez, 2014). For this reason, we echo Collins' (2015) words when she wrote, "Scholars and practitioners think they know intersectionality when they see it. More importantly, they conceptualize intersectionality in dramatically different ways when they use it" (p. 3). This chapter's theoretical exploration ensures that professionals practice good stewardship of Black feminist thought (Davis, 2016), honoring the contributions of Black women when evoking intersectionality as a framework in their praxis. It is only then that we can start to return the labor of Black women from an epistemological death. Moreover, in analyzing the academic gene-alogies of intersectionality, Queer of Color critique, and two spirit critique, this piece better equips those in higher education to select appropriate frame-works to guide their scholarship. Whether scholars think with or beyond intersectionality, it is imperative that they recognize the histories behind these theories in order to envision equitable futures for Queer and Trans People of Color in higher education.

## References

Ahmed, S. (2017). *Living a feminist life.* Duke University Press.

Arvin, M., Tuck, E., & Morrill, A. (2013). Decolonizing feminism: Challenging con-nections between settler colonialism and heteropatriarchy. *Feminist Formations,* 25(1), 8–34.

Beal, F. M. (1970). Double jeopardy: To be Black and female. In T. Cade (Ed.), *The Black woman: An anthology* (pp. 90–100). Signet.

Blockett, R. A. (2017). 'I think it's very much placed on us': Black queer men laboring to forge community at a predominantly White and (hetero)cisnormative research insti-tution. *International Journal of Qualitative Studies in Education,* 30(8), 800–816.

Brockenbrough, E. (2013). Introduction to the special issue: Queers of Color and anti-oppressive knowledge production. *Curriculum Inquiry,* 43(4), 426–440.

Cho, S., Crenshaw, K. W., & McCall, L. (2013). Toward a field of intersectionality stud-ies: Theory, applications, and praxis. *Signs: Journal of Women in Culture and Society,* 38(4), 785–810.

Cisneros, J. (2015). *Undocuqueer: Interacting and working with the intersection of LGBTQ and undocumented* (Publication no. 153863) [Doctoral dissertation, Arizona State University]. ASU Library. https://hdl.handle.net/2286/R.I.34804

Collins, P. H. (2009). *Black feminist thought: Knowledge, consciousness and the politics of empowerment.* Routledge. (Original work published 1990)

Collins, P. H. (2015). Intersectionality's definitional dilemmas. *Annual Review of Sociology,* 41(1), 1–20.

Combahee River Collective. (1983). The Combahee River collective statement. In B. Smith (Ed.), *Home girls: A Black feminist anthology* (pp. 264–275). Rutgers University Press.

Crenshaw, K. (1989). Demarginalizing the intersection of race and sex: A Black femi-nist Critique of antidiscrimination doctrine, feminist theory, and antiracist politics. *University of Chicago Legal Forum, 1989*(8), 139–167.

Crenshaw, K. (1991). Mapping the margins: Intersectionality, identity politics, and vio-lence against Women of Color. *Stanford Law Review, 43*(6), 1241–1299.

Crenshaw, K. (2011). Postscript. In H. Lutz, M. T. H. Vivar, & L. Supik (Eds.), *Framing intersectionality: Debates on a multi-faceted concept in gender studies* (pp. 221–234). Ashgate.

Davis, A. (1981). *Women, race, and class.* Random House.

Davis, A. (2016). *Freedom is a constant struggle: Ferguson, Palestine, and the foundations of a movement.* Haymarket.

Driskill, Q.-L. (2016). *Asegi stories: Cherokee queer and two-spirit memory.* The University of Arizona Press.

Dunbar-Ortiz, R. (2014). *An indigenous peoples' history of the United States.* Beacon.

Duran, A. (2019). Queer and of Color: A systematic literature review on Queer Students of Color in higher education scholarship. *Journal of Diversity in Higher Education, 12*(4), 390–400.

Eaton, A., & Rios, D. (2017). Social challenges faced by queer Latino college men: Navigating negative responses to coming out in a double minority sample of emerging adults. *Cultural Diversity and Ethnic Minority Psychology, 23*(4), 457–467.

Ferguson, R. A. (2004). *Aberrations in Black: Toward a Queer of Color critique.* University of Minnesota Press.

Goode-Cross, D. T., & Good, G. E. (2008). African American men who have sex with men: Creating safe spaces through relationships. *Psychology of Men & Masculinity, 9*(4), 221–234.

Gutzwa, J. A. (2022). "It's survival mode": Exploring how an Indigenous Trans* Student of Color (per)forms identity while transgressing space. *Journal of Diversity in Higher Education.* Advance online publication. https://doi.org/10.1037/dhe0000410

Hancock, A.-M. (2007a). Intersectionality as a normative and empirical paradigm. *Politics & Gender, 3*(2), 41–45.

Hancock, A.-M. (2007b). When multiplication doesn't equal quick addition: Examining intersectionality as a research paradigm. *Perspectives on Politics, 5*(1), 63–79.

Hancock, A.-M. (2016). *Intersectionality: An intellectual history.* Oxford University Press.

Harris, W. G. (2003). African American homosexual males on predominantly White college and university campuses. *Journal of African American Studies, 7*(1), 47–56.

hooks, b. (1981). *Ain't I a woman: Black women and feminism.* South End.

Hughes, K. L. (2015). *The experiences queer college Women of Color have of friendship* (Publication no. 9949334750202959) [Doctoral dissertation, University of Georgia]. http://getd.libs.uga.edu/pdfs/hughes_kim_l_201505_phd.pdf

Hull, A., Bell-Scott, P., & Smith, B. (Eds.). (1982). *But some of us are brave: Black women's studies.* Feminist.

Johnson, E. P. (2001). "Quare" studies, or (almost) everything I know about queer studies I learned from my grandmother. *Text and Performance Quarterly, 21*(1), 1–25.

Jourian, T. J. (2017). "Fun and carefree like my polka dot bowtie": Disidentifications of trans*masculine Students of Color. In J. M. Johnson & G. C. Javier (Eds.), *Queer people of Color in higher education* (pp. 123–144). Information Age.

Jourian, T. J., & McCloud, L. (2020). "I don't know where I stand": Black trans masculine students' re/de/constructions of Black masculinity. *Journal of College Student Development, 61*(6), 733–749. http://doi.org/10.1353/csd.2020.0072

Lange, A. (2017, October 15). *The (mis)use of intersectionality in student affairs: A call to practitioners & researchers* [Web log post]. http://www.itsalexcl.com/blog/2017/10/15/the-misuse-of-intersectionality-a-call-to-student-affairs-researchers-practitioners

Lorde, A. (1984). *Sister outsider: Essays and speeches.* Crossing.

McCall, L. (2005). The complexity of intersectionality. *Signs: Journal of Women in Culture & Society, 30*(3), 1771–1800.

Means, D. R., & Jaeger, A. J. (2013). Black in the rainbow: "Quaring" the Black gay male student experience at historically Black universities. *Journal of African American Males in Education, 4*(2), 124–140.

Miller, R. A., & Vaccaro, A. (2016). Queer Student Leaders of Color: Leadership as authentic, collaborative, culturally competent. *Journal of Student Affairs Research and Practice, 53*(1), 39–50.

Mitchell, D., Jr., & Means, D. R. (2014). "Quadruple consciousness": A literature review and new theoretical consideration for understanding the experiences of Black gay and bisexual college men at predominantly White institutions. *Journal of African American Males in Education, 5*(1), 23–25.

Garvey, J. C., Mobley, S. D., Jr., Summerville, K. S., & Moore, G. T. (2019). Queer and Trans* Students of Color: Navigating identity disclosure and college contexts. *The Journal of Higher Education, 90*(1), 150–178.

Narui, M. (2014). Hidden populations and intersectionality: When race and sexual orientation collide. In D. Mitchell Jr., C Y. Simmons, & L. A. Greyerbiehl (Eds.), *Intersectionality & higher education: Theory, research, and praxis* (pp. 185–200). Peter Lang.

Nash, J. C. (2008). Re-thinking intersectionality. *Feminist Review, 89*(1), 1–15.

Nash, J. C. (2011). "Home truths" on intersectionality. *Yale Journal of Law and Feminism, 23*(2), 445–470.

Nicolazzo, Z. (2016). "It's a hard line to walk": Black non-binary trans* collegians' perspectives on passing, realness, and trans*-normativity. *International Journal of Qualitative Studies in Education, 29*(9), 1173–1188.

Núñez, A-M. (2014). Employing multilevel intersectionality in educational research: Latino identities, contexts, and college access. *Educational Researcher, 43*(2), 85–92.

Patton, L. D. (2011). Perspectives on identity, disclosure, and the campus environment among African American gay and bisexual college men at one historically Black college. *Journal of College Student Development, 52*(1), 77–100.

Patton, L. D., Blockett, R. A., & McGowan, B. L. (2020). Complexities and contradictions: Black lesbian, gay, bisexual, and queer students' lived realities across three urban HBCU contexts. *Urban Education*. Advance online publication. https://doi.org/10.1177/0042085920959128

Patton, L. D., & Simmons, S. L. (2008). Exploring complexities of multiple identities of lesbians in a Black college environment. *Negro Educational Review, 59*(3–4), 197–215.

Russell, E. L. A. (2012). *Voices unheard: Using intersectionality to understand identity among sexually marginalized undergraduate college Students of Color* (Publication no. 49) [Doctoral dissertation, Bowling Green State University]. Higher Education Ph.D. Dissertations. https://scholarworks.bgsu.edu/he_diss/49

Smith, A. (2010). Queer theory and native studies: The heteronormativity of settler colonialism. *GLQ: A Journal of Gay and Lesbian Studies, 16*(1–2), 42–68.

Tillman-Kelly, D. L. (2015). *Sexual identity label adoption and disclosure narratives of gay, lesbian, bisexual, and queer (GLBQ) college Students of Color: An intersectional grounded theory study* [Doctoral dissertation, The Ohio State University]. http://rave.ohiolink.edu/etdc/view?acc_num=osu1429835835

Truth, S. (1851). *Ain't I a woman?* https://www.sojournertruth.com/p/aint-i-woman.html

Tuck, E. (2009). Suspending damage: A letter to communities. *Harvard Educational Review, 79*(3), 409–427.

Tuck, E., & Yang, K. W. (2012). Decolonization is not a metaphor. *Decolonization: Indigeneity, Education & Society, 1*(1), 1–40.

Vega, G. P., Duran, A., McGill, C. M., & Rocco, T. S. (2022). Attending to sexuality in servingness: A phenomenological exploration of the experiences of Latina lesbians at a Hispanic-serving institution. *Journal of Diversity in Higher Education*. Advance online publication. https://doi.org/10.1037/dhe0000434

Waterman, S. J., & Lindley, L. S. (2013). Cultural strengths to persevere: Native American women in higher education. *NASPA Journal About Women in Higher Education, 6*(2), 139–165.

# Part II: Research

# 6. *Metaphorically Speaking: Being a Black Woman in the Academy is Like...*

Christa J. Porter

Critical scholarship exploring Black women's experiences in the academy has increased over the past several decades. Scholars examined how Black women have traversed into and through the academy through the following research foci: historical perspectives of Black women's' trajectories (Gregory, 2001); existence, resistance, and transformation (Hull et al., 1982; Perlow et al., 2018); fatigue and resilience through tenure and promotion (Carter Andrews, 2015; Croom, 2017); mentorship (Ghee & Grant, 2015; Kelly & Fries-Britt, 2022a); self-efficacy (McNeely Cobham & Patton, 2015); and the redefinition of professional socialization and roles (Sulé, 2009, 2023). Researchers must learn from and build upon previous scholarship to further explore Black women's onto-epistemologies, the nuanced ways Black women navigate and negotiate their place and space in the academy (Porter et al., 2023). The purpose of this chapter is to illuminate the narratives of three Black women faculty at historically white institutions using metaphor.

## Intersectionality

The historical and social location of Black women has been (and must continue to be) situated at the nexus of identity and the oppressive structures within which we survive (Collins, 1990; Crenshaw, 1991; hooks, 1981). Black women's experiences in the academy mirror that of our positioning within the history of American society—the historical legacy of marginalization and exploitation Black women have carried as members of society does not change once we enter the ivory towers of academia. Black women hold an *outsider-within status* (Collins, 1986) in the academy as the inter-sections of our minoritized identities as Black women academics relegate us to the margins of the system. Marginalization is compounded as additional identities (and subsequent 'isms) are nuanced such as full-time non-tenure track (NTT) or contingency in academic appointment (Boss et al., 2019), age, marital status, gender identity, sexual orientation, and socioeconomic status. "Because the intersectional experience is greater than the sum of rac-ism and sexism, any analysis that does not take intersectionality into account cannot sufficiently address the particular manner in which Black women are subordinated" (Crenshaw, 1989, p. 140). Crenshaw (1989, 1991) coined the term *intersectionality* in reference to Black women who experienced sexual violence and navigated the structural oppressions present within the justice system in ways that were distinctly different than their white women peers. "When there's no name for a problem, you can't see a problem. When you can't see a problem, you can't solve it" (Crenshaw, 2016). There was no name for what these Black women were experiencing at the intersections of their marginalized identities in the legal system.

Intersectionality as a tool of analysis, however, has been used more recently by scholars to expand the discussion and emphasize unveiling power struc-tures and systems of inequality for People of Color (Collins, 2000; Collins & Bilge, 2016; Dill & Zambrana, 2009). Intersectional analysis explores and unpacks relations of domination and subordination,

> privilege and agency, in the structural arrangements through which various ser-vices, resources, and other social rewards are delivered; in the interpersonal experiences of individuals and groups; in the practices that characterize and sus-tain bureaucratic hierarchies; and in the ideas, images, symbols, and ideologies that shape social consciousness. (Dill & Zambrana, 2009, p. 5)

For Black women faculty in the academy, intersectionality is a critical lens through which to view our experiences. Analyses must also be situated within the context of these systems, power structures, hegemony, and hierarchies that shape the individual and collective consciousness of the academy and those with whom we interact.

## Method

Findings for this chapter are from a larger study on the experiences of Black women faculty at historically white institutions, where my colleagues and I served as researcher participants (Boss et al., 2019; Porter et al., 2020). We—Grace, Danai, and Amanda (pseudonyms)—graduated from a higher education student affairs related doctoral program between 2013 and 2014, we each have held full-time contingent (NTT) and/or tenure-track faculty appointments and have remained in community with one another since beginning our doctoral program in 2010. While we were able locate the literature on Black women's experiences in the academy, we specifically noticed a dearth in scholarship on contingent Black faculty women. This lack of literature provoked us to write ourselves into existence using scholarly personal narratives. Scholarly personal narrative (SPN) as a critical qualitative approach, has been used to assist the scholar-writer affirm their experiences via personal essay organized by categories and themes connected to a larger worldview (Nash, 2004). SPN has served as an optimal technique for Faculty of Color in the academy to not only write themselves into existence, but to also identify themes and implications in their rich narratives that were relevant to one another, future faculty, and those with whom worked alongside Faculty of Color to better understand their experiences and improve the academic climate for Faculty of Color (Fries-Britt & Kelly, 2005; Louis et al., 2016).

In this chapter, I specifically highlight extended excerpts from our individual narratives that contribute to a collective and intersectional analysis using metaphors. As discussed earlier in the chapter, we bear the burden of proof as Black women. We find ourselves having to name, explain, and describe our own experiences as real and true (Crenshaw, 2016). The purpose of conceptual metaphors is to represent one thing with something else; they provide structure into how we understand our experiences (Lakoff & Johnson, 1980). Using metaphor is a meaning-making process; individuals engage metaphors in our daily lives to guide how we relate to others, how we navigate the world, and what we perceive. The coupling of scholarly personal narratives with metaphor not only permitted the space to authentically reflect, but it also challenged us to think more deeply about the tangible ways intersectionality became/becomes real for us as Black women in the academy.

I offered the following prompt:

> Using metaphor(s), how would you describe what it is like to be a Black woman in the academy? What specific experiences influence your description while teaching, researching, or serving as a faculty member? Discuss how intersectionality has influenced the way(s) you show up as a Black woman in the academy? How do you define and identify with intersectionality in your identities?

After compiling the narratives, I reviewed the following four theoretical interventions of intersectionality (Dill & Zambrana, 2009): centering the experiences of People of Color, complicating identity, unveiling power in interconnected structures of inequality, and promoting social justice and change. Our narratives were stored in an online shared folder; we each engaged in member checking for accuracy and each researcher participant reviewed my analysis and interpretation of data. While I was reading our metaphorical analogies, many of our narratives centered on the relationship between identity and power (or inequities in power), so I employed focus coding (Charmaz, 2006) by organizing relevant chunks of data under the two theoretical interventions: (1) complicating identity and (2) unveiling power in interconnected structures of inequality. Complicating identity refers to not only individual and group identities, but also the complex and nuanced relationships between them (Dill & Zambrana, 2009). Unveiling power in interconnected structures of inequality can be described as a force to oppress others and an intangible entity that operates in various domains of society (e.g., hegemonic and interpersonal; Collins, 2000).

## *Findings*

This section is separated into three parts. The first part consists of excerpts from Grace and Danai broadly reflecting on their definitions of intersectionality. The second portion presents the theoretical intervention, complicating identity, in which Amanda, Danai, and Grace articulated the ways intersectionality influenced how they show(ed) up as Black women faculty in the academy. The third and final part of this findings section introduces metaphor through the theoretical intervention, unveiling power in interconnected structures of inequality.

Danai and Grace defined intersectionality respectively,

> I define intersectionality as the thing that makes me more than just another Black woman in the academy. I am a Black woman, but I am also the daughter of a former foster kid whose scrappy, independence taught me to never trust in the system to take care of/care for me but to carve out my own places of belonging. I am a Southerner whose feet tread daily over land where violence was perpetrated over my ancestors and where it was not uncommon to see confederate flags flown high and proud. I am a thousand other things that make my Black womanness simultaneously my own experience and yet still a collective connection. Intersectionality provides me a way of talking both about what it is to be a Black woman and who I am as a Black woman.

Grace reflected,

> When I reflect on intersectionality, my first thought goes to the ways in which I show up as a Black woman with a PhD, and how I experience racism, sexism, and ageism daily as a faculty member. My identities color the way I am received

and at the same time are the lenses through which I exist. As sister Collins discussed, my identities are inextricably linked, thus the marginalization I experience daily, both locally and broadly, are a result of intersectionality as a theoretical framework that encapsulates all the isms.

## Complicating Identity–Influence of Intersectionality as a Black Women in the Academy

Amanda acknowledged,

> For me, navigating the academy is an amalgam of the different positions that I hold. I embrace both intersectionality and intersections of my identity in the academy. Although to be fair, most of the identities that are most salient are those that lack power in the academy: Black, woman, and contingent (NTT). I am also very aware of my being young (I appear younger than I am, constantly being told "oh my gosh, you look like a student" or "my children are older than you" and it being laughed off). Since I've been a faculty member, all these intersections of my identity have been present in ways that I don't believe they were as much as an administrator. There were defined jobs, roles, and responsibilities in administrative life. In faculty life, there's stuff that needs to get done, yet who actually does them is a bit more of a gray area, because they fall under "faculty work." However, these intersections begin to become magnified in the gray area. In my own experience, the women ended up taking on more of the labor of "caring" for the program in terms of recruitment, meeting with students, serving as advisor, developing community, etc. As a contingent faculty member this was assumed to be my sole responsibility, yet isn't faculty life inclusive of program and departmental service as well?

Danai shared,

> The best way I can discuss how intersectionality has influenced the way I show up in the academy is through hyperawareness. My Blackness, womanness, youth, and socioeconomic status are ever present in my mind as I interact with colleagues and students. I find myself constantly considering whether to code switch around both colleagues and students, because I realize there are many who still deem Black vernacular English as lazy and ignorant. Yet, I value authenticity and expressing myself in ways that feel comfortable to me, and often more effectively convey the power of my meaning is also important. But I am not only Black, I am also a woman, and I appear youthful. This trifecta causes me to constantly think about what I must do to get a seat at the table and whether getting to the table is even worth it. This trifecta makes me think about how privileged I am to be in academia, especially now that I am in a tenure-track role, because I know the numbers would suggest I am an anomaly. And I want to redefine the pathway; so that generations of Black and Women of Color academics do not feel like anomalies but can come into academia and find home. Home, a place where they are accepted for who they are fully and what they have

to offer. So, I would say intersectionality places me in a place of questioning if authenticity is attainable for me in the academy.

Grace asserted,

> Specifically, in the academy, because tenure line roles are so coveted, it's almost as if I gained a medal of some sort. Like regardless of my identities, I am "smart" enough and have enough potential to secure one of these spots based on "their" system of judgment and performance. So, I can get in the door and I am now invited to the table. But because of my identities as Black, woman, and young(er), I am still questioned, critiqued, and often marginalized for my ways of knowing, thinking, and producing knowledge based on both my experiences and the experiences of my participants.

Amanda, Danai, and Grace reflected on their marginalized identities, yet the complex relationships, intersections among identities, and situations of power, nuance their experiences even more. Our identities are complicated because they are inextricably linked, interconnected, and cannot exist on their own, nor can our identities exist outside of power structures. The use of metaphor within our scholarly personal narratives challenged us to objectify our realities more clearly.

## Unveiling Power in Interconnected Structures of Inequality– Through the Use of Metaphor

Danai emphasized,

> **Being a Black woman in the academy is putting the wooden spoon over the pot to keep it from boiling over.** It's the everyday microaggressions, death by a thousand cuts of being disregarded, dismissed or invisible that lead me to my metaphor. When I think of my experience I think of a boiling pot just on the brink of overflowing, but realizing I cannot let that happen, I reach for whatever guidance I can to prevent it. I remember hearing long ago, that putting a wooden spoon over a boiling pot would stop it from boiling over. I have tried this a few times, and a couple of those times the pot boiled over anyway. Yet, I still reach for that solution overall. You would think that just turning down the heat would be my first go to, but it rarely seems like a viable option. As it relates to the prompt, I think about all the times I have been at the height of my frustration in academia, particularly tied to my Blackness and my womanness, and I realize, rarely do I think about turning down the heat (do less service, not caring about teaching quality or evaluations, not striving for top-tiered publications), because in my mind I have to do all those things. I must serve students, especially Black and Brown students. I must be great; I cannot let my colleagues or students confirm what I always fear they think: I do not belong. So in lieu of turning down the heat, I reach for the spoon (connecting with a community of peers, prayer, therapy, poetry, dance). Sometimes, I still boil over, but it helps.

Amanda articulated,

> **Being a Black woman in the academy is like using a curling iron in the morning and forgetting whether you turned it off when you've left your home for work (the same thing happens when you question whether you left any electric appliance on).** It's the nagging thought that you might have left the curling iron on and thinking about all the bad things that could happen. Did you leave it near a towel, could it catch fire, would it blow a fuse, etc. It's all the back-and-forth, the "did I?" or "did I not?" that you have to engage in to determine whether you will go back home to ensure that you did indeed turn off the curling iron and be late for work or meeting or whether you hope for the best and that your home is still standing when you get home. Essentially, it comes down to how much risk I am willing to take and the mental acrobatics that I must engage in to reconcile my decision. I've come to think of being a Black woman in the academy in the same way: how much of what I believe, who I am, and how I show up, how much I am willing to risk being seen, heard, and valued in the academy and thinking about all the scenarios that might play out depending on how I "behave." Will I be seen as the proverbial "help," will I be responsible for providing the emotional labor on behalf of the program, will I be viewed as "challenging" when I bring up issues of process, equity, and/or inclusion, will I be viewed as scholarly and just as credible as my white colleagues, will students challenge my authority in the classroom? A very real question that stays just below the surface "will any of these very real possibilities affect whether my annual contract will be renewed?"
>
> Being Black, being a woman and being a non-tenure track faculty member means that I grapple with these "what ifs" all the time as I'm often the only one or one of two Black women in the academic space within my department. When you are thinking about whether you turned something off in your home, most of the time you end up mentioning it to a friend or colleague and they will say, "I'm sure that you did! It's fine." That doesn't make it any easier to get the thought out of your mind. There's still the nagging thought, is it worth the risk? For me, right now, it is worth the risk. I've learned how to show up authentically and recognize the implications and consequences of standing in my truth and integrity. I've learned that while I'm in the academy, I have a responsibility to help change and transform the culture and practices so that they become more equitable and inclusive for Black woman and contingent faculty. It's been because I have a strong community that serve as my sounding boards and allow me to process and vent. Being a Black woman in the academy, finding community is critical.

Grace illustrated,

> **Being a Black woman in the academy is like being a doormat.** The environment and those within it, step on, step over, and force their so(u)les into us, while we hold up, protect, experience wear and tear because of the elements. It is a rarity that someone or something picks us up or dusts us off—from the same elements that/who wear and tear (on) us, we are strengthened, learn to self-clean, and must preserve ourselves for the changing climate(s). I felt this

metaphor daily. It could have been the environment within which I was positioned, or it could have been the toxicity of those persons who sat at the same table. Either way, the feelings of isolation and marginalization were ever-so-present. I was silenced, yet my voice mattered when it was beneficial to others. I was overlooked for opportunities, yet it was my responsibility to increase experiences for students. I was tired, yet I found strength to maximize my efforts for the students and my professional trajectory. I was isolated, yet I found those who remain necessary and great company for the journey. The company I kept then and keep at this point in my career push, pull, encourage, and strengthen.

**Being a Black woman in the academy is like receiving the professoriate badge on a brownie shawl (in the girl scouts)... except the badge is worthless by itself.** It only has meaning and value once its sewn onto the shawl and it's not sown onto the shawl until you receive tenure and promotion. So, you work and write, teach, and publish, and repeat...do all what's necessary and then some, to wear the shawl, but the badge remains in your hand. You are earning and building, creating, and influencing, but without the greater reward until someone else deems you worthy by sewing the badge onto the shawl you wear.

## Discussion and Implications

Collins (2009) challenged researchers engaging in intersectional analyses to reposition identity narratives outward to elucidate social inequalities and structures within which the individuals or group is situated. The purpose of this chapter was to illuminate the scholarly personal narratives of Grace, Amanda, and Danai as we specifically discussed our experiences as Black women faculty in the academy.

The two theoretical interventions permitted me to illuminate a both/and paradigm of Collins' (2009) critique of individuals identifying their research as intersectionality and/or engaging an intersectional analysis—both the individual narratives and the positioning within an inequitable social structure. First, the narrative excerpts I organized under the complicating identity intervention highlighted not only the unique individual and collective identities Black women hold, but also the relationships among them—the ways they are inextricably linked (Collins, 1990) and the ways those identities manifest in the academy. Grace, Danai, and Amanda mentioned their age as being (or appearing) younger than colleagues and the ways youthfulness is demoralized only adding to the marginalization of Black women. Amanda shared that her contingency (NTT) status (and one's responsibility for administrative labor) often relegates her to the margins and is the subject of ongoing microaggressions from her colleagues.

Second, the narrative reflections I organized under the theoretical intervention, unveiling power in interconnected structures of inequality, metaphorically illustrated the social inequalities that exist within the structure of the academy in which Black women hold an outsider-within status (Collins, 1986). Danai compared her experience in the academy to a boiling pot. As a Black woman who is untenured and lacks positional power, she is unable to decrease the academic heat (e.g., pressure or expectations), instead she must place a wooden spoon over the top to sustain her daily existence. Amanda analogized the mental acrobatics and constant reconciliation that Black women endure as like forgetting whether you turned off the curling iron after leaving for work. This consistent questioning however is not simply because Black women feel their identities are underrepresented or valued less than their colleagues; the marginalization of Black women in the academy is systemic and deeply rooted in our historical and social location in American society (hooks, 1981; Garrett & Croom, 2023; Hull et al., 1982). Grace's reflections revealed both the sacrificial investment Black women make and the inequitable evaluation structure we must persist to obtain (and maintain) legitimacy in the academy. Her comparison of our bodies to doormats and us earning (fighting for) a professoriate badge on a brownie shawl captured the juxtapositioning of our outsider-within status (Collins, 1986) and the realities of our resiliency to remain in the academy (Boss et al., 2021).

The longitudinal study of our experiences as Black women in the academy has expanded the work of previous scholarship by examining our experiences in unconventional ways. Coupling scholarly personal narrative with metaphor provided us the language to make meaning of our experiences in an abstract, yet intentional way. Whether a wooden spoon over a boiling pot, turning off a curling iron, being a doormat, or receiving a badge on a brownie shawl, our individual and collective communities were not only crucial in shaping how we interacted with the system, our colleagues, and students, but were also necessary parts of our survival.

## Implications

Two implications from this scholarship on Black women in the academy is through mentoring and individuals who are willing to serve as advocates on behalf of Black women to change the system piece-by-piece. Mentorship of Black women doctoral students into the professoriate by Black women faculty has been evidenced as crucial to their success (Kelly & Fries-Britt, 2022b; Grant & Ghee, 2015). Peer mentorship of Black women faculty who form writing groups, sister circles, accountability groups, and additional ways to commune with one another assist in supporting one's trajectory in the academy (Porter et al., 2022). The onus should not be placed solely on Black women, who are already isolated at their respective institutions, to figure the academic terrain on their own. Academic affairs departments need to formally establish mentoring structures whereby contingent and tenure-track faculty are provided guidance and ongoing support throughout the duration of their academic appointment at the institution. Having a critical contingency of Black women at an institution would help the pairing process, specifically when discussing identity intersections and how one experiences interactions with colleagues and students within their respective departments.

The inequitable social structure of the academy is not going to change itself—the individuals who hold positional and influential power must influence (and be) the change. Despite our strength and resiliency throughout history, Black women faculty do not hold the necessary political power to change the academy. Even when we reach full professorship, Black women's historical legacy of marginalization preclude a positional authority different than their white peers (Croom & Patton, 2012). Black women faculty across rank, must "develop an arsenal of emotional and psychological weaponry against the cumulative effects of the gendered racism and racist sexism that many of us experience" (Carter Andrews, 2015, p. 79). This gendered racial battle fatigue is exhausting, and Black women need others who hold authentic, equitable, and critical intentions, to use their positional and political power and advocate on our behalf within their respective spheres of influence(s).

Being a Black woman in the academy is acknowledging the system for which we are signing up for; we may not physically know what "it" looks like to be at the table, but because of the narratives of those who have paved (and are paving) the way for us, we have some insight. This does not mean, however, we are in complete agreement with the structure, governance, and inner workings of the system; but we do need to understand its/our history. Black women persevered the academy as doctoral students and intentionally continue our trajectories into the professoriate, just as Black women have pushed through hundreds of years of marginalization. In a 1973 interview, Maya Angelou referred to the frightening strength of Black women as like a steel rod running through her body (as cited in Elliot, 1989). The strength Black women have maintained throughout history is powerful to say the least, despite the frightening, inequitable, and exploitive social structures within which we have been forced (and chosen) to occupy.

# References

Boss, G. J., Davis, T. J., Porter, C. J., & Moore, C. M. (2019). Second to none: Contingent Women of Color faculty in the classroom. In R. Jeffries (Ed.), *Diversity, equity, and inclusivity in contemporary higher* education (pp. 211–225). IGI Global.

Boss, G. J., Porter, C. J., Davis, T. J., & Moore, C. M. (2021). Who cares?: (Re)visioning labor justice for Black women contingent faculty. *Journal of African American Women and Girls in Education, 1*(1), 80–94.

Carter Andrews, D. J. (2015). Navigating raced-gender microaggressions: The experiences of tenure-track Black female scholars. In F. A. Bonner II, a. f. marbley, F. Tuitt, P. A. Robinson, R. M. Banda, and R. L. Hughes (Eds.), *Black faculty in the academy: Narratives for negotiating identity and achieving career success* (pp. 79–88). Routledge.

Charmaz, K. (2006). *Constructing grounded theory: A practical guide through qualitative analysis.* SAGE.

Collins, P. H. (1986). Learning from the outsider within: The sociological significance of Black feminist thought. *Social Problems, 33*(6), S14–S22.

Collins, P. H. (1990). *Black feminist thought: Knowledge, consciousness, and the politics of empowerment.* Routledge.

Collins, P. H. (2000). *Black feminist thought.: Knowledge, consciousness, and the politics of empowerment* (2nd ed.). Routledge.

Collins, P. H., & Bilge, S. (2016). *Intersectionality.* Polity.

Crenshaw, K. (1989). Demarginalizing the intersection of race and sex: A Black feminist critique of antidiscrimination doctrine, feminist theory, and antiracist politics. *University of Chicago Legal Forum, 1989*(8), 139–167.

Crenshaw, K. (1991). Mapping the margins: Intersectionality, identity politics, and violence against Women of Color. *Stanford Law Review, 43*(6), 1241–1299.

Crenshaw, K. (2016). The urgency of intersectionality [video file]. https://www.ted.com/talks/kimberle_crenshaw_the_urgency_of_intersectionality.

Croom, N. N. (2017). Promotion beyond tenure: Unpacking racism and sexism in the experiences of Black womyn professors. *The Review of Higher Education, 40*(4), 557–583.

Croom, N. N., & Patton, L. D. (2012). The miner's canary: A critical race perspective on the representation of Black women full professors. *Negro Educational Review, 62 & 63*(1–4), 13–39.

Dill, B. T., & Zambrana, R. E. (2009). *Emerging intersections: Race, class, gender, in theory, policy, and practice.* Rutgers University Press.

Elliot, J. M. (1989). *Conversations with Maya Angelou.* Jackson: University Press of Mississippi.

Fries-Britt, S., & Kelly, B. T. (2005). Retaining each other: Narrative of two African American women in the academy. *The Urban Review, 37,* 221–242.

Garrett, S. D., & Croom, N. N. (2023). Supporting Black womyn associate professors to the full professorship. In C. J. Porter, V. T. Sulé, & N. N. Croom (Eds), *Black feminist epistemology, research, and praxis: Narratives in and through the academy* (pp. 165–176). Routledge.

Grant, C. M., & Ghee, S. (2015). Mentoring 101: Advancing African American women faculty and doctoral student success in predominantly White institutions. *International Journal of Qualitative Studies in Education, 28*(7), 759–785.

Gregory, S. T. (2001). Black faculty women in the academy: History, status and future. *The Journal of Negro Education, 70*(3), 124–138.

hooks, b. (1981). *Ain't I a woman?* South End.

Hull, G. T., Bell-Scott, P., & Smith, B. (1982). *All the women are White, all the Blacks are men, but some of us are brave: Black women's studies.* The Feminist Press.

Kelly, B. T., & Fries-Britt, S. (2022a). *Building mentorship networks to support Black women: A guide to succeeding in the academy.* Routledge.

Kelly, B. T., & Fries-Britt, S. (2022b). Still retaining each other: Sustained mentoring. In B. T. Kelly & S. Fries-Britt (Eds.), *Building mentorship networks to support Black women: A guide to succeeding in the academy* (pp. 5–18). Routledge.

Lakoff, G., & Johnson, M. (1980). *Metaphors we live by.* University of Chicago Press.

Louis, D. A., Rawls, G. J., Jackson-Smith, D., Chambers, G. A., Phillips, L. L., & Louis, S. L. (2016). Listening to our voices: Experiences of Black faculty at predominantly White research university with microaggressions. *Journal of Black Studies, 47*(5), 454–474.

McNeely Cobham, B. A., & Patton, L. D. (2015). Self-will, power, and determination: A study of Black women faculty and the role of self-efficacy. *NASPA Journal about Women in Higher Education, 8*(1), 29–46.

Nash, R. J. (2004). *Liberating scholarly writing: The power of personal narrative.* Teachers College Press.

Perlow, O. N., Wheeler, D. I., Bethea, S. L., & Scott, B. M. (2018). *Black women's liberatory pedagogies: Resistance, transformation, and healing within and beyond the academy.* Springer Nature.

Porter, C. J., Davis, T. J., & Boss, G. J. (2022). Solidifying our 'scholarhood': Growing (up) together as Black women in the academy. In B. T. Kelly & S. Fries-Britt (Eds), *Building mentorship networks to support Black women: A guide to succeeding in the academy* (pp. 69–83). Routledge.

Porter, C. J., Moore, C. M., Boss, G. J., Davis, T. J., & Louis, D. A. (2020). To be Black women and contingent faculty: Four scholarly personal narratives. *The Journal of Higher Education, 91*(5), 674–697.

Porter, C. J., Sulé, V. T., & Croom, N. N. (Eds.). (2023). *Black feminist epistemology, research, and praxis: Narratives in and through the academy.* Routledge.

Sulé, V. T. (2009). Black female faculty: Role definition, critical enactments, and contributions to predominantly White research institutions. *NASPA Journal about Women in Higher Education, 2*(1), 93–121.

Sulé, V. T. (2023). Enact, discard, and transform: Black women's agentic epistemology. In C. J. Porter, V. T. Sulé, *& N. N. Croom (Eds.), *Black feminist epistemology, research, and praxis: Narratives in and through the academy* (pp. 199–205). Routledge.

# 7. Queer Women and Femme Students of Color Seeking Help After Surviving Dating Violence in College

Nadeeka Karunaratne

Though issues of campus interpersonal violence, or sexual and relationship violence, have received heightened national attention in the past decade, higher education policy and practice are limited by the dearth of critical violence research that analyzes the role of intersecting systems of power and the experiences of minoritized students (Harris et al., 2020). Little is known about the experiences of Queer Women and Femme of Color (QWFOC) students who have survived dating violence, particularly their experiences with help seeking from institutional resources (Harris & Linder, 2017). This power-evasive and identity-neutral approach to campus interpersonal violence research limits the ability of higher education administrators, policymakers, and practitioners to adequately address the needs of QWFOC student survivors.

College student dating violence survivors typically have low rates of help seeking (20–23%) from formal resources like mental health services, campus police, and Title IX offices (Cantor et al., 2020; H. Cho & Huang, 2017). The sparse existing literature on help seeking clearly lacks an analysis of the influences of race *and* sexuality. For instance, some scholars note that cultural practices of silence may deter help seeking from Women of Color student survivors (Agbayani-Siewert & Flanagan, 2000; Ragavan et al., 2021). Further, queer women students may face barriers to accessing help, such as isolation, lack of awareness of dynamics of abuse and available resources, and fear of discrimination from service providers (Bloom et al., 2016). Despite these distinct bodies of literature, few researchers examine the intersectional help-seeking experiences of Queer Students of Color.

## Theoretical Framing and Chapter Purpose

Intersectionality, a theoretical framework that can be employed to understand how interlocking systems of oppression function to influence individuals' lived experiences, stems from Black feminist activist-scholars (Crenshaw, 1989). The term was coined by Kimberlé Crenshaw in 1989, who later outlined three forms of intersectionality through the analysis of the experiences of Women of Color survivors of interpersonal violence (Crenshaw, 1991). *Representational intersectionality* allows for an analysis of how the portrayal of Women of Color in cultural imagery, like popular culture, contributes to their devaluation and the violence committed against them. *Political intersectionality* refers to the failures of both antiracist and feminist movements (e.g., Civil Rights Movement, mainstream antiviolence movement) to center the needs of Women of Color. *Structural intersectionality* highlights how the dominant norms of whiteness are institutionalized into laws and services that marginalize Women of Color (Crenshaw, 1991).

Driven by intersectionality and the aforementioned gaps in existing research, the following question guides this critical qualitative study: What are the help-seeking experiences of Queer Women and Femme Students of Color after surviving dating violence during college? In this chapter, I aim to highlight how the theory of intersectionality, specifically the three forms of intersectionality, can be used as a lens to analyze the experiences of minoritized college students.

## Method

"Um, I think I do have a question for you. Hopefully it's not too personal. Did you ever come out to your parents and how was that experience for you?" Gina (pseudonym), a QWFOC dating violence survivor, asked me this question toward the end of our second interview together. While we had spent most of this interview talking about her healing from dating violence, interlaced throughout both of our conversations were discussions about navigating restrictive gender norms, parental expectations, and biphobia. After I shared about my recent experience coming out to my Sri Lankan immigrant mom, Gina responded: "Thank you for sharing that. I really appreciate it... I'm still exploring my queer identity within the Latine community."

Gina's question and subsequent gratitude embody the power of a critical methodology rooted in healing (Karunaratne, 2023). Critical qualitative inquiry guided this study, as it allowed for the investigation of the interconnectedness of individuals' experiences and structures of power (Pasque et al.,

2012), aligning with intersectionality. In this chapter, I use intersectionality to analyze the narratives of 16 students who identify as queer, lesbian and/ or bisexual—a subset of participants from a larger study with 35 Women and Femme Students of Color who experienced dating violence in a past relationship during college. Using narrative inquiry, data were generated in the larger study with 35 undergraduate students attending one of three large public universities in the western United States. More specifically, participants engaged in two virtual semi-structured interviews (Olson, 2011) and a photo-elicitation method (Lapenta, 2012) centered on their healing. The first interview focused on their backgrounds and experiences of dating violence, including the context of the abuse, their immediate responses, and the impacts on their academics and social lives. The second interview, which included the photo-elicitation activity, centered help seeking and healing. Participants self-identified as Asian, Black, Filipina, Filipino American, Hapa, Hispanic, Latinx/Latina/Latine, Mestiza/x, Mexican, Mexican-American, Mixed, Multiracial, and Pakistani/Indian. Students' gender identities included gender queer, nonbinary, nonbinary femme, and woman and their class years ranged from first to fifth.

As a Queer Woman of Color, I regularly share the political and personal facets of my identities and experiences with participants, engaging in a form of vulnerability that allows for deeper connection with students. I also employ trauma-informed and healing-centered research approaches to foster students' healing through this research (Karunaratne, 2023). My identities and experiences influence how I conceptualized and analyzed this research—serving Queer Student Survivors of Color as a prevention educator, trauma-informed yoga instructor, and a cultural center coordinator allowed me to witness firsthand the structures that failed to consider or appropriately respond to these students' needs. My experiences as a trauma-informed yoga instructor directly influence my engagement with students as I aim to create spaces that foster healing through attention to the nuanced effects of trauma and multiple forms of oppression on students' lived experiences (Karunaratne, 2023).

Intersectionality can serve as a "way of thinking about and conducting analyses" (S. Cho et al., 2013, p. 795). Therefore, I employed intersectionality (Crenshaw, 1989, 1991) as an analytic tool to illuminate how various structures of oppression, like racism and homophobia, are interlocking, ultimately influencing how QWFOC seek help from dating violence experiences. Aligning with critical qualitative approaches, reflexive thematic analysis acknowledges the role of the researcher in cocreating knowledge, allowing for recognition that "data are not coded in an epistemological vacuum" (Braun & Clarke, 2006, p. 84). In my first round of coding, I primarily used inductive codes that centered students' meaning-making, including in vivo codes or codes using participants own words (e.g., "Women of Color are dehumanized"); emotions codes (e.g., scared), and values codes which signified values, attitudes, or beliefs representing participants' perspectives (e.g., survivors are silenced; Saldaña, 2021). I also relied on structural coding that allowed me to categorize narratives (e.g., self-awareness increased, self-awareness decreased), concept coding exploring macro levels of meaning (e.g., homophobia), and causation coding that labeled participants' beliefs about events and their causes (e.g., intergenerational trauma; Saldaña, 2021).

I then engaged in a second round of deductive coding using the three forms of intersectionality (i.e., political, representational, and structural). I looked both for explicit and implicit mentions of systems of oppression operating in students' lives (Bowleg, 2008). During this process, I analyzed interviews at the "latent level" to move beyond the "semantic" or surface content of data to understand the underlying ideas present in students' narratives (Braun & Clarke, 2006, p. 84), in alignment with intersectional analyses (Bowleg, 2008). After an initial round of analysis, I shared a document that contained a summary of my analyses and invited participants to provide written or verbal feedback. I also practiced dialogic engagement with other education scholars and Women of Color professionals who work in campus interpersonal violence advocacy. Incorporating participants' feedback, I categorized codes and generated themes, which I present below.

## Findings

In terms of seeking help from formal resources on campus, only one of the 16 students engaged with reporting through Title IX, and no students chose to report to local or campus law enforcement. Further, only two students engaged with their confidential campus advocacy office. Most (14) students did seek out therapy in some form—nine through campus resources and five via off-campus services. Using the three forms of intersectionality (i.e., representational, political, and structural), I highlight QWFOC students' help-seeking experiences after surviving dating violence in college.

### Representational Intersectionality

Though much of the (White) feminist literature discusses the negative consequences of representations of violence against women broadly, Crenshaw (1991) offered the argument that discussing violence against women broadly is not enough to understand the experiences of Women of Color and the overlapping forms of oppression that shape their experiences of interpersonal violence. Much of existing scholarship centers the ways in which dehumanizing depictions of Women and Femmes of Color position them as more vulnerable to violence (INCITE!, 2016). However, in this study, students explicitly spoke about the ways they internalized these representations to influence their help seeking after experiencing violence. The representations of QWFOC in cultural imagery and societal discourse can contribute to their dehumanization and marginalization, which *representational intersectionality* can be used to understand (Crenshaw, 1991).

In considering disclosure of their abusive experiences and seeking help, QWFOC survivors feared 1) being blamed and 2) not being taken seriously; these fears were directly linked to the images and discourses surrounding QWFOC in popular culture, media, and society generally. Students' *fear of being blamed* for their abuse was directly linked to portrayals of QWFOC as hypersexual and promiscuous (Haynes et al., 2020; Museus & Saelua, 2014). Given these racist and heteronormative representations, the violence QWFOC survivors experience is seen as their fault (Donovan & Williams, 2002). This fear of being blamed because they were viewed as hypersexual and promiscuous made many survivors in this study hesitant to seek help. For example, Liza highlighted stereotypes of promiscuity that deeply influenced her experiences of dating violence: "Being a Black queer woman, there's this really toxic stereotype like we're automatically more promiscuous or open to sexual things." Due to this and other stereotypes, Liza felt she would not be believed for her abuse because people from whom she sought help would "be like, 'Oh, you're always like this.'"

Students also *feared they would not be taken seriously* if they sought help for their experiences of dating violence because of the normalized depictions of violence against QWFOC individuals that made violence seem "predestined," a term Blue used. Blue felt that abuse against Women and Femmes of Color is "not taken seriously." Blue went on to share, "It's just seen to me as like inherent to our station." Linking this representation of violence against Women of Color with Blue's help seeking, Blue questioned, "How do you even handle that when there's no one to take it seriously?" Consequently, like Blue, many survivors felt they should be silent about their experiences and not seek help.

In addition to fearing not being taken seriously because of the normalization of violence against QWFOC individuals, student survivors also felt violence against White women was taken more seriously than harm to Women and Femmes of Color. Highlighting this, multiple students discussed the disproportionate media coverage of harmed or missing White women in comparison to Women and Femmes of Color. Several students spoke about a recent case of a White woman who went missing, which then became "global news." Gina shared, "Meanwhile, Women of Color, especially Indigenous women and darker-complexion women, go missing every day. And that's not talked about." These societal representations of QWFOC and the violence they experience served to minimize students' own experiences of dating violence and functioned as a barrier to help seeking. Media discourse embodied the social hierarchy that values White women's bodies over those of Women of Color (Crenshaw, 1991). The marking of their bodies as violable, a philosophy stemming directly from the enslavement of Black people, Native American genocide, and the historical exploitation of immigrants (INCITE!, 2016), was visible to student survivors. Due to these representations, students feared their abuse would not be taken seriously if they sought help, which ultimately limited their help seeking. Analysis using representational intersectionality demonstrated that decisions to seek help, which can dictate healing for survivors, are not solely individual-level decisions. Rather, students' responses to dating violence are influenced by societal representations of QWFOC individuals.

## Political Intersectionality

Students' help seeking after dating violence was influenced by (1) White feminist practices engrained in many campus resources designed to support survivors and (2) community norms. This influence can be understood through *political intersectionality*, which refers to how Women and Femmes of Color are positioned in communities and political groups (e.g., feminism, antiracism) that often do not consider their needs and experiences at the intersection of multiple identities and corresponding forms of oppression (Crenshaw, 1991).

Most students did not feel comfortable seeking help from structures on campus that were intended for survivors, such as Title IX offices; this hesitation was linked to the nature of *available support that heavily centered reporting processes* (Shepp et al., 2023). The heavy focus on reporting as a response to interpersonal violence stems from the legacy of the White feminist movement (Kim, 2018). The mainstream antiviolence movement (i.e., second-wave feminism) historically focused on promoting carceral approaches to interpersonal violence response, including collaboration with law enforcement and reliance on the criminal punishment system (Kim, 2018; Richie, 2012). Mainstream organizers advocated for the addition of domestic violence to criminal codes, increased criminal penalties for interpersonal violence, and mandatory arrest policies, which fuel(ed) the growth of the carceral state and harm Communities of Color (Kim, 2018). These carceral responses to interpersonal violence in the United States, broadly, are mirrored on college campuses (Shepp et al., 2023). Of course, reports of violence to local or campus law enforcement directly link to carceral structures outside of higher education. However, even Title IX structures align with carceral logics of punishment without focusing on survivors' needs for safety and healing (Shepp et al., 2023).

In this study, QWFOC participants critiqued the punitive responses to interpersonal violence that their institutions offered. Many students emphasized their concerns with reporting their experiences of dating violence, particularly due to the negative views about policing and incarceration they held that were often rooted in their intersecting identities. Students often feared law enforcement and did not believe in punishment as a helpful response to dating violence. For example, Charlotte shared the tension they felt between "rehabilitation versus punishment." Sharing their concerns, Charlotte explained the need for "accountability outside of Title IX and the police, especially us being the Black community." Charlotte emphasized the need for rehabilitation through programs and counselors that helped the "person who was harming" take accountability for and learn from their behavior. Charlotte also highlighted the need to focus on ensuring the survivor feels safe within community spaces and on campus, rather than focusing on punishing the "person who was harming." Other students also voiced a need for restorative approaches to dating violence that center on uplifting survivors' needs for safety and justice and holding those who harm accountable for their actions. Elaborating on her rationale for preferring restorative approaches over punishment, Bee shared, "I really do believe hurt people hurt people." Bee, like many other students, did not see a benefit in punishing those who have also experienced harm in their lives. The existing reporting structures, infused with White feminist values, left little options for QWFOC to feel adequately supported in their needs.

Given the inadequacies of institutional violence-specific resources, some students sought help from identity-specific resources on campus, such as the lesbian, gay, bisexual, transgender, and queer (LGBTQ) center and cultural centers. Describing how they would spend time in the lounge area of the center, Frida described the LGBTQ Center on their campus as "a comfort space." Liza also shared that her campus's LGBTQ Center had "resources leading to like outside therapists or sliding scale therapists" off campus. These identity-specific spaces on campus served as important resources for QWFOC students seeking help for their dating violence experiences. These spaces supported students with their identity development, fostered connection to community, and offered healing programs.

However, *not all racial, ethnic, or cultural spaces felt safe for survivors.* Alejandra highlighted a sexual assault incident that occurred within her cultural student organization. While student leaders of the organization provided a resource list to the survivor, Alejandra noted, "They really didn't do much besides like help guiding her through what to do." In particular, they did not address the larger conditions that allowed the violence to occur in the first place or provide intersectional education for members, doing little to shift the culture for QWFOC. When Communities of Color practice values promoting silence around issues of abuse, sex, and dating, they perpetuate larger structures of intersectional oppression that Women and Femmes of Color face. This lack of recognition of the unique experiences of the women and femmes in their communities is what Crenshaw highlighted as one facet of political intersectionality (Crenshaw, 1991). For example, Crenshaw (1991) described how antiracist movements often only center the needs of Men of Color, ignoring those of women and femmes in their communities. Many of these community norms stem from practices inherited through settler colonialism and the necessity to assimilate to survive in the United States because "[i]n order to colonize a people whose society was not hierarchical, colonizers must first naturalize hierarchy through instituting patriarchy" (Smith, 2005, p. 23). Further, violence perpetrated by state agents, like the police and immigration enforcement, foster a general ethos of the need to be silent about issues of interpersonal violence so as not to draw attention to one's family or community and because of the inability to turn to these formal entities for support (Richie, 2012).

Political intersectionality highlights the influence of White feminist values and community practices on QWFOC survivors' help seeking. Given existing reporting structures did not represent their priorities or fulfill their needs for healing, QWFOC students often chose not to seek help for their dating violence experiences. Consequently, many students had to seek help from identity-based spaces on campus to find healing. However, due to community norms around silence about issues of violence, these spaces could sometimes be harmful.

## Structural Intersectionality

Molly highlighted a common sentiment shared by many students, which resulted in many survivors not seeking help from formal campus resources: "We are grouped in with White women. Like that is an assumption that people make that we face the same struggles, but I don't think that's necessarily true." *Structural intersectionality* can be used to analyze the ways that dominant norms of whiteness are embedded into institutional structures, programs, and policies that marginalize QWFOC students who experience dating violence (Crenshaw, 1991). Students described the challenges they experienced seeking help and finding healing through formal resources, primarily because their healing needs as QWFOC were not supported by institutional structures. The healing journeys of QWFOC students were rooted in cultural epistemologies, practices, and meaning making, which were (1) communal and (2) related to identity development—healing needs often unaddressed by institutional resources.

In contrast to the individualistic perspectives of healing that western philosophy promotes (Singh, 2009), students in this study described *healing as communal in nature*. Students specifically spoke about healing being fostered by communities of Women of Color, Nonbinary People of Color, and Queer People of Color. Sofi explained that their community of Women of Color and nonbinary people brought them a lot of healing. Sofi spoke about valuing the communal knowledge and experiences of Women of Color in their healing process. Sofi shared, "What brings me comfort and has brought me a lot of healing have been my community of Women of Color and nonbinary folk." Sofi went on to say, Women of Color give "this support and [are] who I can go to for love and help and everything." Sharing space with others holding similar identities allowed students to further understand their own identities, reciprocally process shared lived experiences, and foster healing. However, students often had to create these spaces for themselves, as institutional violence services did not offer identity-specific healing programs.

Students also described how *cultivation of their identities was an important aspect of their healing*. For instance, Molly shared, "As a Queer Nonbinary Person of Color, really grasping and understanding these identities of mine has helped contribute literally to my healing." Molly connected their exploration of their identities to become more self-assured, linking both to their healing: "I have become more self-assured, but that's because I've explored my identity more." Additionally, after learning about the history of Chicana lesbians in her city, Lizette explained:

> It has definitely made me feel less alone and more included into a community that I didn't know I even had. Like the lesbian community is already small as it is. So, to find even like a smaller group that relates to your culture is even more of a feeling of coming home, like a feeling of becoming closer to myself. And a feeling of less isolation in my cultural belongings.

Through learning about communities of Chicana lesbians, Lizette felt affirmed in her cultural background as well as in her sexual identity. Highlighting the power of this spiritual connection, Lizette said she experienced "a feeling of coming home" and "a feeling of becoming closer to myself." For many students, understanding their complex identities supported their senses of self and in turn fostered their healing. Some students also spoke about the political aspect of their survivorhood, which allowed them to better understand the connections between patriarchy, homophobia, racism, and dating violence, and helped them to foster a stronger appreciation for their identities.

Despite the connection between identity exploration and healing, students experienced many challenges finding providers who could support them regarding their sexual and racial identities. Sofi's first therapist "had some religious undertones" that made Sofi feel uncomfortable exploring their queer identity. Highlighting intersectionality, even when survivors found therapists who could support their sexual identity exploration, they were not always able to offer support around their racial and ethnic identities. For example, Megan expressed "cultural differences make it very difficult" to find a therapist with whom they resonate as Megan described their experiences with a White queer therapist as "awful, it was just not good." Students like Megan highlighted the importance of mental health providers being able to affirm their intersecting identities, especially when working to process experiences of dating violence.

Structural intersectionality illuminates the ways current campus services often do not address the healing needs of Women and Femme Survivors of Color. Student participants were motivated to engage in their healing and have innate knowledge and practices within themselves and their communities that can foster their healing. However, structural support from their institutions is necessary to fully achieve their healing goals.

## *Discussion and Implications*

The framework of intersectionality is a powerful tool for understanding the help seeking of QWFOC students from experiences of dating violence. In this research, intersectionality allowed me to center the experiences of QWFOC students and to deconstruct the ways in which interlocking systems of domination, such as racism, homophobia, and sexism, influenced their lives. As students' narratives highlight, representations of QWFOC influenced students' help-seeking practices. Consequently, these representations must be discussed and deconstructed in order to support students fully. Analysis of students' narratives also demonstrated that the structures aimed to address interpersonal violence on campuses are not designed for the needs of QWFOC student survivors. Institutional policymakers and leaders must work to address the unique experiences and needs of minoritized students. For example, in contrast to punitive structures, institutions should institute rehabilitation and restorative justice processes that would allow students who harm others to take accountability for and learn from their behavior. Support services should integrate identity development into programming and create communal spaces for QWFOC students to promote healing. Further, collaboration between violence support services and identity-based centers on campus is needed to truly support the healing of student survivors with multiple minoritized identities.

In scholarship, by employing power-conscious frameworks that consider how dating violence is intertwined with racism, homophobia, and other structures of domination, researchers can illuminate the full landscape of campus dating violence to better prevent and respond to violence. For instance, scholars can complicate their exploration of survivors' disclosure and help-seeking processes to focus on how larger systems of oppression influence decisions to disclose and seek help, rather than continuing to focus on individual factors as the current body of literature does (Cantor et al., 2020).

Intersectionality can be employed to understand that while there may be similarities in the dynamics of dating violence among all people, the differences are crucial to addressing and eradicating violence (Crenshaw, 1991). My use of intersectionality in this study corresponds with a refusal of a single-axis framing of dating violence and brings the full intersectional subordination of QWFOC into the conversation on campus dating violence (Haynes et al., 2020; MacKinnon, 2013). Finally, the use of intersectionality to guide this research foregrounds the practical social justice implications (Duran & Jones, 2019; Harris & Patton, 2019) of this work. This research aims to address the gap in scholarship and practice surrounding QWFOC survivors, ultimately intending to support their retention and persistence in higher education (Wood et al., 2020).

## References

Agbayani-Siewert, P., & Flanagan, A. Y. (2000). Filipino American dating violence: Definitions, contextual justifications, and experiences of dating violence. *Journal of Human Behavior in the Social Environment, 3*(3–4), 115–133.

Bloom, T., Gielen, A., & Glass, N. (2016). Developing an app for college women in abusive same-sex relationships and their friends. *Journal of Homosexuality, 63*(6), 855–874.

Bowleg, L. (2008). When Black + Lesbian + Woman ≠ Black Lesbian Woman: The methodological challenges of qualitative and quantitative intersectionality research. *Sex Roles*, 59(5–6), 312–325.

Braun, V., & Clarke, V. (2006). Using thematic analysis in psychology. *Qualitative Research in Psychology*, 3(2), 77–101.

Cantor, D., Fisher, B., Chibnall, S., Harps, S., Townsend, R., Thomas, G., Lee, H., Kranz, V., Herbison, R., & Madden, K. (2020). *Report on the AAU campus climate survey on sexual assault and misconduct*. Association of American Universities. https://www.aau.edu/sites/default/files/AAU-Files/Key-Issues/Campus-Safety/Revised%20Aggregate%20report%20%20and%20appendices%201-7_(01-16-2020_FINAL).pdf

Cho, H., & Huang, L. (2017). Aspects of help seeking among collegiate victims of dating violence. *Journal of Family Violence*, 32(4), 409–417.

Cho, S., Crenshaw, K. W., & McCall, L. (2013). Toward a field of intersectionality studies: Theory, applications, and praxis. *Signs: Journal of Women in Culture and Society*, 38(4), 785–810.

Crenshaw, K. (1989). Demarginalizing the intersection of race and sex: A Black feminist critique of antidiscrimination doctrine, feminist theory and antiracist politics. *The University of Chicago Legal Forum*, 1989(1), 139–167.

Crenshaw, K. (1991). Mapping the margins: Intersectionality, identity politics, and violence against Women of Color. *Stanford Law Review*, 43(6), 1241–1299.

Donovan, R., & Williams, M. (2002). Living at the intersection: The effects of racism and sexism on Black rape survivors. *Women & Therapy*, 25(3–4), 95–105.

Duran, A., & Jones, S. R. (2019). Using intersectionality in qualitative research on college student identity development: Considerations, tensions, and possibilities. *Journal of College Student Development*, 60(4), 455–471.

Harris, J. C., Cobian, K., & Karunaratne, N. (2020). Re-imagining the study of campus sexual assault. In L.W. Perna (Ed.), *Higher education: Handbook of theory and research* (Vol. 35). Springer.

Harris, J. C., & Linder, C. (Eds.). (2017). *Intersections of identity and sexual violence on campus: Centering minoritized students' experiences*. Stylus.

Harris, J. C., & Patton, L. D. (2019). Un/doing intersectionality through higher education research. *The Journal of Higher Education*, 90(3), 347–372.

Haynes, C., Joseph, N. M., Patton, L. D., Stewart, S., & Allen, E. L. (2020). Toward an understanding of intersectionality methodology: A 30-year literature synthesis of Black women's experiences in higher education. *Review of Educational Research*, 90(6), 751–787.

INCITE! Women of Color Against Violence. (2016). *Color of violence: The INCITE! anthology*. Duke University Press.

Karunaratne, N. (2023). Toward a methodology of healing: Promoting radical healing among student survivors through research. *Journal of Women and Gender in Higher Education*, 16(1), 39–51.

Kim, M. E. (2018). From carceral feminism to transformative justice: Women-of-Color feminism and alternatives to incarceration. *Journal of Ethnic & Cultural Diversity in Social Work, 27*(3), 219–233.

Lapenta, F. (2012). Some theoretical and methodological views on photo-elicitation. In E. Margolis & L. Pauwels (Eds.), *The SAGE handbook of visual research methods* (pp. 201–213). Sage.

MacKinnon, C. A. (2013). Intersectionality as method: A note. *Signs: Journal of Women in Culture and Society, 38*(4), 1019–1030.

Museus, S. D., & Saelua, N. A. (2014). Realizing the power of intersectionality research in higher education. In D. Mitchell, Jr., C. Simmons, & L. Greyerbiehl (Eds.), *Intersectionality & higher education: Theory, research, & praxis* (pp. 68–77). Peter Lang.

Olson, K. (2011). *Essentials of qualitative interviewing.* Left Coast Press.

Pasque, P. A., Carducci, R., Kuntz, A. M., & Gildersleeve, R. E. (2012). *Qualitative inquiry for equity in higher education: Methodological innovations, implications, and interventions.* Wiley Periodicals.

Ragavan, M., Syed-Swift, Y., Elwy, A. R., Fikre, T., & Bair-Merritt, M. (2021). The influence of culture on healthy relationship formation and teen dating violence: A qualitative analysis of South Asian female youth residing in the United States. *Journal of Interpersonal Violence, 36*(7–8), NP4336-NP4362.

Richie, B. E. (2012). *Arrested justice: Black women, violence, and America's prison nation.* New York University Press.

Saldaña, J. (2021). *The coding manual for qualitative researchers* (4th ed.). SAGE.

Shepp, V., O'Callaghan, E., & Kirkner, A. (2023). The carceral logic of Title IX. *Journal of Women and Gender in Higher Education, 16*(1), 4–24.

Singh, A. A. (2009). Helping South Asian immigrant women use resilience strategies in healing from sexual abuse: A call for a culturally relevant model. *Women & Therapy, 32*(4), 361–376.

Smith, A. (2005). *Conquest: Sexual violence and American Indian genocide.* Duke University Press.

Wood, L., Voth Schrag, R., & Busch-Armendariz, N. (2020). Mental health and academic impacts of intimate partner violence among IHE-attending women. *Journal of American College Health, 68*(3), 286–293.

# 8. Navigating Multiple Oppressions: The Intersectional Experiences of a Chinese American College Student with Dis/abilities[1]

YAN WANG AND BETH L. GOLDSTEIN

Despite the continued growth of the Asian American population in the United States (U.S.; U.S. Department of Health and Human Services Office of Minority Health, 2019), Asian Americans are still societally overlooked, underrepresented and underserved (Eligon, 2020; Museus, 2014). The invisibility of Asian Americans in policy and research arenas attributed to their assumed economic success (Lee, 2015; Moses et al., 2018; Museus & Kiang, 2009). The blurred economic, cultural and societal diversity of Asian Americans obscures significant issues with discrimination and privilege.

The intersecting identities of Asian Americans with dis/abilities make them invisible both in Asian American studies and dis/ability studies (Cooc, 2018; Cooc & Yang, 2017; Hasnain et al., 2020; Mereish, 2012). In Asian American studies, researchers struggle to dismantle a homogenized approach to a highly diverse census category (Museus et al., 2013) that includes people of Indian, Pakistani, Chinese, Japanese, Korean, Southeast Asian and many other origins. Asian American study scholars also challenge the model minority stereotype imposed on students of Asian descent, who are described as academically high achieving. However, this model minority is not a "privilege to be considered normal, but a privilege to be considered exceptional (in comparison to other non-white minority groups)" (Cheng, 2013, p. 75, as cited in Lee et al., 2017, p. 501). It pits students of Asian descent against other People of Color—African Americans in particular—in a rather vicious way insofar as it blinds society writ large to the discrimination both groups face (Tai & Kenyatta, 1999). In dis/ability studies, researchers often focus on the overrepresentation of African Americans and Latino students in special education (Blanchett, 2006). Asian Americans with dis/abilities are often ignored (Cooc, 2018).

The concept of dis/ability is not a biological and genetic term; rather, it is socially constructed, like race. Race and dis/ability co-construct each other within the lived experience of People of Color. As Annamma et al. (2013) state, "for [S]tudents of [C]olor, race does not exist outside of ability and ability does not exist outside of race; each is being built upon the perception of the other" (p. 6). Therefore, this chapter utilizes intersectional and critical frameworks: intersectionality, disability critical race theory and intersectional invisibility, to examine the experience of one female Chinese American college student with dis/abilities during her educational journey. We unpack how particularities of racism, ableism and patriarchy co-affect her lived experience. We also highlight how she finds strength through navigating the systems of oppression and privilege. We conclude with educational policy implications.

## Literature Review

### Social Construction of Dis/ability

Researchers have refuted the ideologies that dis/ability, like race, is a biological fact (Erevelles & Minear, 2010; Gillborn, 2015). Linton (1998) argues that variations existing in human behavior are but the meaning we make of those variations. Erevelles and Minear (2010) argue dis/ability is "a socially constructed category that derives meaning and social (in)significance from historical, cultural, political and economic structures that frame social life" (p. 132). Annamma et al. (2013) further explicate that the concept of dis/abilities is "grounded in hegemonic notions of normalcy" (p. 19) with inherent consequences for power and resource inequalities.

Blanchett et al. (2005) used the term "double jeopardy" (p. 71) to describe how demographic disproportionality and the failure of urban schools contribute to Students of Color's dire situation. Students of Color with dis/ability experience double jeopardy of discrimination by virtue of being socially constructed as both raced and dis/abled. As Ferri and Connor (2005) note:

> Dis/ability has become a more socially accepted, even normalized category of marginalization for [S]tudents of [C]olor. Examining these discourses of exclusion simultaneously highlights how deeply racialized notions of ability are entrenched in our culture—so much so that segregation of "the disabled" has also meant segregating [S]tudents of [C]olor. (p. 454)

## Experiences of Asian Americans with Dis/abilities

A dearth of literature investigates the experiences of Asian Americans with dis/abilities, highlighting their experienced discrimination and the obscured diversity within this group. Through quantitative research methods, Cooc (2018) concluded that the national data had underestimated the number of Asian American students in special education; when they do get referred for support services, it is usually later than their White peers. The model minority stereotype plays an essential role in teachers' decision-making process. Teachers assume Asian American students do not have learning dis/abilities because of their respectful and obedient manners (Park, 2019). Teachers also speculate that Asian American students should excel not only in science, technology, engineering, and mathematics but also in English proficiency, overlooking the linguistic and cognitive diversity of these students (Wang et al., 2021).

Mereish (2012) found that Asian Americans with learning, emotional, or physical dis/abilities reported more everyday discrimination and greater psychological and physical distress than those without. Furthermore, those with severe physical dis/abilities reported even greater discrimination and distress. Hasnain et al.'s (2020) review of research on Asian Americans with dis/abilities reiterates that the diversity within the Asian American community is severely oversimplified; there is no account of how ethnicity, age, gender, religion, refugee or immigrant status, etc., impact their experience as people with dis/abilities. Second, the predominance of quantitative studies obscures their nuanced lived experience and narratives.

This study, therefore, directly addresses the lived experience of Emma, a Chinese American female college student with both mental and physical dis/abilities. Through critical frameworks, we illuminate the importance of intersectionality and heterogeneity in defining her experience. Significantly, this research concerns how Emma both negotiates and is construed by U.S. education, Chinese American community, and her country of origin. By incorporating how a transnational life impacts her experiences, we further suggest the complexity of international intersectionality.

## Theoretical Framework

### Intersectionality

Intersectionality recognizes that people have different dimensions to their identities (gender, race, ethnicity, etc.); how people interact with and are positioned by the society is influenced by the societal valuation of these identities.

Therefore, intersectionality "helps us understand the multidimensional ways people experience life" (Dill et al., 2007, p. 630). Crenshaw (1989) asserts that because "intersectional experience is greater than the sum of racism and sexism, any analysis that does not take intersectionality into account cannot sufficiently address the particular manner in which Black women are subordinated" (p. 140). Intersectionality challenges the "uncritical and disturbing acceptance of dominant ways of thinking about discrimination" (Crenshaw, 1989, p. 150). Collins and Bilge (2016) state that "Intersectionality adds additional layers of complexity to understandings of social inequity, recognizing that social inequality is rarely caused by a single factor ... intersectionality encourages understandings of social inequality based on interactions among various categories" (p. 26). An intersectional lens enables us to examine how oppression and social inequality resulting from different dimensions of identity can impact the life of Asian Americans with dis/abilities.

## Disability Critical Race Theory (DisCrit)

Developed by Annamma et al. (2013), disability critical race theory (DisCrit) aims to unravel how race plays a role in the lives of people with dis/abilities. By exploring the mechanisms by which race and ability are socially constructed and interdependent, it exposes the process by which People of Color are simultaneously raced and disabled. It also explicates how the social construction of dis/ability is inherently racial (Waldman et al., 2022), rooted in dominant notions of normalcy where deviations from White, middle-class, able-bodied norms are viewed as socially subordinate (Annamma et al., 2013). Recognizing the misfit of Students of Color with dis/abilities in multiple social categories, Annamma et al. (2013) argue,

> We believe that [S]tudents of [C]olor who have been labeled with dis/abilities live in the same complex world where they do not fit neatly into any one category. However, for [S]tudents of [C]olor, the label of dis/ability situates them in unique positions where they are considered "less than" white peers with or without dis/ability labels, as well as their non-disabled [P]eers of [C]olor. In brief, their embodiment and positioning reveal ways in which racism and ableism inform and rely upon each other in interdependent ways. (p. 5)

## Intersectional Invisibility

Purdie-Vanghns and Eibach (2008) postulate that because people with two or more subordinate identities do not fit the prototypes of their constituent subordinate groups, they will experience intersectional invisibility—historical, cultural, political, and legal invisibility. "Situating prototypicality in this real-world ideological context provides a basis for examining how and why intersecting subordinate-group identities affect people's lives" (Purdie-Vanghns & Eibach, 2008, p. 387). While Purdie-Vanghns and Eibach focused on the subordinating power of androcentrism, ethnocentrism and hetero-centrism, we argue to add ableism to unravel the intersectional invisibility of people with dis/abilities. In addition, when people move internationally, they encounter divergent systems of oppression as each country may differently designate privilege and marginality. We therefore further add internationalism as significant to intersectional invisibility for people with multiple oppressed identities when they travel transnationally.

These three frameworks are interconnected. People experience intersectional invisibility because they have multiple identities, and it is the lack of understanding of the intersectionality of their multiple identities that contributes to their invisibility. Disability critical race theory challenges the one-sided perception of people with dis/abilities and urges us to see how the intersection of race and disability contributes to their lived experience. Combining these three connected theoretical frameworks reveals the interwoven oppressions that impact Emma's experience. By adopting the three theoretical frameworks together, we are able to understand how she was made marginal and invisible yet also stronger through her intersectional identities.

## *Method*

This research is part of a larger qualitative research project investigating Chinese American college students' ethnic identity development and college experience. The project used semi-structured interviews and informal socialization for data collection. It focused on 13 participants from a large university in the Midwestern United States, recruited from Chinese language classes from 2014 to 2019.

Emma (pseudonym) was the only participant with visible physical dis/abilities, resulting from her premature birth. She used a wheelchair due to congenital spastic cerebral palsy and relied on her left hand for daily functioning. She was born to a Chinese immigrant family. She has an elder sister. Emma has a strong passion for history. She won many contests in history when she was in high school and earned her bachelor's and master's degree in history. Emma studied abroad in China during undergraduate school. She became well known by people at her host institution because she was very social and took every opportunity to communicate with people. Emma is currently pursuing her doctor's degree in history at an American university, focusing on the Chinese Cultural Revolution. YW has known Emma since

2012. Unlike most participants, who were interviewed twice, Emma was interviewed six times, each around one hour. She also had numerous informal socializations with YW, such as having dinner together, studying together and home visits. Emma's sister, parents, and college friend were also interviewed. Interview transcriptions and field notes were analyzed thematically using axial and clustered coding (see Creswell, 2013, for coding schemes).

Critical race hermeneutics (CRH) "uses critical race theory (CRT) to revise the best aspects of critical hermeneutics, creating a methodology for the theoretical study of race and white supremacy;" it emphasizes "how communication is distorted by a white supremacist social structure, turning discursive exchanges into everyday forms of racialized material, psychic, and symbolic violence" (Allen, 2021, p. 18). In interpreting text, CRH guides researchers to use "conflict theory...[and] see white supremacy as the historical (and geographical) context" (Allen, 2021, p. 20). Recognizing how whiteness and ableism have been constructed as norms against which non-white and dis/abled people are judged, and inspired by the critical attention to race in data analysis proposed by CRH, we also attend to ableism to analyze how it becomes a norm to judge and evaluate people with dis/abilities through seemingly well-intentioned discourses. We highlight how discourses toward people with dis/abilities in a White and ableist supremacy society can be distorted to uphold discriminatory norms. We believe this attention to both race and ability will make intelligible how normative discourses can reproduce structural White and ableist supremacy. We pose the hegemonic norms as problems needing interrogation.

## Findings

Emma lived with discrimination; her life was fragmented in the U.S., Chinese American community and China. She experienced marginalization, subordination and invisibility in unique ways in each social context. She was inferiorized because of her dis/abilities, and at the same time, her ability and gender were racialized due to her Chinese heritage. These identities created her intersectional invisibility across various social contexts. As she moved transnationally, the varied systems of oppression complicated her experience and exposed her to international invisibility.

### Inferiorizing Dis/ability

Emma experienced discrimination from people around her, especially from people of Chinese descent. Her sister testified that "some of the people who were most unkind to Emma were Chinese. They basically say very mean and horrible things to her because of her dis/ability." Emma remembered a Chinese American classmate calling her "half smart for half of the year, but dumb for the next half" when she was moved from advanced math class to regular math class. She recalled being called "retarded" numerous times by her peers. Given that smartness is a construct just like whiteness (Leonardo & Broderick, 2011), her peers' perceptions of Emma as mentally retarded do not "exist in an objective state, but are understood only through society's cultural, historical perspectives, and in practices that create and reproduce them" (Kasa-Hendrickson, 2005, p. 57). That Emma frequently suffered from hurtful remarks echoes what Leonardo and Broderick (2011) state "like the derogation of [P]eople of [C]olor under white supremacy, smart supremacy derides the 'intellectually disabled' figure. The discourse of derision is daily for both marginalized groups" (p. 2224).

"Well-intentioned" microaggressions also inflicted pain on Emma. She vividly recounted one Chinese American leader of the youth Bible class at her Chinese American church, who publicly singled her out: "我们当基督徒的就更知道应该怎么爱像Emma这样的残疾人。" (Translation: "We Christians need to know how to love people like Emma, who has dis/abilities"). Emma was shocked upon hearing this. She felt like "有点出戏了" ("being put in the spotlight"). Despite his good intention, the leader had marginalized Emma. By separating her from "we" (i.e., the abled and Christians) who need to love her, he positioned her as inferior and dependent. The leader's comment, "people like Emma," excluded her from her Chinese American community despite her Chinese ancestry. Rather than seeing her as a whole person, the youth leader names her as a person with dis/abilities learning to be a Christian. The "savior" mentality that people like Emma need to be loved demonstrates the intersectional hegemony of ableism and Christianity. Emma was made hypervisible and invisible simultaneously. Intersecting religious, ableist and ethnic prejudices made her atypical in a context she expected to be safe and affirming.

By attending to ableist supremacy in understanding seemingly benign discouses, we can understand how the following recollection is distorted by an ableist social structure which discriminates against Emma in a subtle way.

甚至有的时候，我和妈妈在超市买东西，碰到一位阿姨。她就会："哦，Emma回来了？ 哦，Emma，你特别厉害，你现在在做什么呢？特别厉害，你可以一个人在大学.

Translation: Similar things happened even when my mother and I were in the grocery store. We met an [Chinese] acquaintance. She said, "oh, Emma, you came back [from college]. You are so incredible. What are you doing right now? You are amazing. You can study in college by yourself."

Upon hearing this, Emma shouted in her head, "Wait, shut up. I already know you know all of this. Please stop talking about it." Reflecting on her reaction, Emma shared,

> So that's a very bad reaction, right? I don't like really welcome it,.... 我不能避免这些东西，我一辈子别人都会这样看我，"哦，   Emma怎么这么奇怪，怎么这么厉害？又是残疾情况，又是中国人，还上了大学。"所以有的时候不能避免，就是尽量ignore.   一个反应是藏起来，一个反应是ignore就是do my best to ignore.
>
> Translation: So, that's a very bad reaction, right? I don't like really welcome it. … I cannot avoid things like that. People would see me this way all my life: "Oh, how come Emma is so different and high achieving? She has dis/abilities; she is Chinese and goes to college." Sometimes I cannot avoid such comments, so I try to ignore them. One reaction is to hide; another is to ignore, to do my best to ignore.

Emma was acutely aware of the implication of the comment "she has dis/abilities…and goes to college." Such "compliments" insidiously question her intelligence. This is strikingly similar to the "Black Genius" (McGee, 2018) rhetoric where Black students' high academic performance is considered as extraordinary. While the "Black Genius" rhetoric reinforces White racial superiority by positioning Whites as more intelligent than Blacks, the statement "she has dis/abilities…and goes to college" not only reinforces the White racial superiority but ableism superiority, indicating that Students of Color with dis/abilities are even "less than" White students with or without dis/abilities.

Emma's recollection of people of Chinese descent inflicting discrimination echoes the research on Chinese people's negative attitude toward people with dis/abilities (Chan et al., 2002; Chen et al., 2002; Lam et al., 2006). Lam et al. (2006) assert that because Chinese society values harmony and karma, "[d]is/ability is seen as disharmony, and therefore hardly tolerable among Chinese. …[A] dis/ability is a result of divine intervention, punishment for one's transgression in the previous life" (p. 272). Knowing the implications of dis/ability in Chinese culture, Emma and her family experienced much internal shame. Her mom expressed great guilt for Emma's dis/ability. She attributed Emma's dis/ability to her wrongdoings, manifesting the influence of the logic of karma in Buddhism (Lam et al., 2006). Emma aspired to have Harry Porter's "invisible cloak, [so as] to blend in as much as possible." She tried her best not to bother people. Her friend testified "you can tell she feels all the time 不要麻烦别人 (Translation: "don't want to bother people")…and feels a little apologetic about asking for help."

These entrenched ideas travel internationally and play a role in Chinese Americans' (especially recent immigrants) negativity toward people with dis/abilities. Emma experiences international invisibility when Chinese ethnic beliefs about shaming migrate across national borders. Furthermore, this same ethnic community is also influenced by the United States' hegemonic ideologies of whiteness, smartness and religion that further alienate Emma. Hence, people of Chinese descent living in the U.S. unintentionally inflict pain on Emma through overlapping yet distinct hegemonies in their two cultures–Chinese and American.

## Racializing Ability

### Being Avoided

While the inferiority of dis/abled people is too often entrenched in people of Chinese descent's mind, non-Chinese people racialize Emma's dis/ability. Her race and dis/ability intersect to render her to be avoided and exoticized. Emma recalled White people often avoided interaction with her through comments like "I don't know what to do with you, or how to talk to you, how to approach you and how to befriend you." She stated, "There is also problems with 美国白人。我自己觉得他们也有问题。比如说在超市，小朋友盯着眼睛看着我，然后父母就说: 'oh, that's not polite, don't stare'" (Translation: "There are also problems with American Whites. I think they have problems [with people with dis/abilities] too. For example, in the grocery store, if a kid stares at me, the parents would quickly say 'oh, that's not polite, don't stare.'"). White parents transmitted a message to their White child that people like Emma, who uses a wheelchair, must be avoided. Emma was simultaneously singled out and then quickly avoided. While we do not know exactly what was transpiring, we speculate that Emma's intersectional identities as an Asian female with dis/abilities played a role in the White parents' avoidance of her. This raced, gendered and disabled gaze and avoidance recall Yancy's (2017) argument that the white gaze "replicates the history of whiteness as terror" because it is used to reduce the Black body to "an eater of shit, and a drinker of urine…a monster, something freakish, abnormal, and capable of the most disgraceful acts" (p. xxxi). Through the White parents' raced, gendered and disabled gaze, Emma was fragmented and thus deprived of humanity.

*Being Exoticized*

In other contexts, Emma became the focus. Emma explained,

> It is sort of a mixture of curiosity and fascination. So there is [name of the spouse of one of her white professors], …she was like staring at me and she would not stop talking to me，都搞得我师弟吃醋了 ("which made my classmate jealous").

Instead of being avoided as in the previous incident, Emma became the spotlight, another microaggression that Students of Color experience (Davis et al., 2004).

*Model Minority*

Asian American students with dis/abilities' needs and struggles are obscured by the model minority stereotype (Park, 2019). Emma's interaction with her peers further demonstrates how this stereotype has marginalized her.

During high school, Emma was staying with students in special education during physical education classes. Here is the conversation between them,

> 我就看见他们在看电影，然后他们就说 "oh, I don't know why..." 就是他们有点不懂，那个电影的概念，我就想，哦，可以跟他们解释，我就说，"这是那个山的altitude,因为山太高了，所以就没有oxygen-，所以他们就不能呼吸"。有一个[黑人]女孩子就说，"why are you using such a White word?"
> Translation: I saw them watching a film. They [one of them] [seemed a little confused] asked, "oh, I don't know why.… " So they [he/she] did not understand the concept in that film. I was like, I can explain it to them [him/her]. So I said, "that is the altitude of the mountain because it is too high, so there is no oxygen, and they cannot breathe." One [Black] girl said immediately, "why are you using such a White word?"

Emma used the word "altitude," and this action was deemed as "acting White" (Ogbu, 2004) because "altitude" is believed by the Black girl to be a White word. Being accused of "acting white," Emma was dismissed by her peers in special education: "smartness" was racially coded as "not normal" from her peers' perspective. Emma was caught between the "shifting boundaries between normal and abnormal," and the ways "in which race contributes to one being positioned on either side of the line" (Annamma et al., 2013, p. 10).

Emma's Chinese identity rendered her discursively atypical among her dis/ability peers, an example of how racism and ableism circulate interdependently to uphold notions of normalcy (Annamma et al., 2013; Waldman et al., 2022). Students of Color with dis/abilities "are forced to divide loyalties as social conflict is presented as a choice between grounds of identity" (Crenshaw et al., 1995, p. 354). They must align with groups that do not fully share their identities (Watts & Erevelles, 2004). Thus, Emma was forced to choose to stand with Asian Americans or Whites (honorary) despite not having fully shared experience or acceptance with either of them.

Other times, her college peers chose to overlook her dis/ability, attributing her exemplary academic performance to her race. Emma shared a conversation in her Chinese class:

像做这个presentation,他们就会说,"哦，觉得很难,背不住,"我也觉得要花很多的时间准备，但是做完了报告以后，他们也会说,"哦，你的报告比我长多了，是因为你是中国人。"
Translation: Like doing presentations, they [her peers] would say, "oh, this is hard; I cannot memorize it." I need to spend a lot of time preparing it too. But after the presentation, they would say, "Your presentation is much longer [better] than mine because you are Chinese."

Her peers instantly erased Emma's hard work and the difficulties she had to overcome as someone with dis/abilities. Her dis/ability was immediately invisible; her race became her salient identity. The model minority silences the possibility that Asian American students with dis/abilities have academic challenges (Park, 2019; Wang et al., 2021).

Acutely understanding this imposed model on Asian Americans, and not willing to succumb to the "retarded" label against people with dis/abilities, Emma experienced tremendous pain in navigating these two conflicting stereotypes. She said,

所以我就一直觉得，我不能走路，但是我脑袋还可以，我没有那么傻，所以我要很努力。要,要表现比较好。让老师喜欢我，让同学接受我…来破开一个典型，但是我破开的典型不是说,OK, it's not saying that all Chinese people are smart, I want to break the stereotype. It's the stereotype that it's more along … you know, 残疾人都是傻子。
Translation: Even though I cannot walk, I always think my brain is good. I am not that dumb. So I need to work hard, to perform well and let my teachers and classmates like me…[I want to] break the stereotype, but not the stereotype that all Chinese people are smart. I want to break the stereotype. It's the stereotype that it's more along, you know all dis/abled are dumb.

To "prove the stereotype [model minority] right" (McGee, 2018, p. 10), and simultaneously, to prove the stereotype of people with dis/abilities wrong, Emma strived hard to excel academically. Emma was mentally and physically exhausted by doing this; racism and ableism contributed oppressively to her suffering. Yet she also found strength and affirmation in navigating the systems of oppression and privilege. She got the Fulbright scholarship to study abroad in Taiwan and was accepted to a prestigious university to continue her doctoral study in history.

## Play the Dis/ability Card

In high school, Emma was struggling to complete an assignment her teacher assigned, which was to do a three-dimensional brain project requiring a lot of hand coordination. When she eventually took the courage to ask for an alternative assignment, her teacher bluntly refused her, saying, "No. I am trying to be supportive. I am trying to get you out of your comfort zone." Emma was offended:

> She assumed I wanted an easier assignment just because... she made that assumption and she immediately said no. and I got upset, right? and I didn't know how to tell her, you know, 这不是，我不是想占便宜，但是她就是明显的以为我想占便宜嘛，想偷懒 (Translation: This is not that I want to take advantage, but she obviously believed this was what I wanted, because I was lazy)

Emma's intersectional identities as Asian and a person with dis/abilities potentially pushed the teacher to assume that Emma was playing the dis/ability card. She assumed that Emma, as a model minority, was taking advantage of her dis/ability to get an easier assignment. Therefore, she felt it right to refuse Emma's request. But her refusal is more than a lack of awareness of the needs and struggles of students with dis/abilities (Wolanin & Steele, 2004). She was "racializing ability" (Annamma et al., 2013, p. 2) in that she correlated Emma's race with her supposed ability. This has seriously impacted Asian American students' success in school (Hwa-Froelich & Westby, 2003; Lee, 2006).

This teacher's attitude had severe ramifications for Emma in her later educational journey. Emma shared, "Every time that I have to speak up for myself—in seminar discussions, in private meetings with my professors and advisors, at the library, or even at the restaurant—I have to chase her voice out of my head first." This fear of being refused accommodation loomed large in Emma's mind. "是不是别的老师也会像这个老师一样？" (Translation: Will other teachers be like that teacher?) I have flashbacks, right? It is a psychological thing." This psychological burden pushed Emma to be extremely harsh to herself academically. "I should not tell anybody that I am struggling with this reading or this research. My writing has to be perfect; every word has to be perfect." This mental exhaustion to prove herself echoes Banks's (2017) finding that Students of Color are burdened in the classroom that "(they) had to prove that (they) knew just as much as the rest of the other students in the classroom" (p. 102) to circumvent other people's subjectivity. Emma's experience illustrates the core of DisCrit theory: the socially constructed concept of race and ability interacts so that students like Emma are simultaneously raced and dis/abled (Annamma et al., 2013). She was navigating the world of being an Asian and being a person with dis/ability, and neither social world could fully recognize her needs and struggles.

Across these scenarios, the model minority stereotype against Asians (Lee, 2015), the exoticization of Asian women (Uchida, 1998), as well as the inferiority imposed on people with dis/abilities discursively make her hypervisible and yet also invisible. These are never neutral constructs but "what any of us make of them" (Biklen & Kliewer, 2006, p. 182). When Emma is constructed by others as the exotic Asian female, the smart model minority, the shamed or inferior dis/abled person, each diminishing stereotype both draws attention (hypervisibility) and creates distrust and distancing (invisibility). Emma struggles with these raced, gendered, and disabled gazes as dehumanizing of her personhood. At the same time, she was made stronger by asserting who she was through challenging the system of oppression and privilege.

## Intersectionality of Ableism, Sexism, and Patriarchy

The intersection of sexism and patriarchy with ableism was heightened when Emma visited her country of origin–China. Her intersectional identities attracted much attention. Chinese people were surprised to learn that Emma studied at a university. Their curiosity revealed that despite the existence of many people with dis/abilities in China (Zheng et al., 2011), they are not widely seen in public. Part of their absence was due to poor accessibility. Emma experienced many difficulties accessing the dining room, residence hall, and library, even within the university. The hegemonic ableism in China seriously limited her mobility there.

The patriarchal society, valuing men over women, heavily influences how Chinese people subordinate and exclude Emma. Emma met a mother with her toddler boy one evening at her host institution. After some brief conversations, the mother made a comment that seriously troubled Emma:

男孩妈妈: 美国没有独生子女政策吧? 你有没有弟弟哥哥什么的?
Emma: 没有啊, 我只有一个姐姐。
(然后她一听只有一个姐姐，她的表情就是好像我很可怜，或者觉得我父母很可怜。)
男孩妈妈: 啊? 你没有弟弟? 你也没有哥哥? 只有一个姐姐?
Emma: 是啊, 只有一个姐姐。
(然后她就看她的宝宝)
男孩妈妈: 我这个儿子是第二个。他还有一个哥哥。
(反正我记得她的表情就是好像同情心的表情。)
Translation: Toddler's mother: There is no One-Child policy in the US, right? Do you have any brothers?
Emma: No. I only have one elder sister.

(The mother was very sympathetic upon hearing this. Her facial expression transmitted a message that she felt sorry for me and for my parents.)

Toddler's mother: What? Don't you have any brothers? Only a sister?

Emma: Yes. Only a sister.

(The mother looked at her child.)

Toddler's mother: This is my second son. He has an elder brother.

(I remembered her sympathy toward my family and me vividly.)

Miller et al. (2004) argue that people with dis/abilities are often regarded as objects of pity (as cited in Harpur, 2009, p. 163). Here Emma was pitied by that mother, not only because she was in a wheelchair but because she had no brothers. To some extent, the mother believed that not having a brother generates more pity than having physical dis/abilities. What is hidden in their brief conversation is how the Chinese patriarchal society, which devalues women, undermines Emma's self-worth. The mother perceived her as not valuable to her family because Emma could not carry the family line. Her family's suffering deserves sympathy since only a son might have offset their pity. By attending to a critical interrogation of ableism in people's discourses, the exchange, especially the mother's body language, reveals how entrenched ethnic ableism, sexism and patriarchy define Emma's experience. Despite the shared commonalities of oppressive systems, different cultures socially construct these concepts uniquely. As Emma travels internationally, she encounters exclusion and invisibility resulting from the different social ideologies in each country; thus, we argue, she experiences international invisibility due to how her intersectional identities are situated differently in each country.

## Conclusion

This chapter utilizes intersectionality, DisCrit and intersectional invisibility to explore the lived experience of one female Chinese American college student with dis/abilities. As she moves between the U.S. society, the Chinese American community and China, systems of oppression such as ableism, white supremacy, sexism and patriarchy work together to create her marginalization and intersectional invisibility. Within U.S. society, stereotypes against Asians and the dis/abled complicated Emma's experience. By others, her intersectional identities as Asian and dis/abled were not recognized as interactive; instead, she was positioned on two ends of a spectrum, either perceived as model or dumb. Being stereotyped as a "smart Asian" put her in tension with both Black and White peers and led teachers to treat her "qualitatively (different) than white students with disabilities" (Annamma et al.,

2013, p. 7). Instead of being seen as a whole person, Emma was constantly seen as fragments. This fragmentation deprives Emma of humanity.

From within Chinese culture, patriarchal values jeopardized Emma's sense of self, as did the shaming around dis/ability as societally disharmonious. The different operations and dynamics of such systems of oppression in the U.S. and China render her vulnerable to be invisible in unique ways. In other words, due to how Chinese society operationalizes dis/ability, patriarchy and gender, Emma was subjected to a different set of invisibility that she would not have in the U.S. This cross-border invisibility we term "international invisibility."

Despite the experienced discrimination, marginalization and invisibility, Emma was not a passive victim. She became stronger as she navigated the intricacies of oppression. The embodiment of an Asian and a person with dis/abilities pushed her to challenge the systems of oppression and become resilient in facing discrimination and marginalization.

Inspired by critical race hermeneutics, we attended to ableism to analyze the seemingly well-intentioned remarks made to people with dis/abilities along with their intersectional behaviors. Race, gender, and dis/ability are not biological facts but social constructions in response to a society's response to "difference" from the norm (Mirza, 1998). The existence of normalcy needs to be challenged through a "critique of the structures of 'normativity' that are produced in an ableist and racist society" (Watts & Erevelles, 2004, p. 292). Thus, dis/ability must be understood as a "political and social category" (Annamma et al., 2013, p.19) that interacts with other such categories to mark and situate people's lives.

While our research highlights the lived experience of one Chinese ethnic with dis/abilities, it has several implications for practice and research. First, our research challenges the common perception that as "honorary white," Asian Americans do not experience discrimination and racism. Practitioners must address Asian American students' struggles with racism in order to better support them. Second, our paper allows people to see how racism, ableism, sexism and patriarchy conspire against Asian Americans with dis/abilities. Practitioners must keep intersectionality in mind when supporting Asian American students with dis/abilities, rather than seeing them from a "single story" perspective. Third, by documenting the ways that the particularities of Chinese culture shaped one student's experiences, this research argues for attention to the diversity within the Asian American population that has consequences for students. Future research should challenge the homogenized approach in studying Asian Americans. Finally, this case study depicts how a person with multiple marginalized identities navigates the systems of oppression and privilege and can become stronger and more resilient in spite of it.

## Note

1 We choose to use the term dis/ability instead of disability because we believe the word "disability" signals a negativity that comes to define individuals as primarily "unable" to navigate society. By using "/" we aim to disrupt this misleading conception, as it simultaneously conveys the mixture of ability and dis/ability (Annamma et al., 2013) and challenges the hegemony of normalcy. In other words, no one is disabled unless there is a uniform definition of normalcy.

## References

Allen, R. L. (2021). Critical race hermeneutics: A theoretical method for researching the unconscious of white supremacy in education. In C. E. Matias (Ed.), *The handbook of critical theoretical research methods in education* (pp. 15–30). Routledge.

Annamma, S. A., Connor, D., & Ferri, B. (2013). Dis/ability critical race studies (DisCrit): Theorizing at the intersections of race and dis/ability. *Race, Ethnicity and Education, 16*(1), 1–31.

Banks, J. (2017). "These people are never going to stop labeling me": Educational experiences of African American male students labeled with learning disabilities. *Equity & Excellence in Education, 50*(1), 96–107.

Biklen, D., & Kliewer, C. (2006). Constructing competence: Autism, voice and the "disordered" body. *International Journal of Inclusive Education, 10*, 169–188.

Blanchett, W. J. (2006). Disproportionate representation of African American students in special education: Acknowledging the role of white privilege and racism. *Educational Researcher, 35*(6), 24–38.

Blanchett, W. J., Mumford, V., and Beachum, F. (2005). Urban school failure and disproportionality in a post-Brown era: Benign neglect of the constitutional rights of Students of Color. *Remedial and Special Education, 26*(2), 70–81.

Chan, C. C. H., Lee, T. M. C., Yuen, H.-K., & Chan, F. (2002). Attitudes towards people with disabilities between Chinese rehabilitation and business students: An implication for practice. *Rehabilitation Psychology, 47*(3), 324–338.

Chen, R., Brodwin, M. G., Cardoso, E., & Chan, F. (2002). Attitudes toward people with disabilities in the social context of dating and marriage: A comparison of American, Taiwanese, and Singaporean college students. *Journal of Rehabilitation, 68*(4), 5–11.

Collins, P. H., & Bilge, S. (2016). *Intersectionality*. Polity Press.

Cooc, N. (2018). Exploring the underrepresentation of Asian American students in special education: Evidence from California. *Exceptionality, 26*(1), 1–19.

Cooc, N., & Yang, M. (2017). Underrepresented and overlooked: A review of Asian American children with disabilities. *Multiple Voices for Ethnically Diverse Exceptional Learners, 17*(1), 1–17.

Crenshaw, K. (1989). Demarginalizing the intersection of race and sex: A Black feminist critique of antidiscrimination doctrine, feminist theory, and antiracist politics. *University of Chicago Legal Forum, 1989*(8), 139–167.

Crenshaw, K., Gotanda, N., Peller, G., & Thomas, K. (1995). *Critical race theory: The key writings that formed the movement.* The New Press.

Creswell, J. W. (2013). *Qualitative inquiry research design: Choosing among five approaches* (3rd ed.). Thousand Oaks.

Davis, M., Dias-Bowie, Y., Greenberg, K., Klukken, G., Pollio, H. R., Thomas, S. P., & Thompson, C. L. (2004). A fly in the buttermilk: Descriptions of university life by successful undergraduate students at a predominately White Southeastern university. *Journal of Higher Education, 74*, 420–445.

Dill, B. T., McLaughlin, A. E., & Nieves, A. D. (2007). Future directions of feminist research: Intersectionality. In S. N. Hesse-Biber (Ed.), *Handbook of feminist research* (pp. 629–637). Sage.

Eligon, J. (2020). Why the fastest growing population in America is the least likely to fill out the census. *The New York Times.*

Erevelles, N., & Minear, A. (2010). Unspeakable offenses: Untangling race and dis/ability in discourses of intersectionality. *Journal of Literary & Cultural Disability Studies, 4*, 127–145.

Ferri, B. A., & Connor, D. J. (2005). Tools of exclusion: Race, dis/ability, and (re)segregated education. *Teachers College Record, 107*(3), 453–474.

Gillborn, D. (2015). Intersectionality, critical race theory, and the primacy of racism: Race, class, gender, and dis/ability in education. *Qualitative Inquiry, 21*(3), 277–287.

Harpur, P. (2009). Sexism and racism, why not ableism? Calling for a cultural shift in the approach to disability discrimination. *Alternative Law Journal, 34*(3), 163–167.

Hasnain, R., Fujiura, G. T., Capua, J. E., Bui, T. T. T., & Khan, S. (2020). Disaggregating the Asian "other": Heterogeneity and methodological issues in research on Asian Americans with disabilities. *Societies, 10*(3), 58, 1–19.

Hwa-Froelich, D., & Westby, C. (2003). Frameworks of education: Perspectives of Southeast Asian parents and Head Start staff. *Language, Speech, and Hearing Services in Schools, 32*, 299–319.

Kasa-Hendrickson, C. (2005). "There's no way this kid's retarded": Teachers' optimistic constructions of students' ability. *International Journal of Inclusive Education, 9*, 55–69.

Lam, C. S., Tsang, H., Chan, F., & Corrigan, P. W. (2006). Chinese and American perspectives on stigma. *Rehabilitation Education, 20*(4), 269–279.

Lee, S. J. (2006). *Up against whiteness: Race, school, and Immigrant Youth.* Teachers College Press.

Lee, S. J. (2015). *Unraveling the "model minority" stereotype: Listening to Asian American youth*. Teachers College Press.

Lee. S. J., Park, E., & Wong, J. S. (2017). Racialization, schooling, and becoming American: Asian American experiences. *Educational Studies, 53*(5), 492–510.

Leonardo, Z., & Broderick, A. A. (2011). Smartness as property: A critical exploration of intersections between whiteness and dis/ability studies. *Teachers College Record, 113*(10), 2206–2232.

Linton, S. (1998). *Claiming dis/ability: Knowledge and identity*. New York University Press.

McGee, E. (2018). "Black genius, Asian fail": The detriment of stereotype lift and stereotype threat in high-achieving Asian and Black STEM students. *AERA Open, 4*(4), 1–16.

Mereish, E. H. (2012). The intersectional invisibility of race and dis/ability status: An exploratory study of health and discrimination facing Asian Americans with disabilities. *Ethnicity and Inequalities in Health and Social Care, 5*(2), 52–60.

Mirza, H. S. (1998). Race, gender and IQ: The social consequence of a pseudo-scientific discourse. *Race, Ethnicity and Education, 1*(1),109–126.

Moses, M. S., Maeda, D. J., & Paguyo, C. H. (2018). Racial politics, resentment, and Affirmative Action: Asian Americans as "model" college applicants. *The Journal of Higher Education, 90*(1), 1–26.

Museus, S. D. (2014). *Asian American students in higher education*. Routledge.

Museus, S. D., & Kiang, P. N. (2009). Deconstructing the model minority myth and how it contributes to the invisible minority reality in higher education research. *New Directions for Institutional Research, 142*, 5–15.

Museus, S. D., Maramba, D. C., & Teranishi, R. T. (Eds.). (2013). *The misrepresented minority: New insights on Asian Americans and Pacific Islanders, and the implications for higher education*. Stylus.

Ogbu, J. U. (2004). Collective identity and the burden of "acting White" in Black history, community, and education. *The Urban Review, 36*, 1–35.

Park, S. (2019). Beyond underrepresentation: Construction dis/ability with young Asian American children to preserve the "model minority" stereotype. *Asia-Pacific Journal of Research in Early Childhood Education, 13*(3), 73–95.

Purdie-Vaughns, V., & Eibach, R. P. (2008). Intersectional invisibility: The distinctive advantages and disadvantages of multiple subordinate-group identities. *Sex Roles, 59*(5), 377–391.

Tai, R. H., & Kenyatta, M. L. (1999). *Critical ethnicity: Countering the waves of identity politics*. Rowman & Littlefield.

Uchida, A. (1998). The orientalization of Asian women in America. *Women's Studies International Forum, 21*(2), 161–174.

U. S. Department of Health and Human Services Office of the Minority Health (OMH). (2019). *Profile: Asian Americans*. Author.

Waldman, K., Stickley, A., Dawson, B. A., & Oh, H. (2022). Racial discrimination and dis/ability among Asian and Latinx populations in the United States. *Dis/ability and Rehabilitation, 44*(1), 96–105.

Wang, J. J., Redford, L., & Ratliff, K. A. (2021). Do special education recommendations differ for Asian American and White American students? *Social Psychology of Education, 24*(4), 1065–1083.

Watts, I. E., & Erevelles, N. (2004). These deadly times: Reconceptualizing school violence by using critical race theory and disability studies. *American Educational Research Journal, 41*(2), 271–299.

Wolanin, T. R., & Steele, P. E. (2004). *Higher education opportunities for students with disabilities.* The Institute for Higher Education Policy.

Yancy, G. (2017). *Black bodies, White gazes: The continuing significance of race in America.* Rowman & Littlefield.

Zheng, X., Chen, G., Song, X., Liu, J., Yan, L., Du, W.,... & Zhang, J. (2011). Twenty-year trends in the prevalence of disability in China. *Bulletin of the World Health Organization, 89*, 788–797.

# 9. Latina/x Identities and Oppression in Higher Education: A Case in a Hispanic-Serving Institution

HILDA CECILIA CONTRERAS AGUIRRE

In the United States (U.S.), higher education institutions have increased the enrollment of women and minority students at the bachelor level; however, theoretical and practical implications affecting underserved students and minority faculty members remain. Hispanic-Serving Institutions (HSIs) are accredited degree-granting public and private postsecondary institutions with at least 25% or more of full-time undergraduate Hispanic students (used interchangeably with Latinx throughout the chapter) designated by the U.S. Department of Education (Hispanic Association of Colleges and Universities [HACU], 2021). HSIs play a vital role in registering 62% of Latinx under-graduates of whom 48% are women (*Excelencia* in Education, 2023a, 2023b). In 2021–22, the number of HSIs reached 571, representing 19% of all post-secondary institutions (*Excelencia* in Education, 2023b). The representation of Latinas in higher education from the undergraduate to faculty levels are illustrated in Figure 9.1.

Figure 9.1 highlights the important role that HSIs have in Latina stu-dents' college degree attainment. For example, in 2020, Latinas earned 43% of all degrees attained by women (*Excelencia* in Education, 2023a). Also, the huge gap between Latinas' bachelor completion and the percentage of Latinas with faculty positions is remarkable. The percentage of Latina faculty representation at HSIs remains unclear.

This chapter included Latina/x students' and faculty members' voices due to their shared, divergent, and continued experiences of marginalization prevalent in academia. It also addressed the importance and function of iden-tity for this specific group of Latina/x people. Studies on the role of identity

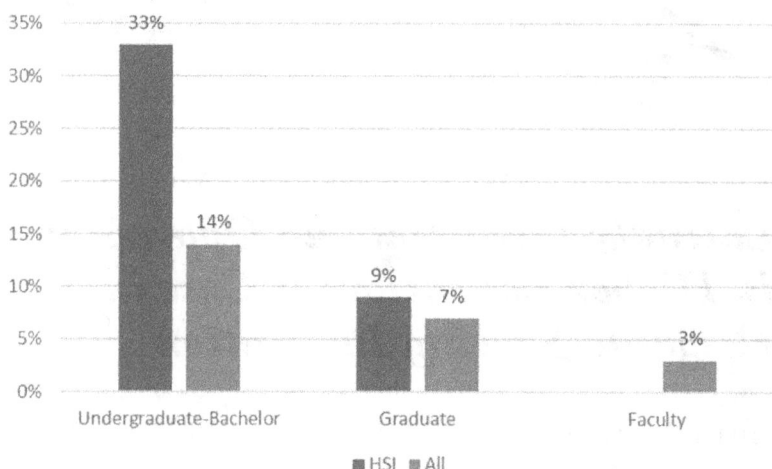

**Figure 9.1.** Representation of Latina Undergraduates and Graduate Students at HSIs and All Institutions–Latinas' Representation as Faculty

Note. *Excelencia* in Education, 2023b. Author's image.

on people's performance, relationships with others, and perspectives of themselves and others are vast (Hurtado & Gurin, 2004; Lawler, 2015). Several scholars have focused their research on studying the identity of minorities in STEM to address persistence (e.g., see Contreras Aguirre et al., 2020; Rodriguez et al., 2020; Verdín et al., 2018). Identity helps classify people considering their race, class, gender, sexuality, and physical aspects; environment also plays a critical role in the way one identifies with a group. Therefore, a person's identity is the combination of multiple identities (Hurtado & Gurin, 2004; Lawler, 2015). Latinx with Mexican heritage "maintain multilayered aspects of ethnic identities" (A. García, 2002, p. 157). Primarily, due to the geographical proximity between the U.S. and Mexico and the close ties with the extended family living in Mexico (A. García, 2002; Hurtado & Gurin, 2004).

Historically, dominant groups, commonly from middle-class backgrounds, have set the norm and rules of what is normal, even in terms of identity development. For example, perceptions of feeling less worthy than others is a common experience that oppressed individuals go through (Hurtado & Gurin, 2004; Lawler, 2015). "All individuals seek to feel good about the groups they belong to" (Hurtado & Gurin, 2004, p. 44) but is not always easy to feel good about it, especially when society imposes certain appearances on women, creating issues with self-image. Also, Lawler (2015) noticed how working-class people "do not look right and they do not act right" (p. 125) under the eyes of middle-class privileged individuals who normalize good taste in appearance and behaviors. As Peña (2022) put it, "being first-generation and Black or Brown and poor means we start our journey on foot while others ride aboard a train" (p. 47). This quote provides a clear example of Crenshaw's (1991) concept of intersectionality and its contribution to this chapter on how these multiple, socially constructed demeaned identities (e.g., Latina/x, first-generation, and low-income) contribute to individuals experiencing marginalization and oppression in academia.

## Context

The study took place at an HSI situated in the U.S.-Mexico border area. This HSI, identified as Hill University, enrolls approximately 14,000 students, of which 58% are Latinx, 71% are state residents, and 75% are full-time students. Undergraduates represent 81% and graduate students represent 18% of all students enrolled at Hill University. Hill University's main campus offers 97 bachelor's, 68 master's, 29 doctoral degrees, 24 graduate certificates, and one education specialist. Faculty demographics show that 54% are in tenure and tenure-track lines, 73% are in full-time positions, 67% are non-minority individuals, and 53% are women. Latinas/x who participated in this study were members of a mentoring program targeting Latinx students that promotes community building through emotional, cultural, academic, and professional support (Contreras Aguirre & Romero, 2023). Therefore, participants self-identify as Latinas/x, particularly Mexican Americans, Chicanas, and Mexicanas. Participants shared their unique experiences in navigating higher education from three different perspectives: undergraduate and graduate students are on an academic journey while the faculty members are experiencing the professional world of higher education. The study explores the multiple identities and oppressive environments that a group of Latina/x students and faculty members, who were participants in a mentoring program, found in higher education contexts. The research question guiding this study examined: How did Latinas' identities and college environment influence the college experiences of this selected group of Latinas/x?

## Literature Review

### Latina Identity Development

According to Lawler (2015), the word *identity* means identical, and we are all equal with others and share multiple aspects in our everyday lives, shaping our personal identity. Identity is also directly influenced by the socialization that happens with family members (Hurtado & Gurin, 2004). People find their uniqueness when they differentiate themselves from others. Individuals want to be unique, so they emphasize small differences until these differences become characteristics that define them. Social identity is related to how a person self-identifies with a group they consider valuable (Tajfel, 1978). Social identities include gender, ethnicity, class, and race. To socially situate themselves, individuals use a psychological process that is composed of social categorization (i.e., social and physical characteristics important in particular contexts), social comparison (i.e., differences with other groups in terms of status, richness, and poverty), and psychological work (i.e., achieve a sense of uniqueness; Hurtado & Gurin, 2004). Chicanos and Latinx individuals with roots in Mexico feel that there is a mixture of cultural, historical, political, and linguistic experiences and that feeling is even more palpable at the U.S.-Mexico border. Latinx/Chicanos value their ancestors by using Spanish to produce intellectual work, contributing to their social visibility (Hurtado & Gurin, 2004). When there is a positive cultural adaptation that reflects the social identity of Latinx, the intersection of multiple identities is exercised by people. The recognition of mestizaje or the interbreeding of people considered to be of different racial types, which according to Segato (2010), in the version of the elites, is thus a unitary path for the nation towards its whitening and Eurocentric modernization. This aforementioned example illustrates how Latinx identities are complex and ever-changing over time and context. Identities are also created through narratives, which usually contain characters, actions, and backgrounds. Through narrative traditions, individuals put together various facets/episodes of their lives to produce their own ongoing story and consequently, their own narrative. That narrative/story becomes each one of us, "I am like this" (Lawler, 2015, p.21).

## The Oppressive Climate in Higher Education

Minorities such as Women of Color, and in particular Latinas, face multiple challenges at U.S. higher education institutions, first as college students both as undergraduates and graduate students and later as academics (Contreras Aguirre et al., 2020; Flores, 2023; Gonzalez et al., 2013). In particular, Latinx students bring their personal, social, and cultural experiences that are heavily influenced by their families, immigration status, economic affluence, and network in the form of access to information, resources, and people to college (Espinoza & Garfield, 2023; Rodriguez et al., 2021). Skills and knowledge are needed to persist and take advantage of all opportunities that universities offer students. Students need to develop skills to navigate higher education which will facilitate a smooth transition from high school, community college to four-year institutions (Doran, 2023; Herrera et al., 2022). However, hostile climates persist on campuses for different reasons, the most common having to do with being Women of Color in STEM or not physically looking like other students and faculty may be the cause of discrimination (Herrera et al., 2022; Peña, 2022). Similar patterns of inequalities are seen at every step of the ladder from undergraduates to faculty. One of the most salient characteristics is that most Latinx are first-generation individuals, which shapes the experience of Latinx even in occupying faculty positions (Covarrubias, 2022; Peña, 2022). Espinoza and Garfield (2023) noted how minority first-generation faculty find it difficult to interpret the rubric for tenure track evaluations which are mostly inconsistent and ambiguous.

The multiple identities of the participants in this study include gender, ethnicity, culture, socioeconomic status, and being first-generation to experience college. The identities of the women and non-binary individual are explored in conjunction with the oppressive environments within academia, and when combined, experiences and particular situations are perceived as negative. The participants experience a lack of cohesive student support, a lack of Hill University's motivation to entice Latinx graduate students, and a lack of institutional leadership that understands the complexities of Latinx identity formation in relation to higher education. Despite participants experiencing such an oppressive environment at the intersection of who they are and what they represent, they adopt behaviors and strategies to improve such situations. Some strategies include participating in formal or informal mentoring practices with students and/or faculty and finding allies with people who share similar values and ethnicity (Contreras Aguirre et al., 2020; Covarrubias, 2022; Peña, 2022).

### Intersectionality: The Case of Latinx

Intersectionality, a term coined by Crenshaw (1989, 1991), introduces multiple, interlocking forms of oppression including racism, sexism, classism, and ableism, which combined with oppressive actions further support toxic practices, aggravating the perceived negative experiences of those with marginalized identities. Research on minoritized groups such as Latinx individuals exposes multiple factors that influence the experiences of individuals who identify with these groups (Contreras Aguirre et al., 2020; Settles, 2006). Among other aspects, these experiences are often discriminatory acts based on prototyping people due to their sex and race (Carbado et al., 2013). For example, the federal designation of Latinos, recently Latinx or Latine, grouping Mexican, Latin American, Caribbean, and Spanish populations into the same category creates identity issues for these individuals (G. García, 2019). Other problems have to do with Latinx individuals being educationally, socially, and economically oppressed and suffering stigmatization as people with less intellectual value (Lacayo, 2016; Rivera, 2008). Another example of multiple identities is exposed in García-Louis (2022)'s study noting that the view of the U.S. Latinx community as synonymous with Mestizx (or people of Indigenous and Hispanic descent) marginalizes the experiences of Afro-Latinx and Indigenous Latinx people. For these reasons, the cultural and racial diversity of the Latinx community in the U.S. and the legacy of colonialism must be considered when analyzing the experiences of Latinx people. These are just a few examples of the implications that intersectionality has on individuals that contribute to shaping and defining their everyday experiences.

## *Method*

I conducted the study with a qualitative inquiry approach in which nine participants recruited from a mentoring program, and who decided voluntarily to participate, shared their experiences related to their identities and college climate through *pláticas* and *testimonios*. According to Fierros and Delgado Bernal (2016), pláticas are conversations that have the potential for people who relate culturally to make meaning of the pláticas by sharing life experiences and creating a space for soul healing. In turn, testimonios are narrative approaches to experiential reflections that communicate a perspective or call for action intentionally and/or politically (Reyes & Rodríguez 2012; also see Chapter 17 for an explanation of testimonios). All participants were from different academic programs and at different levels of their educational and professional journeys. The group's commonalities were ethnicity, gender, and first-generation status. Table 9.1 highlights other participant characteristics. Five individual pláticas with faculty and one graduate student and two group pláticas with undergraduates and graduate students were held during some of the data collection, in which participants shared personal experiences, and stories (Fierros & Delgado Bernal, 2016). Participants also reflected on their identities and how their intersecting identities shape their academic approach and interpersonal relationships. I collected the data by recording the interviews and then used Rev.com to develop transcripts of the interviews. Following the transcript development, I utilized Dedoose, a qualitative data analysis software to review the transcripts. My analysis of data consisted of reading the pláticas or conversations several times, and other documentation to identify patterns. The research started with the unitization of the data, that is, identifying pieces of information that have meaning by itself, once all data were unitized, I used the content analysis approach to find patterns and grouped the information forming categories and themes (Lincoln & Guba, 1985). I developed different types of codes including initial open codes to help classify all data, and axial codes that group initial open codes within each transcript. The excerpts categorized by the axial codes were used to help address the purpose of the study and research question (Saldaña, 2013).

**Table 9.1.** Participant Demographics

| Pseudonym | Gender | Academic Program | Student/Faculty |
|---|---|---|---|
| Estrella | Woman | Counseling & Community Psychology | Undergraduate student |
| Paola | Woman | Mathematics | Undergraduate student |
| Regina | Woman | Social Work | Graduate student |
| Ari | Woman | Plant and Environmental Science | Graduate student |
| Hola | Non-binary | Astronomy | Graduate student |
| Lila | Woman | Communication Studies | Faculty |
| Luna | Woman | Social Work | Faculty |
| Jay | Woman | Sociology of Education | Faculty |
| Siba | Woman | Bilingual Education | Faculty |

## *Findings*

This section presents how participants reflected on their experiences in higher education and on their most salient identities as Latinas/x, women, non-binary, and first-generation individuals in their roles as undergraduate students, graduate students, and faculty members. Latinas/x from undergraduates to faculty members mentioned several aspects that were detrimental to the appropriate adjustments and development in the postsecondary context. The following categories cover the experiences of Latina/x participants in aspects such as invisibility in traditionally White spaces, oppressive environment experiences as Latinas/x, and isolation aspects contrasting with cultural aspects.

## Feelings of Invisibility in Traditional White Spaces

The lack of visibility in the higher education landscape was commented on during the pláticas and testimonios. Participants mainly highlighted the overwhelming representation of White faculty in postsecondary institutions, where students and faculty feel unseen. An undergraduate student, named Estrella, a Junior double majoring in counseling, community psychology, and Spanish mentioned, "It's [higher education] a, a different space, you know, where most professors are White, and you don't really see yourself in other people." She highlighted the need to have more Latinx faculty at Hill University. Lila, a faculty member from the communication studies department seconded this feeling and added:

> I don't think I was necessarily shocked at the fact that academia is still very White. And our department is very White... so I don't know to me that doesn't come as a shock anymore because truly anywhere I go with academia, that's always what I encounter anyway.

Despite the different areas of higher education, two participants, an undergraduate student and a faculty member, noted similar observations surrounding White faculty representation compared to other ethnicities and races, especially at this HSI. Additionally, Paola, a first-year student in mathematics, added a comment on the unequal representation of Latinx people in the campus environment, highlighting the difference in the representation of faculty and service people: She said:

> I don't know, it's awkward and it's really sad because I, I see like all the White faculty instead of like Hispanic faculty and, but then...go to the dining hall and uh, from the kitchen I can hear all the cumbias and salsa and everyone just playing like Latino music and all the faculty, everyone else is White.

All three experiences reflected Latinas/x's point of view of institutional contexts in locations where racially minoritized individuals have become the majority, and still, universities look unchanged, with an overrepresentation of White faculty and administrators in leadership positions. The last quote highlighted the role of Latinx people predominantly in the service industry compared to jobs as academics.

## Navigating Oppressive Environments Due to Latinas/x's Multiple Identities

The oppressive contexts that Latina/x participants perceive in higher education made them feel vulnerable and feel a lack of empathy for the identities they represent such as being both Latinas/x and non-traditional students, and Latinas/x and first-generation faculty. The identities they represent are absent on the university campus landscape, policies, and practices. Regina, a master's student in social work mentioned:

> I guess the struggles that I've had in continuing my education is that the educational system is very westernized, very Eurocentric. And it doesn't take into consideration that students, especially graduate students, take on many roles. Other than just being specifically a student, you know, like me, I am a mother, I am a stepmother and a wife. And so, I feel like I've struggled in trying to continue my education in a system that's not really tailored to…like me.

Regina clarified her many struggles in continuing her education besides her other commitments. The intersection of a heavily Western and Eurocentric academic system and her roles as a woman, mother, Latina, and student leave in her the feeling that higher education was not for her because she was not a traditional student. A faculty member, named Jay, from sociology of education, shared a similar perspective about higher education as an alienated place for minoritized individuals. She expressed, "Let's start from the very beginning. Institutions were not created for or by people that look like you and me." She emphasized the contrast between higher education to educate the elite, men, and wealthy and people from a minority background, brown, and first-generation. Both the graduate student and the faculty member agreed with the idea that institutions do not know how to deal with different student and employee profiles. This situation is particularly alarming due to the increased diversity of students and the integration of professors from historically marginalized backgrounds into higher education institutions. Both participants blamed institutions in general, for lacking systemic change and updated institutional policies that benefit People of Color. Such changes must include embracing diversity and valuing people who bring other experiences to college.

## Isolation vs Expected Cultural Relevant Aspects

All participants regardless of the level (e.g., undergraduate, graduate students, and faculty) had not felt a sense of belonging. Students mentioned their peers with whom they interact daily as indifferent to developing relationships and creating community, one of the more salient aspects of Latino culture. Ari, a graduate student in plant and environmental science conveyed:

> The graduate student population in the department is mostly international from the Middle East. So, they tend to be a lot more cliquey with each other…

So it has been really difficult to try to form any sort of, I guess conversation with them.

Like Ari's experience in graduate school, highlighting what she values as a woman and Latina, Hola, a doctoral student in astronomy, also mentioned the struggle in connecting with students based on cultural similarities. Hola commented:

> I feel like that is (cultural similarities) probably the most challenging aspect of being a graduate student because it's very hard for me to stay motivated when I feel like there's so many other, like familial factors and things that I have to take into account that I don't see any of my peers ever worrying about.

Aligned with the experience of Ari and Hola, Estrella opined, "I feel like most students are Hispanic or Latina and still there's not really a sense of unity or community between us except for like Chicano program." These Latina/x students experienced isolation at the department and institutional levels mostly because of cultural differences. Latina/x faculty also felt isolated due to a phenomenon created by the pandemic where people limited their personal interactions. In those times, institutions opted for organizing all interactions through Zoom meetings. Faculty members felt affected by this situation and still saw it as problematic. Siba a faculty member from bilingual education and Luna, said respectively, "It has been very isolating, you know, since I started in 2020, I know a lot of us did stay isolated" and "Definitely the isolation...Like, we only see each other once every couple of weeks on Zoom...but I don't ever see anybody on campus." Student and faculty's experiences with this individualized approach happening in higher education contrasted with the Latino community-based focus that participants value and would like to see as students and scholars. The need for community and mutual support is often discussed by Latinx students and faculty, who despite being numerous at HSI, there is a disconnection and lack of interaction among Latinx individuals.

## Discussion

The study explored the research question concerning how this selected group of Latinas/x's identities and the college environment at Hill University influenced their college experiences. Built on Crenshaw's theorization of intersectionality, Latina/x individuals reflected on their experiences and identity formation in higher education as students and scholars. This study highlights Latina/x's multiple identities intersected with hostile, unwelcomed, and alienated higher education settings. Most participants were aware of

Latinas/x's underrepresentation in college, in particular in STEM academic programs, both as students and professors and in leadership positions. Being that Hill University is an HSI, students were expecting to find a stronger Latinx identity within the institution with more Latinx faculty representation. However, several participants expressed feeling invisible in what has been, and continue to be, traditionally White spaces. Like other institutions, at Hill University, approximately 60% of students are Latinx and 67% of the faculty are White. Given this disparity and the location of Hill University on the U.S.-Mexico border, participants problematized their presence and reflected on what Hurtado and Gurin (2004) identified as social comparison. During this social comparison, participants realized the difference in status and social class of both Whites and Latinx causing stigmatization of feeling powerless and less than others (Lacayo, 2016; Rivera, 2008).

In addition, the findings highlighted the multiple identities of Latina/x participants, first related to the several layers of ethnic identity (A. García, 2002) if they self-identify as Mexican Americans, Chicanas, or Mexicanas. Also important is gender identification as most commonly women and nonbinary individuals are the targets of machismo and discriminatory-related issues (Herrera et al., 2022; Peña, 2022). The second layer is tied to the participants' social class and the prejudices of the middle class toward the working class even in aspects such as women's appearance and norms of taste and behavior (Hurtado & Gurin, 2004; Lawler, 2015). And the third layer is linked to the first-generation status, which reflects the struggles to navigate the college-level system both as students and academics (Covarrubias, 2022; Peña, 2022). Latina/x participants' experiences in college are heavily influenced by how they see themselves in terms of ethnicity, gender, social class, and first-generation roles. Latina/x participants' intersection of identities shapes how they perceive themselves and others and the types of marginalizing experiences they encounter (Crenshaw, 1989, 1991). Among these experiences is navigating the college's oppressive contexts which a participant noted the hardship of combining family duties with being a graduate student. Lacking support, empathy, and appropriate resources to deal with time management and stress could help alleviate those difficulties. The cultural aspects of the Latina/x participants greatly influence their interactions with others, attitudes, and behaviors (Contreras Aguirre et al., 2020; Settles, 2006). The participants were not the exception and highly value the connection and community they may develop with peers and colleagues. However, several participants did not perceive such a community and neither group support in other Latinx people on campus. One of their strategies was to be part of the mentoring program where participants were recruited. In this program, students and faculty found allies and a sense of compañerismo (companionship) that is usually absent in other academic programs. Tajfel (1978) noted that social identity is developed when people identify with a group and that group is valuable. Also important is that part of that identification becomes who we are, that is, the social identity along with the auto-created story contributes to explaining who that person is (Lawler, 2015). In contrast, participants' feelings of isolation were commonly experienced and mentioned by both students and faculty members.

This study contributes to the current literature on how Latinas/x in their roles as undergraduates and graduate students, and faculty members at an HSI reflected on their multiple identities to reach their academic and professional goals. Particularly, the intersection of being women, non-binary, and Latinas in STEM academic programs and roles of power generates oppressive environments. In this study, Latinas/x made sense of their presence in unfamiliar spaces as first-generation individuals, expressed isolation feeling alienated from their needs, and doubted to recognize how others value what minorities bring to postsecondary education, and consequently, the workforce.

## Implications for Practice

The projections indicate an increase in the Latinx student college population, and consequently, an expansion of Latinx faculty at HSIs in the near future. Therefore, HSIs must develop and implement validating practices and approaches on behalf of their Latinx students and faculty population. Some of these practices may include (1) wider use of different types of mentoring to further support students' pathways; (2) improved communication strategies and targeted informative sessions to encourage Latinx to advance their studies, and (3) more discussions, forums, and pláticas that promote understanding of the intersection between the Latina/x (multiple) identities and their struggles to see themselves in higher education and beyond. All of them should be implemented at HSIs and promoted by HSIs leaders to create a more welcoming, encouraging, and supportive HSI environment.

## References

Carbado, D. W., Crenshaw, K. W., Mays, V. M., & Tomlinson, B. (2013). Intersectionality: Mapping the movements of a theory. *Du Bois Review: Social Science Research on Race, 10*(2), 303–312.

Contreras Aguirre, H. C., González, E., & Banda, R. (2020). Latina college students' experiences in STEM at HSIs: Framed within Latino critical race theory. *International Journal of Qualitative Studies in Education, 33*(8), 810–823.

Contreras Aguirre, H. C., & Romero, C. (2023). Advancing Latinx faculty and students in academia through femtoring/mentoring. In A. Wilkerson & S. Samuels (Eds.), *Best practices and programmatic approaches for mentoring educational leaders* (pp. 35–47). IGI Global.

Covarrubias, R. (2022). Continuing cultural mismatches. Reflections from a first-generation Latina faculty navigating the academy. In T. L. Buenavista, D. Jain, & M. C. Ledesma (Eds.), *First-generation Faculty of Color: Reflections on research, teaching, and service* (pp. 150–161). Rutgers University Press.

Crenshaw, K. (1989). Demarginalizing the intersection of race and sex: A Black feminist critique of antidiscrimination doctrine, feminist theory, and antiracist politics. *University of Chicago Legal Forum, 1989*(8), 139–167.

Crenshaw, K. (1991). Mapping the margins: Identity politics, intersectionality, and violence against women. *Stanford Law Review, 43*(6), 1241–1299.

Doran, E. (2023). Toward a new understanding of Hispanic-serving community colleges. *Community College Review, 51*(2), 285–305.

Espinoza, K., & Garfield, T. (2023). "It's me, do you have a second?": How testimonios and personal narratives of mentorship and friendship help a tenure-track Latina navigate the academy. *Educational Studies, 59*(3), 280–298.

*Excelencia* in Education. (2023a, March). *Latinas at Hispanic-Serving institutions (HSIs)*. https://www.edexcelencia.org/pdf-Latinas_at_Hispanic-Serving_Institutions

*Excelencia* in Education. (2023b, March). *Hispanic-Serving institutions (HSIs): 2021–22*. https://www.edexcelencia.org/media/2105

Fierros, C., & Delgado Bernal, D. (2016). Vamos a pláticar: The contours of pláticas as Chicana/Latina feminist methodology. *Chicana/Latina Studies: The Journal of Mujeres Activas en Letras y Cambio Social, 15*(2), 98–121.

Flores, A. (2023). *The Latina doctoral student experience: A qualitative phenomenological study* (Unpublished dissertation). Texas State University, San Marcos, Texas. Electronic Theses and Dissertations.

García, A. M. (2002). *The new Americans–The Mexican Americans*. Greenwood Press.

García, G. A. (2019). *Becoming Hispanic-serving institutions: Opportunities for colleges and universities*. Johns Hopkins University Press.

García-Louis, C. (2022). Suficiente, enough: Reckoning with the complexities of a colonial past that racializes LatinXs as MestizXs. *Journal of Hispanic Higher Education, 22*(3), 291–306.

Gonzales, L. D., Murakami, E., & Núñez, A-M. (2013). Latina faculty in the labyrinth: Constructing and contesting legitimacy in Hispanic serving institutions. *Educational Foundations, 27*, 65–89.

Herrera, F. A., Rodriguez-Operana, V. C., Kovats Sánchez, G., Cerrillos, A., & Marquez, B. (2022). "It was hard, and it still is...": Women of Color navigating HSI STEM transfer pathways. *AERA Open, 8*(1), 1–15.

Hispanic Association of Colleges and Universities (HACU). (2021, March). *2021 Hispanic higher education and HSIs facts*. https://www.hacu.net/hacu/HSI_Fact_Sheet.asp

Hurtado, A., & Gurin, P. (2004). *Chicana/o identity in a changing US Society: Quién soy? Quiénes somos?* University of Arizona Press.

Lacayo, C. (2016). Latinos need to stay in their place: Differential segregation in a multi-ethnic suburb. *Societies, 6*(3), 1–18.

Lawler, S. (2015). *Identity: Sociological perspectives*. Polity Press.

Lincoln, Y., & Guba, E. (1985). *Naturalistic inquiry*. Sage.

Peña, L. G. (2022). *Community as rebellion: A syllabus for surviving academia as a Woman of Color*. Haymarket Books.

Reyes, K., & Rodríguez, J. (2012). Testimonio: Origins, terms, and resources. *Equity & Excellence in Education, 45*(3), 525–538.

Rivera, G. (2008). *His panic: Why Americans fear Hispanics in the U.S.* Penguin.

Rodriguez, S. L., Lu, C., & Ramirez, D. (2020). Creating a conceptual framework for computing identity development for Latina undergraduate students. In E. M Gonzalez, F. Fernandez, & M. Wilson (Eds.), *An asset-based approach to advancing Latina students in STEM* (pp. 25–39). Routledge.

Rodriguez, S., Pilcher, A., & Garcia-Tellez, N. (2021). The influence of familismo on Latina student STEM identity development. *Journal of Latinos and Education, 20*(2), 177–189.

Saldaña, J. (2013). *The coding manual for qualitative researchers*. Sage.

Segato, R. L. (2010). Los cauces profundos de la raza Latinoamericana: una relectura del mestizaje. *Crítica y Emancipación, 2*(3), 11–44.

Settles, I. (2006). Use of an intersectional framework to understand Black women's racial and gender identities. *Sex Roles, 54*, 589–601.

Tajfel, H. E. (1978). *Differentiation between social groups: Studies in the social psychology of intergroup relations*. Academic Press.

Verdín, D., Godwin, A., Kirn, A., Benson, L., & Potvin, G. (Eds.). (2018). Understanding how engineering identity and belongingness predict grit for first-generation college students. *Proceedings of the Collaborative Network for Engineering and Computing Diversity Conference*. https://docs.lib.purdue.edu/enegs/75

# 10. Liminality as a Necessary Companion to Intersectionality

LISA DELACRUZ COMBS AND RENEE L. BOWLING

This chapter stems from work conceptualizing liminality as a framework (Bowling & Combs, 2023; also see Chapter 3 of this volume for other work on liminality). In describing our work to others, a common response has been, "Oh, you're studying intersectionality." To us as graduate students with liminal experiences, the two concepts ere distinct, and we conceived of liminality as a companion construct to intersectionality. However, their distinctions are not yet clearly distinguished nor is the relationship between intersectionality and liminality well understood. Our awareness of the need to further differentiate liminality from intersectionality led us to write this chapter and to seek evidence-based differentiation. One of our hypotheses and driving areas of agreement was that liminality held great possibility as a generative framing device for people with liminal identity experiences. Simultaneously, LDC was actively engaged in her dissertation work focused on liminality. Throughout data collection, she was consistently surprised by how often participants mentioned intersectionality when describing how they made meaning of liminality as a concept. Participants expressed a conflation of intersectionality and liminality which parallels the experience we have had as authors. It is from this place of conflation that we begin to connect and bridge across these concepts.

In this chapter we introduce liminality through the findings of an empirical grounded theory study to nuance the theoretical conversation around intersectionality. Much intersectionality scholarship is missing reflection on the ways in which human experiences of intersectionality are liminal, or in-between, which we are certainly not the first to have noticed, but for which we have offered an initial equity-minded conceptual framing (Bowling & Combs, 2023). Herein, we propose that an understanding of liminality can be complementary to the uses and applications of intersectionality as a lens to understand students' identities and experiences in higher education. We ask, can one do justice to intersectionality work ethically without an understanding of liminality? As scholars with in-between identity experiences ourselves, we have been interested to explore the contours between these two concepts. A fortuitous opportunity arose while writing this chapter to incorporate the initial empirical findings from LDC's grounded theory study, which adds important student voices to this developing area of scholarship and praxis.

## What is Liminality?

Originally conceptualized within the anthropology discipline (Turner, 1979), liminality is a term used to describe a threshold existence or an in-between space across two distinct points, in this case, social identity categories or experiences. College students who feel like they do not fit into any one group or category may experience ambiguity, leading to a greater likelihood of liminal identity encounters. Though not an exhaustive list, examples of students who may be inclined to have liminal experiences include multiracial students, gender non-binary students, students from interfaith families or who straddle socioeconomic statuses, students with invisible/temporary disabilities, and international, veteran, and bisexual students.

As a conceptual device alongside intersectionality, liminality has three components (Bowling & Combs, 2023). The first asserts that liminality does not focus on an end goal or arrival point. It is a threshold existence or encounter that may be temporary, and which requires nuance and complexity in its definition and application. In other words, liminality does not focus on destination but rather embodiment. We intentionally do not assign value to the in-between space, acknowledging that liminal identity experiences may be positive or negative depending on students' perceptions, context, and environment. They may be welcomed or ascribed, visible or invisible. The second component is the cornerstone of this chapter, deliberately framed by the principles of intersectionality. We argue that liminality is best understood through the lens of interconnected systems of power in acknowledgement that liminality does not function in isolation. This chapter explores the relationship between intersectionality and liminality in greater depth. Finally, liminality must be recognized as a lived experience in higher education spaces, including in connection to experiences of intersectionality. This validation can lead to an increased sense of belonging, critical thought and reflection, and reimagining of possibilities within higher education structures. Perhaps most importantly, liminality provides a conceptual tool to reframe what may be value-laden (e.g., positive, neutral, negative, or mixed) student experiences.

## Related Concepts

When situating liminality in a larger conversation within scholarship across multiple disciplines, tangential concepts emerge. Turner (1979), working with his wife, originally conceptualized liminality as an in-between space informed by anthropology and studies of religious rites of passage. Bhabha (1994) introduced cultural hybridity across time and space with an explicit focus on implications for the colonizer/colonized relationship. Anzaldúa (1987) operationalized an in-between space rejecting binaries with her focus on borderland theory. Borderlands is strongly connected to borders, physical existence, and immigration; therefore, we are cautious in applying it across and between different identity groups. In Okello's (2022) piece regarding how carcerality and whiteness inform pedagogy, he addressed liminality in conjunction with limbos, which Black feminist scholar James (1999) referred to as a vulnerable and isolated state. Okello (2022) drew parallels between limbos and liminality, calling attention to the "betwixt and between marginal states" (p. 7).

It is useful to draw upon Wijeyesinghe's (2012) intersectional model of multiracial identity where she depicted multiracial identity as reminiscent of a galaxy. This image captures shifts and interactional changes over time, emphasizing the "messiness" over the concrete or static. Galaxies orbit one another, contain multiple smaller galaxies, and take shape in various sizes and forms within the larger context of systems or space. The multiplicity of conceptualizations that capture the shared experiences of being in-between demonstrates the relevance of liminality to nuance intersectionality. The expansive nature of liminality's application across identity experiences, from its original anthropological conceptualization to contemporary applications, make it a helpful supplement to better understand intersectionality.

## Embodied Liminality

We come to this chapter from our individual and combined scholarship and our personal identities and experiences of liminality. LDC identifies as a multiracial Woman of Color and operates from a liminal embodiment, continuing to disrupt racial rigidity in higher education and examine ideas related to critical mixed race studies and poststructural feminist perspectives in her work. From this poststructural third wave perspective, power is always a part of the framing. RLB works transnationally in K-12 and higher education and has multicultural and multireligious family influences. Her work explores worldview diversity and intercultural learning, student identity development, campus climates and belonging. For her, power is omnipresent but may not always be the fulcrum on which liminality hinges; for example, language, ethnicity, or nationality may have primary significance for individuals' threshold identities and experiences.

We originally connected as graduate students around disparate experiences of liminality and shared a mutual desire for ways of thinking about in-betweenness across and between social identity groups that might lead to coalition-building: the building of bridges across difference, rather than walls. We felt this as a need not just in society but in higher education to avoid continued bifurcation into ever more isolated groups. We began co-writing by bringing together the literature on multiraciality and international student identity development, seeking to center common minoritized student experiences. Our commitment to this work is personal and on behalf of students of multidimensional identities who experience and/or live in the in-between.

## Method

While co-writing this chapter conceptually, LDC was simultaneously engaged in conducting a research study of a diverse set of undergraduate students and used Keating's (2013) interconnectivity theory as a theoretical framework to investigate liminality. While a discussion of the relationship between intersectionality and liminality was not the focus of the study, this author was surprised by the participants repeatedly raising the topic of intersectionality in their interviews. We conferred as co-authors about this unexpected but welcome confluence between the study and our conceptual work together, and LDC chose to amend her interview protocol to expressly include prompts about intersectionality that would allow her to follow this emergent line of inquiry. Thus, this chapter presents further development of our conceptual work around liminality in relation to intersectionality that is empirically-informed by findings nested in a larger research study of college students' liminal identity experiences.

LDC's study on liminality employed grounded theory and specifically situational analysis (Clarke et al., 2017) as the qualitative methodology. Situational analysis is an extension of Strauss and Corbin's (1994) grounded theory methodology with the specific aim to examine the nuances of a complex situation. In this study, the situation under investigation was college students' liminal identity experiences. The purpose of the larger study was to generate a student development theory focused on the shared meanings of liminality as a third wave construct. LDC defined liminal identity experiences as an in-between embodiment related to existing beyond rigid social identity categories. The research questions that guided this larger study were:

1. What are the thematic meanings that college students have around liminality as a social experience?
2. How do college students who experience liminality build community with other peers?

LDC recruited participants by sharing a call on social media, multicultural center listservs, and with colleagues that work in higher education. Those that wanted to participate in the study filled out an intake form to express their interest and share more about their social identities. Participation criteria included undergraduate students that self-identified as having a liminal experience, with examples given that included race, gender, religion, sexuality, class, and ability. Participants were selected by utilizing maximum variation to have a variety of perspectives and social identities represented in the sample (Jones et al., 2016), resulting in 13 participants.

Data collection methods included two in-depth individual, semi-structured interviews and visual maps. LDC elicited visual maps from participants in formats of their choosing, such as word clouds, Pinterest boards, and concept maps, about how they made sense of liminality as a college student, based on a personal artifact from their liminal experience. While acknowledgment of intersecting systems of power was part of the conceptual framework, intersectionality was not explicitly referenced in the interview protocol. However, nine out of the 13 participants brought up intersectionality in the discussion about liminality without being prompted. These nine participants were thus included for the purposes of this chapter (see Table 10.1). Intrigued by this pattern, and as part of her iterative process in consultation with RLB, LDC chose to adjust the interview protocol to include a follow-up question about the relationship between liminality and intersectionality. This question was only included when a participant mentioned intersectionality in their interview. For the purposes of this chapter, the researcher pulled the nine masked responses about intersectionality and employed open coding (Saldaña, 2016) to find common themes across the data.

**Table 10.1.** Participant Identities and Characteristics

| Pseudonym | Year in Undergraduate Studies | Major | Liminal Identity Experiences | Discussed Intersectionality |
|---|---|---|---|---|
| Iago | 3rd Year | International Studies | Gender, sexuality, cultural identity, invisible disabilities, bilingual | Y |
| Aless | 2nd Year | Psychology and Criminology | Non-binary and queer | N |
| Orepheus | 1st Year | Architecture | Pansexuality, genderqueerness, queerness, biracial experiences, invisible disabilities | N |
| Sol | 1st Year | English and African American Studies | Gender identity and sexuality | Y |
| AJ | 3rd Year | Psychology | Biracial, bisexual, non-binary, invisible disability, and social class liminal identities | Y |
| Theia | 5th Year | Women and Gender Studies | Invisible chronic illnesses/ disabilities, trans femme but still perceived as male, and have been born into wealth and also homeless. | Y |
| Laila | 3rd year | Psychology | Biracial, Jewish mother and Christian father | Y |
| Rosaline | 3rd Year | English | Bisexuality, mixed race, disability | Y |

| Pseudonym | Year in Undergraduate Studies | Major | Liminal Identity Experiences | Discussed Intersectionality |
|---|---|---|---|---|
| Rose | 2nd Year | Fine Arts | Being a multicultural (hispanic/white) woman as well as being bisexual | Y |
| Candance | 3rd Year | City and Regional Planning | Being bisexual, as well as having had to straddle the line between being a boy and a girl during gender transition | Y |
| Nicole | 2nd Year | Biology | Multiracial | N |
| Jae | 1st Year | Spanish/ Sociology | Gender nonbinary, a mestizo (multiracial as in Native American and white) latine, living in a mixed-citizenship status family, child of an immigrant, having an invisible disability | N |
| Grace | 3rd Year | Biomedical Sciences and Gender and Women's Studies | Bisexual | Y |

## *Findings: Contributions to Understanding Lived Experiences of Intersectionality*

In this section, we offer three themes to discuss liminality's contributions to understanding lived experiences of intersectionality. The first is imagery of intersectionality and liminality to set the stage of how the participants conceptualized these two concepts. The second theme focuses on how liminality is a complementary tool that facilitates nuanced and fluid applications of intersectionality. With our final theme, we discuss an asset-based approach to intersectionality.

## Imagery of Intersectionality and Liminality

We open the discussion of our findings with a grounding in the participants' descriptions of liminality and intersectionality. The participants, hereafter referred to by pseudonyms, observed a conflation between these ideas and expressed excitement at the opportunity to differentiate between the two concepts. When asked a follow-up question to explain the difference, both Theia, a trans femme student who straddles multiple social classes, and Grace, a bisexual student, responded, "Oh that's such a good question." Participants verbally generated imagery in the interviews to illustrate the distinction. For example, they referred to intersectionality as the cross section of two roads and liminality as an in-between space between two worlds. Rosaline, a multiracial and bisexual student with a disability, described this contrast when she said:

> When I think of intersectionality, I think, like standing at the corner of two different streets. And, like you're not technically on one street or the other street. And I guess that's liminality, too, because you're in the middle. You're not categorized by either one or the other.

For Rosaline, intersectionality inspired the image of a crossroad, resembling Crenshaw's (1989) original conceptualization, whereas liminality represented the middle ground or expanding beyond two streets. Similarly, AJ, a biracial, bisexual, non-binary student with invisible disabilities and liminal class identities, used color theory to illustrate the difference between the concepts:

> Yeah. So, I feel like, not to be like color theory but, like liminality, I feel like is more occupying a blend of the spaces like somewhere in that middle ground; whereas intersectionality is like a simultaneous like overlapping of those experiences.

In other words, liminality evoked blending or smudging in contrast to the discrete edges of intersectionality.

The imagery of liminality as blurring or smudging echoes Keating's (2013) work on interconnectivity as threshold theorizing that invites others to engage expansive possibilities beyond binaries. A potential limitation of intersectionality is that with systems of power as the focal point people either access power (privilege) or do not (oppression), resembling the rigidity of discrete edges or crossroads that the participants also described. This binary view can reinforce deficit thinking and is often zero-sum, where to rebalance power, some other group must be disempowered, which plays out in the language of deconstruction and dismantling. Certainly, power is real, has for far too long been invisibly tied to whiteness, and must be intentionally interrogated for which intersectionality theory is imperative. We argue that liminality can complement intersectionality as a power-aware conceptual framework and a necessary lens to understanding the complexities of lived experiences of in-betweenness. Keating (2013) explicitly stated, "[I]ntersectionality in itself is not enough. We need to range widely. We need multiple stories and multiple tools" (p. 37). Liminality can be one of these tools.

## A Fluid Lens

As authors, like Harris and Patton (2019) we argue that intersectionality is often misapplied as an individual lens. A more accurate interpretation of the theoretical base would be to say that a person navigates intersectional systems that affect the way they experience and move through the world. Often, however, the conceptualization of intersection gives the impression of these systems and people's related identities as being fixed axes with a singular point of connection. Participants echoed this point by emphasizing that intersectionality is the interaction *of two or more* systems of power, whereas liminality is the embodied experience of existing across or between within *one* social identity category. Candace, a bisexual trans student, emphasized this point when she said, "Liminality identity might… It's just a little bit more like focused on how you fit into one identity, whereas, like intersectionality, is more of how multiple identities interact." Participants such as Laila, a biracial third-year college student with a Jewish mother and Christian father, further expanded upon how liminality encompasses being in-between within one identity category when reflecting upon her identities. For example, she described intersectionality through the lens of interactions of oppressive structures from a Black woman's perspective which accounts for *two interacting systems* of oppression, racism and sexism. Her biracial identity, however, demonstrates the fluidity *within one identity category*, her race. This does not negate that people can have multiple liminal identity experiences at once. However, in many people's experience, the ways in which systems intersect are not fixed, nor are they limited in the number of axes or dimensions, but are connected to contextual cultures, history, and power (Dill, 2009). Individual human experiences of intersectionality may be dynamic, shifting in relation to time, space, place, and relative identity salience, as the model of multiple dimensions of identity brought into focus (Jones et al., 2012). Indeed, "individuals inhabit multiple social locations that are lived and experienced simultaneously" (Jones et al., 2012, p. 698): students experience intersectional systems in liminal ways. Liminality can serve as a companion tool for more nuanced and fluid applications of intersectionality to lived experience, especially for students who find themselves in-between within one or more identity categories.

## An Asset-Based Approach

As a complementary framing device, the application of liminality provides students with an asset-based approach to dynamically viewing their multi-dimensionality while acknowledging the very real challenges of existing in-between in a society that systemically privileges monoracism (Johnston & Nadal, 2010) and monoculturalism. In addition to understanding the negative impact of bisecting systems of power, students may explore not only what they have lost but what they might find by being located between shifting cultures and power dynamics. Individual dynamic and nuanced experiences of in-betweenness come into view.

The positive aspects of liminality were recognized by the students in the study. Students' liminal experiences can be lonely, confusing, and misunderstood by others, but "liminality can be seen as a benefit," as Iago, a queer, gender non-conforming, bilingual student with invisible disabilities, reasoned in their interview. AJ referred to the blend in the middle as generative, a space where "sometimes...you get a new identity." Participants variously referred to the process as one of integration or a collision of worlds where one world enters another. Characterized by ambiguity, Theia stated, "liminality to me is...about the gray and the unknown," where "things don't always quite mesh together perfectly." Later on, she elaborated, "That's also what makes things interesting." Her comment demonstrates these students' internal processing and intercultural sensitivity: their ability to analyze differences and identify the beneficial aspects of their liminal identities, not only the challenges. Related work with global nomad or third-culture students found liminality to be these students' constant experience (Schaetti & Ramsey, 1999), with some of their resulting strengths outlined as adaptability, open-mindedness, and intercultural communication and social skills (Pollock et al., 2010; Quick, 2010). These assets associated with liminal experiences are also commonly identified with leadership. Put another way, students with liminal identity experiences are adept at reading the room, navigating novel social scenarios, identifying allies, and code-switching.

With liminality as the vantage point, students can acknowledge how power is operational in their communities and environments and gain vocabulary for describing how identities may be fluid, dynamic, and even hybrid within themselves, with various combinations holding potential for community cultural wealth (Yosso, 2005). Liminality thus centers the marginal experience of multiplicity. It provides a framework for a "both, and" viewing of one's identity from multiple perspectives: without assigning judgment, with an "eyes wide open" view of intersectional systemic realities, while creating possibility for dynamic expressions over the life course. What excites us is that once students began using liminality to frame their experiences, they are then able to identify with others' similar experiences *from different identities* to validate each other's struggles and strengths.

## Concluding Thoughts on Findings

While it may be possible to add more axes or dimensions to the existing conceptualization of intersectionality, we are in favor of attention to and acknowledgment of some experiences of intersectionality as liminal. Liminality may be used to nuance intersectionality's dynamism, not as a competing framework, but as a complementary framing device aligned with third wave student development theorizing. In physics, compound lenses leverage convergence and divergence to add complexity to the perspective that lenses capture, and intersectionality and liminality may co-operate conceptually in a similar way. Intersecting systems of power are important to keep in the range of focus; so, too, are students' experiences of in-betweenness.

## Reimagining Possibilities: Implications for Theory, Research, and Praxis

The aim of this chapter was to augment applications of intersectionality by connecting it to relevant liminality scholarship that reflects the way many students experience the world. Without deliberate attention to liminality, discussions of intersectionality overlook significant and common experiences that are marginalized when educators only consider discrete identity categories. We centered the experiences of multiracial, multicultural, and other students who experience shifting identities and affiliations such as veteran, immigrant, religious, or parent. We conclude with implications for theory, research, and praxis that further illuminate the interconnected nature of intersectionality and liminality.

In our previous work, we suggested researchers and practitioners adopt liminality as a companion frame to recognize how power co-operates with in-betweenness. Using liminality as a compound lens with intersectionality may empower students and those who work with them from an asset-based approach. We desire this contribution to be generative for both theory and practice. By being power-aware but focused on possibility, the focus can be on what is additive from the identities one is in-between, even when experiences of liminality may themselves be difficult or painful. There is a hopeful arc to liminality as a framing device that allows one to dynamically revisit and reframe past, present, and future experiences. Rather than fixed, it presents the individual with a contextually rich opportunity to negotiate their identity, to decide and redecide which aspects to foreground, which to treasure, and whether to land in one spot or flow freely between aspects of identities and communities in a given moment or context. We believe this highlights the agency of individuals who often find themselves neither here nor there involuntarily, and as such it is a tool for positively negotiating liminal existence and interactions in the world.

It is also our hope for this chapter to be useful to scholars and practitioners who study and work across and between populations of students with liminal identities. This is especially important for students whose identities have historically been marginalized and for whom intersectionality is personally relevant. We have suggested the utility of this complementary framing for coalition-building (Bowling & Combs, 2023) and expressly envision it not only as applicable to multiracial students but to other populations as well that may experience liminality.

In the introduction to this chapter, we asked whether one could do justice to intersectionality work ethically without an understanding of liminality. To be clear, in the context of higher education, we mean work with students in all their variability. Because liminal identity experiences are, at least presently, marginal—most people are either this or that, not in-between or both—it would be impossible to center the margins without attending to liminality. We invite scholars and practitioners to consider liminality as a complementary tool to intersectionality for understanding students' stories and helping them to frame their assets, agency, and possibilities for connection and belonging through shared experiences of liminality.

## References

Anzaldúa, G. (1987). Borderlands/La frontera: The new mestiza. Aunt Lute Books.
Bhabha, H. (1994). *The location of culture*. Routledge.
Bowling, R. L., & Combs, L. D. (2023). Liminality as a third wave conceptual framework. *Journal of Student Affairs Research and Practice. 60*(4), 537-549. https://doi.org/10.1080/19496591.2022.2150974

Clarke, A. E., Friese, C., & Washburn, R. S. (2017). *Situational analysis: Grounded theory after the interpretive turn.* Sage.

Crenshaw, K. (1989). Demarginalizing the intersection of race and sex: A black feminist critique of antidiscrimination doctrine, feminist theory and antiracist politics. *University of Chicago, Legal Forum, 1989*(8), 139–167.

Dill, B. T. (2009). Intersections, identities, and inequalities in higher education. In B. T. Dill & R. E. Zambrana (Eds.), *Emerging intersections* (pp. 229–252). Rutgers University Press.

Harris, J. C., & Patton, L. D. (2019). Un/doing intersectionality through higher education research. *The Journal of Higher Education, 90*(3), 347–372.

James, J. (1999). *Shadowboxing: Representations of Black feminist politics.* St. Martin's Press.

Johnston, M. P., & Nadal, K. L. (2010). Multiracial microaggressions: Exposing monoracism in everyday life and clinical practice. In D. W. Sue (Ed.), *Microaggressions and marginality: Manifestation, dynamics, and impact* (pp. 123–144). Wiley & Sons.

Jones, S. R., Kim, Y. C., & Skendall, K. C. (2012). (Re-)framing authenticity: Considering multiple social identities using autoethnographic and intersectional approaches. *The Journal of Higher Education, 83*(5), 698–724.

Jones, S. R., Torres, V., & Arminio, J. (2016). *Negotiating the complexities of qualitative research in higher education: Fundamental elements and issues.* Routledge.

Keating, A. (2013). *Transformation now! Toward a post-oppositional politics of change.* University of Illinois Press.

Okello, W. K. (2022). "What are you pretending not to know?": Un/doing internalized carcerality through pedagogies of the flesh. *Curriculum Inquiry, 52*(4), 405–421.

Pollock, D. C., Van Reken, R. E., & Pollock, M. V. (2010). *Third culture kids: The experience of growing up among worlds: The original, classic book on TCKs.* Hachette UK.

Quick, T. L. (2010). *The global nomad's guide to university transition.* Summertime.

Schaetti, B. F., & Ramsey, S. J. (1999). The global nomad experience: Living in liminality. *Mobility.* https://transitiondynamics.wordpress.com/resources-and-products/articles-and-publications/198-2/

Saldaña, J. (2016). Goodall's verbal exchange coding: An overview and example. *Qualitative Inquiry, 22*(1), 36–39.

Strauss, A., & Corbin, J. (1994). Grounded theory methodology: An overview. In N. K. Denzin & Y. S. Lincoln (Eds.), *Handbook of qualitative research* (pp. 273–285). Sage.

Turner, V. (1979). Betwixt and between: The liminal period in rites de passage. In W. A. Lessa & E. Z. Vogt (Eds.), *Reader in comparative religion: An anthropological approach* (pp. 234–242). Harper Collins.

Wijeyesinghe, C. (2012). The intersectional model of multiracial identity: Integrating multiracial identity theories and intersectional perspectives on social identity. In C. Wijeyesinghe & B. W. Jackson (Eds.), *New perspectives on racial identity development: Integrating emerging frameworks* (pp. 81–107). New York University Press.

Yosso, T. J. (2005). Whose culture has capital? A critical race theory discussion of community cultural wealth. *Race, Ethnicity and Education, 8*(1), 69–91.

# 11. Backward Thinking: Exploring the Relationship Among Intersectionality, Epistemology, and Research Design

Daniel Tillapaugh and Z Nicolazzo

Scholarship on intersectionality, particularly in educational research, often focuses on the intersecting identities of participants (e.g., Jones & Abes, 2013; Tillapaugh, 2012). Despite this focus, Renn (2010) argued that some scholars' use of intersectionality inadvertently created "some slippage of the term among educational researchers" (p. 7). The lack of exploration regarding the interrogation of power implicit in intersectionality, how it influences one's multiple identities and how it mediates one's interactions with others, troubles us as scholars. Informed by Bowleg's (2008) foundational work on the complex challenges of intersectionality research, we believe intersectional thinking that begins and ends with research participants' identities misses an important step, which is how intersectionality is implicated in, and thus influences, the research design. We argue that one's epistemological grounding, how one conceptualizes truth and power and the ways in which scholars influence each other's thinking about their research projects, has a direct impact on the fecundity of the research content. These are the topics around which we frame our analysis within this chapter. In doing so, we find it important to engage in *backward thinking,* or the idea that one not only needs to leverage intersectionality with participants and in data analysis but also prior to seeking participants, specifically in terms of one's epistemology, reflexivity, and overall research design.

In this chapter, we pose the following questions, which serve as a guide to our backward thinking:

1. What happens when one thinks about intersectionality as a concept influencing study design and the research process itself?
2. How might thinking about intersectionality as affecting what happens before data collection and analysis be an important lens for better addressing the multifaceted political aspects of research?
3. What could an investigation of intersectionality of researchers' epistemological groundings offer the field of educational research, particularly for higher education?

In asking these questions, we seek to expand our collective thinking about the concept of intersectionality by reflecting on how it impacts the design of research studies as well as how one thinks about the research one does. By doing so, we argue that not only do researchers and participants benefit, but the potential effect(s) of one's research may be positively influenced as well. In other words, by engaging in backward thinking regarding intersectional research, we allow for greater visibility for highly marginalized student populations, thus increasing our visibility of their (and our) lives.

## *Epistemology Defined*

Epistemology, or the theory of knowledge, comprises "the relationship between what we know and what we see [and] the truths we seek and believe as researchers" (Lincoln et al., 2011, p. 103). Seen in this way, a researcher's epistemological grounding is always already embedded in a relationship between oneself (e.g., one's social identities) and something or someone else. Although concerns about truth, power, values, and knowledge are central to one's epistemology, these are understood not solely through internal thought but as a result of didactic interactions between an individual and others in one's social context, including between researcher(s) and participant(s). For higher education researchers, this means one comes to one's own epistemic beliefs as a result of interacting with research participants as well as other scholars.

Epistemes may range from positivism—the belief in absolute and objective truths that can be established through scientific inquiry—to poststructuralism—the belief that categories of identification are constantly in flux and do little to convey specific meaning about that which is being explained (Lincoln et al., 2011). Furthermore, some epistemologies foreground participants and their voices (e.g., constructivism), while others place primary emphasis on exposing and interrogating overarching systems of societal power, privilege, and oppression (e.g., criticalism; Lincoln et al., 2011).

Although research studies have traditionally been rooted in one episteme (e.g., constructivism), some scholars (e.g., Abes, 2009; Kincheloe, 2001) have begun to recognize how epistemologies overlap, converge, and can work in collaboration to provide a more complete and complex understanding of data. Because how one thinks about knowledge is rooted in how our identities intersect with one another, we must reflect on and understand how our chosen epistemes inform our own worldview as researchers but also as people. For this theoretical analysis, we as authors discuss how researchers can work together across epistemological perspectives to enhance the research process and resulting analysis.

## *Intersectionality Defined*

Dill and Zambrana (2009) framed intersectionality "as an analytical strategy—a systematic approach to understanding human life and behavior that is rooted in the experiences and struggles of marginalized people" (p. 4). Citing the increasing emergence of studies on intersectionality in higher education, Jones and Abes (2013) maintained, "with an explicit focus on locating individuals within larger structures of privilege and oppression, intersectionality as an analytic framework for understanding identity insists on... a more holistic approach to identity" (p. 135). By centering the conversations of social identities in an intersectional view, scholars begin to interrogate the "interconnected structures of inequality" (Dill & Zambrana, 2009, p. 5) by which power and privilege are granted (or not granted) based on the intersections of one's social identities, as well as how these systems are maintained and replicated within society (Berger & Guidroz, 2009; Crenshaw, 1995). Elaborating on this point, Weber (1998) highlighted that one's own internalized understanding of one's identity (e.g., gender, race) "depends on one's *simultaneous* location in the race, class, gender, and sexuality hierarchies" (p. 26). As a result, power intrinsically plays a role in the identity politics at both an individual and collective/societal level (Crenshaw, 1995; Weber, 1998).

### *The Concept of Systemic Power*

The notion of power is deeply implicated in intersectionality. Baca Zinn and Dill (1996) argued that intersections of identity create a confluence of privilege and oppression for individuals. Shields (2008) expanded on this idea, stating that the intersection of identities "instantiate social stratification" whereby identities "may be experienced as a feature of individual selves, but [they] also reflect... the operation of power relations among groups that comprise that identity category" (p. 302). In their work, Dill and Zambrana (2009) offered four domains by which power structures subordinate others based on dimensions of their identities and maintain systems of inequality. These included the following:

1. The structural domain, which consists of the institutional structures of the society including government, the legal system, housing patterns, economic traditions, and educational structure.
2. The disciplinary domain, which consists of the ideas and practices that characterize and sustain bureaucratic hierarchies.
3. The hegemonic domain, which consists of the images, symbols, ideas, and ideologies that shape social consciousness (Collins, 2000).
4. The interpersonal domain, which consists of patterns of interaction between individuals and groups. (p. 7)

Any discussion of intersectionality without due consideration given to the implications and effects of systemic power misses the proverbial mark. Rather than talking about intersectionality, which includes the ways in which power mediates the lived experiences of people based on dominant and/or subordinated identities, the lack of focus on the effects of systemic power often leads researchers to equate intersectionality with how people's various identities come together at the individual level (Bowleg, 2008; Nash, 2008) or the exploration of individuals' multiple identities without considering their social contexts and the influence of power on their experiences and, thus, the livability of their lives (Butler, 2004).

### *Intersectional Identities* ⟸⟹ *Intersectional Research*

Who a researcher is—one's worldview, life experiences, and social identities—often influences the research one undertakes (Jones et al., 2006; Stewart, 2010). Moreover, a researcher rarely if ever conducts data collection and analysis in isolation. Instead, researchers work within a community of scholars, examples of which include not only the conferences at which research results are disseminated but also the personal interactions researchers have with one another to discuss and work through the particularities of one's work. Therefore, not only is there a synergistic relationship between who one is as a researcher and one's work but also how one interacts with others in a community of scholars and one's work. In other words, while we are not suggesting every research project needs to have multiple researchers, we are suggesting that researchers' identities do influence the ways in which they make meaning and view their own research from a variety of epistemological foundations (e.g., those of our colleagues).

Dill (2009) stated, "Intersectional work is dependent upon collaborations, alliances, and networks among scholars with similar intellectual interests, visions, ideas, and values" (p. 234). Additionally, Kincheloe (2011) suggested researchers bring together multiple ways of thinking and collecting data as a way to engage in inquiry with emancipatory aims. Here, it becomes clear that who one is as a researcher and how one interacts with others in the community of scholars directly influences the way one thinks, constructs, and enacts research. As examples of how these intersectional relationships enhance one's research, we as authors will now reflect on how our own thinking has been altered as a result of our ongoing dialogue and collaboration with each other.

## The Evolution of Dan's Research

As a qualitative researcher, I (DT) have come to understand the importance of reflexivity and its role within my work. Being a White, gay, cisgender male from a middle-class, rural farm family in upstate New York, I know that my own lived experiences and multiple social identities play a significant role in how I make meaning of myself and others. My research interests are really passion areas of mine that stem from my personal life. The feminist slogan of "the personal is political" (Hanisch, 2006, p. 1) resonates with me in that my research is informed by my personal life and vice versa. My interest in intersectionality in higher education stems from my interest in student development and my critique that much of the traditional theories used in practice in higher education subjugate and splinter aspects of one's identities into fragmented parts rather than encouraging one to take a holistic approach. To me, intersectionality provided an outlet for understanding one's multiple identities within the context of the larger systems of power in which one lives.

My line of research has been largely focused on how sexual minority men in college make meaning of their multiple identities, particularly their sense of masculinities and sexuality (see Tillapaugh, 2012). As a researcher who tends to identify as a constructivist, I embrace the notion of social construction of identities. Therefore, in my research, I place an emphasis on understanding data (e.g., students' personal narratives) in the social contexts in which they live as well as examine the construction of knowledge between the participants and myself (Charmaz, 2006). Exploring my own meaning making process of my social identities illuminated important aspects of my positionality, which certainly helped me check some biases and assumptions; certainly reading key works on intersectionality and research (see Crenshaw,

1995; Dill & Zambrana, 2009; Bowleg, 2008; McCall, 2005; Stewart, 2010) also informed my epistemological stances and the ways I wanted to conduct my research using intersectionality as an analytical lens. At the same time, my peer review team—of which Z was a member—also played an important role in the evolution of my work.

Z's role within my research shifted my work forward tremendously, particularly in thinking critically about aspects of identity, especially the location of power and difference. As a critical researcher entrenched in critical trans politics—a critical theoretical perspective centered on increasing the life chances of trans*[1] individuals via broad-based coalitions and movements for social change (Spade, 2015)—I appreciate Z's interrogation of aspects of my work that I often take for granted or on which I did not push back. The tensions between our different theoretical paradigms may be present, but they have allowed for a blending—an epistemological bricolage (Kincheloe, 2001), of sorts—that has certainly helped my own thinking around intersectionality. As a constructivist, I appreciated the aspects of one's multiple identity development within the work but often would find myself bringing in aspects of Z's critical approaches to the systemic parts of my research. For example, in discussions of heteronormativity experienced by many of my participants in college, conversations with Z heightened my ability to dig into how heteronormativity tended to be replicated within the LGBT (lesbian, gay, bisexual, transgender) community and its advocacy for same-sex marriage rather than issues that may take higher priorities for others within our community (e.g., employment nondiscrimination laws, immigration laws for same-sex partners, access to health care for trans* people). This epistemological bricolage has provided a more nuanced and complex examination into the ways in which intersectional approaches to research can provide significant implications for practice, policy, theory, and research in higher education, which we discuss further in this chapter.

## The Evolution of Z's Research

When positioning myself (ZN) within my research, I often struggle to provide "something other than a list of attributes separated by those proverbial commas (gender, sexuality, race, class), that usually mean that we have not yet figured out how to think [about] the relations we seek to mark" (Butler, 2011, p. 123). Although I am a queer, trans* researcher with an invisible disability who, due to my educational attainment, has transcended the lower middle-class background I was thrown into when my parents divorced, stating these identities does little to shed light on who I am. Similarly, stating that Dan, as a gay cisgender man, has influenced my work also seems devoid of meaning. I am not saying that social identities do not matter. Quite the opposite; I am suggesting that they matter too much to just string them together with commas and think one has explored fully one's positionality.

In reflecting on my work with Dan, what does seem important is that we simultaneously converge regarding some identities (e.g., we are both White) while diverging across other categories of difference (e.g., Dan is cisgender and I am trans\*). Additionally, we negotiate dominant and subordinate identities, both individually and between us. As such, my relationship with Dan, which has spanned more than a decade, has set the stage for us to support each other as our identities shift over time as well as challenge how our thinking, life experiences, and social identities mediate our worldviews and how we make meaning of our research. Specifically, Dan's commitment to constructivist grounded theory (Charmaz, 2006) has reminded me of the importance of listening to the voices of my participants and building strong, reciprocal relationships with them. Concurrently, in keeping with the tenets of critical trans politics (Spade, 2015), I also maintain a focus on interrogating the genderism in which the trans\* students with whom I research are culturally embedded to increase the livability of our lives. Furthermore, Dan has impressed upon me the importance of focusing on my own feelings, reactions, and responses throughout the research process. As a result of this new affective orientation toward my research, I am continually drawn back to my participants and the process of working alongside of them rather than solely foregrounding the systemic forms of oppression on which my critical theoretical perspective centers.

## Thinking Through Intersectionality Together

It is evident in reflecting on our own experiences as researchers that our work has been enhanced by recognizing not only the connections we have to our lines of inquiry but also to each other as scholars. Nevertheless, because we have slightly different epistemological groundings (e.g., I [DT] am a critical constructivist and Z a criticalist), which tend to foreground different things (e.g., constructivism foregrounds participants' voices while criticalism foregrounds a thorough critique of social inequity), we have to negotiate what our working together means. For example, we want study participants to share their stories in whatever way they make meaning of them (a constructivist tenet), but we also realize that how they tell these stories, and the context in which these stories are placed, are often laced with elements of power, privilege, and oppression (a critical tenet). Put another way, participants' stories may be studded with elements of power, privilege, and oppression that they may not know how to articulate or make meaning of but may be highlighted by a critical analysis. As such, our working together in an intersectional way has mandated that we address questions regarding how each of us approaches research, the ways we structure research questions, and how we collect and analyze data. Furthermore, we were constantly cycling back to how our social identities, life experiences, and social contexts were mediating our responses both to each other and our work. For example, the salience of my (ZN) trans* identity allowed me to recognize a theme of gender policing grounded in transphobia that emerged from the data obtained in DT's research (Tillapaugh & Nicolazzo, 2015). Our own vantage points as researchers have been informed by our multiple identities and the institutional and societal systems in which we are embedded, which is consistent with taking an intersectional approach to the research process. Although thinking through intersectionality requires consistent and intense reflection in all phases of the research process, we have found the resulting effects to be worthwhile.

Due to the lack of emphasis on power as a mediating force in educational research on intersectionality, we now turn to do some backward thinking on its influence on the research process prior to data collection and analysis. In doing so, it is important to recognize the way power has the potential to influence participants despite them not articulating the connection. In other words, the constellation of identities for any given researcher (see Iverson, 2014), along with one's epistemological and methodological choices for any given study, influence the following: which participants seek to join a study, which participants are selected, what experiences they share, how they share their experiences, and what meaning is made from their sharing on behalf of the researcher, participant(s), and for them as co-constructors of knowledge. For example, my (ZN) epistemological choice to use critical trans politics (Spade, 2015) likely had an influence in who I was able to recruit for my dissertation study as well as the meaning(s) me and my participants reached as a result of our collaboration. How one talks about one's work, the questions one uses to frame one's inquiry, and the places one seeks (and does not seek) participants not only impacts what data one collects (and does not collect), but they also are directly related to one's personal identities as an individual and researcher as well as one's interactions among one's scholarly community.

These are not idle decisions, and they are not without consequence. Power not only mediates the direction in which a study goes and how meaning making in the data analysis process occurs. Additionally, power also affects how the research is perceived, the extent to which it is welcomed, by whom it is welcomed, and the access one may or may not get to publish and/or present in certain venues. Scholars have pointed out that the complex intersections of personal identities and overarching social contexts (e.g., neoliberalism) may influence one's ability to be recognized as a knowledge producer in the academy (Elia & Yep, 2012; Pasque et al., 2012). Furthermore, although researchers on the margins certainly do gain access to publish their work, questions of in what venue, at what cost, and if such access acts as a form of "buffer zone" (Kivel, 2007; Spade, 2010) that occludes the continued pervasiveness of systemic oppression (e.g., sexism, genderism, heterosexism, ableism, classism) embedded within the institutions through which such knowledge is shared persist. As Dill (2009) reinforced, research on intersectionality should actively call for and maintain social justice and the disruption of these pervasive systems of oppression for the benefit of those marginalized within society. For example, Tierney's (1997) commentary on whether gay scholars should look to publish in mainstream journals or queer publications, and the effects of such decisions, shows how power mediates not only how one approaches research and the research process but the extent to which one's research is viewed as valid, appropriate, and useful by others in one's respective field of study.

## *Implications for Educational Research*

What does all of this mean for those individuals interested in conducting research through the lens of intersectionality? We believe the process of backward thinking has several important implications for one's individual and collective work. Taking an intersectional perspective in one's work is deeply enriching and rewarding in that everyone has multiple competing identities and multiple ways of thinking. Thus, intersectional approaches seem natural as a means of engaging in and with research. At the same time, conducting research informed through the lens of intersectionality is extremely difficult to do (Jones & Abes, 2013).

As researchers and scholars, one needs to engage those aspects of oneself through reflexivity by considering one's positionality as well as one's work with collaborators, when possible, to help examine and illuminate potential biases. Additionally, one needs to also have a keen awareness of the contexts in which participants live and learn and become well-versed in considering those while engaged in data analysis. For example, one of my (DT) participants, a first-generation Cambodian American gay male from a working-class family, discussed his experiences of taking out additional student loans to provide money to his family back home for their expenses, working two part-time jobs, and thus not being connected to student organizations on campus. In the interviews, the student discussed this as being connected to his Buddhist upbringing, but I, from my positionality of being from a White middle-class background, felt as though these behaviors were indicative of the student's social class. During the study's focus group, I asked the student directly about his social class and its potential impact on his college experience; the student once again pressed back and said his faith had more to do with his personal engagement with family and college and that his social class played very little into his identity. This experience was significant because it pointed to what McCall (2005) referred to as *intracategorical complexity*, or the ways differing identities within a social group (i.e., gay men) create uniquely textured experiences that desire to be teased apart. This encounter also reminded me that ultimately, the power I had as a researcher could easily have been used to manipulate the student's truth that his faith was more salient than his social class. As a result, I had a transformative learning experience related to his own reflexivity as well as how his meaning-making of his shared experiences and my understanding of that same data were *both necessary* in providing a fuller, more complex, and more complete picture for the research study.

McCall's (2005) notion of intracategorical complexity also connects to Warner's (2008) discussion of master categories versus emergent categories in intersectional research. Warner stated, "Before researchers make the assumption that the master category validly represents all or most groups, the researcher must first establish the merit of that assumption" (p. 458). As with the aforementioned example, my (DT) positionality ultimately played into an incorrect assumption around the master category of the participant. The participant's religious beliefs combined with his racial identification as well as his status as a first-generation American played a much more significant role in his own master narrative than his socioeconomic status. Through the act of suspending my own judgment and engaging with my participant around his own meaning making of his intersectional identities, his truth was validated rather than my own incorrect assumptions. By engaging in reflexive work, I (DT) came to understand that it is essential that individuals become vigilant in understanding their own reflexivity as it relates to how they think about research, who they are, and how they approach their work.

Another implication of using intersectionality in educational research is to understand the political ramifications of that work on a micro and macro level. Truly intersectional research must address the micro and macro levels in concert with one another to frame one's multiple social identities in the larger context of systems of inequality in which one is a part (Dill & Zambrana,

2009; Jones & Abes, 2013). This relates back to Bowleg's (2008) point that "intersectionality researchers are charged with the responsibility of making the intersections between ethnicity, sex/gender, sexual orientation (to name just a few) and the social inequality related to these identities, explicit" (p. 322). Similarly, Choo and Ferree (2010) posited, "The complexity of multiple institutions that feed back into each other—both positively and negatively—can become obscured when the macrostructures of inequality are separated from the microstructures of social construction of meaning" (p. 146). When thinking backward, it becomes critical to situate one's work at both the micro and macro levels to allow for the visibility inherent at illuminating the phenomenon being studied. As Warner (2008) cautioned, "One of the central issues in the study of intersectionality is that of visibility—who is granted attention, who is not, and the consequences of these actions for the study of social issues" (p. 462). Therefore, care must be taken as one sets forth with one's research to ensure that questions of visibility are addressed in the name of research that interrogates social structures and attempts to forward human dignity and social equity.

## Conclusion

In articulating the importance of intersectionality, Dill and Zambrana (2009) stated the following:

> We argue that intersectionality challenges traditional modes of knowledge production in the United States and illustrate how this theory provides an alternative model that combines advocacy, analysis, theorizing, and pedagogy—basic components essential to the production of knowledge as well as the pursuit of social justice and equality. (p. 1)

As researchers who are heavily invested in intersectional approaches to research, we agree with this statement. Yet, rather than just thinking about how intersectionality can be used as an analytical tool, we place emphasis on the notion of backward thinking, or identifying how intersectionality is essential to thinking through one's epistemological, axiological, and/or ontological groundings. These aspects of one's thinking are foundational for the ways in which research studies are framed and carried out. Whether one does research alongside other researchers, in collaboration with participants, or by oneself, backward thinking is one strategy to engage in deeper reflection about the research *process* rather than just using intersectionality as a lens for analyzing research *content*. In doing so, scholars are able to provide richer and more complex analyses of their research—both the process by which research was done and the data co-constructed with participants—and to promote equity and justice for those participants with whom one researches.

## Note

1 The use of the asterisk in the word *trans\** is used to symbolize the multiplicity of gender identities, expressions, and embodiments within the trans\* community. For more information about the use of the asterisk in the term trans\*, see Tompkins (2014) and Nicolazzo (2017).

## References

Abes, E. S. (2009). Theoretical borderlands: Using multiple theoretical perspectives to challenge inequitable power structures in student development theory. *Journal of College Student Development, 50*, 141–156.

Baca Zinn, M., & Dill, B. T. (1996). Theorizing difference from multiracial feminism. *Feminist Studies, 22*, 321–331.

Berger, M. T., & Guidroz, K. (Eds.). (2009). *The intersectional approach: Transforming the academy through race, class, and gender.* University of North Carolina Press.

Bowleg, L. (2008). When Black + lesbian + woman ≠ Black lesbian woman: The methodological challenges of qualitative and quantitative intersectionality research. *Sex Roles, 59*(5–6), 312–325.

Butler, J. (2004). *Undoing gender.* Routledge.

Butler, J. (2011). *Bodies that matter: On the discursive limits of "sex."* Routledge.

Charmaz, K. (2006). *Constructing grounded theory: A practical guide through qualitative analysis.* Sage.

Choo, H. Y., & Ferree, M. M. (2010). Practicing intersectionality in sociological research: A critical analysis of inclusions, interactions, and institutions in the study of inequalities. *Sociological Theory, 28*, 129–149.

Collins, P. H. (2000). *Black feminist thought: Knowledge, consciousness, and the politics of empowerment* (2nd ed.). Routledge.

Crenshaw, K. W. (1995). Mapping the margins: Intersectionality, identity politics, and violence against Women of Color. In K. W. Crenshaw, N. Gotanda, G. Peller, & K. Thomas (Eds.), *Critical race theory: The key writings that formed the movement* (pp. 357–383). New Press.

Dill, B. T. (2009). Intersections, identities, and inequalities in higher education. In B. T. Dill & R. E. Zambrana (Eds.), *Emerging intersections: Race, class, and gender in theory, policy, and practice* (pp. 229–252). Rutgers University Press.

Dill, B. T., & Zambrana, R. E. (2009). Critical thinking about inequality. In B. T. Dill & R. E. Zambrana (Eds.), *Emerging intersections: Race, class, and gender in theory, policy, and practice* (pp. 1–21). Rutgers University Press.

Elia, J. P., & Yep, G. A. (2012). Sexualities and genders in an age of neo-terrorism. *Journal of Homosexuality, 59,* 879–889.

Hanisch, C. (2006). *The personal is political.* http://www.carolhanisch.org/CHwritings/PersonalisPol.pdf

Iverson, S. V. (2014). Identity constellations: An intersectional analysis of female student veterans. In D. Mitchell, Jr., C. Y. Simmons, & L. A. Greyerbiehl (Eds.), *Intersectionality and higher education: Theory, research, and praxis* (1st ed., pp. 135–145). Peter Lang.

Jones, S. R., & Abes, E. S. (2013). *Identity development of college students: Advancing frameworks for multiple dimensions of identity.* Jossey-Bass.

Jones, S. R., Torres, V., & Arminio, J. (2006). *Negotiating the complexities of qualitative research in higher education.* Routledge.

Kincheloe, J. L. (2001). Describing bricolage: Conceptualizing a new rigor in qualitative research. *Qualitative Inquiry, 7,* 679–692.

Kincheloe, J. L. (2011). Critical ontology. In K. Hayes, S. R. Steinberg, & K. Tobin (Eds.), *Key works in critical pedagogy: Joe L. Kincheloe* (pp. 201–217). Sense.

Kivel, P. (2007). Social service or social change? In INCITE! Women of Color against violence (Eds.), *The revolution will not be funded: Beyond the non-profit industrial complex* (pp. 129–149). South End.

Lincoln, Y. S., Lynham, S. A., & Guba, E. G. (2011). Paradigmatic controversies, contradictions, and emerging confluences, revisited. In N. K. Denzin & Y. S. Lincoln (Eds.), *The Sage handbook of qualitative research* (4th ed., pp. 97–128). Sage.

McCall, L. (2005). The complexity of intersectionality. *Signs: Journal of Women in Culture and Society, 30*(3), 1771–1880.

Nash, J. C. (2008). Re-thinking intersectionality. *Feminist Review, 89,* 1–15.

Nicolazzo, Z. (2017, February 1). To use or not use the asterisk [Blog post]. https://znicolazzo.weebly.com/trans-resilience-blog/-to-use-or-not-to-use-the-asterisk.

Pasque, P. A., Carducci, R., Kuntz, A. K., & Gildersleeve, R. E. (2012). *Qualitative inquiry for equity in higher education: Methodological innovations, implications, and interventions* (ASHE Higher Education Report). Jossey-Bass.

Renn, K. A. (2010). LGBT and queer research in higher education: State and status of the field. *Educational Researcher, 39,* 132–141.

Shields, S. A. (2008). Gender: An intersectionality perspective. *Sex Roles, 59,* 301–311.

Spade, D. (2010). Be professional! *Harvard Journal of Law & Gender, 33,* 71–84.

Spade, D. (2015). *Normal life: Administrative violence, critical trans politics, and the limitations of law* (2nd ed.). Duke University Press.

Stewart, D. L. (2010). Researcher as instrument: Understanding "shifting" findings in constructivist research. *Journal of Student Affairs Research and Practice, 47*(3), 291–306.

Tierney, W. G. (1997). *Academic outlaws: Queer theory and cultural studies in the academy.* Sage.

Tillapaugh, D., & Nicolazzo, Z. (2015). "It's kind of apples and oranges": Gay college males' conceptions of gender transgression as poverty. *Journal of Critical Scholarship on Higher Education and Student Affairs, 1*(1), 67–81.

Tillapaugh, D. W. (2012). *Toward an integrated self: Making meaning of the multiple identities of gay men in college* (Unpublished doctoral dissertation). University of San Diego, San Diego, CA.

Tompkins, A. (2014). Asterisk. *TSQ: Transgender Studies Quarterly, 1*(1–2), 26–27.

Warner, L. R. (2008). A best practices guide to intersectionality in psychological research. *Sex Roles, 59,* 454–463.

Weber, L. (1998). A conceptual framework for understanding race, class, gender, and sexuality. *Psychology of Women Quarterly, 22,* 13–22.

# Part III: Praxis

# 12. The Unlikely Allies Conference: An Intersectional Approach to Diversity Training Between White and Black Women in Academia

NICOLE M. WEST

Although diversity, equity, inclusion, and belonging (DEIB) offices, positions, and initiatives in higher education are burgeoning, many institutions attend to campus climate concerns with broad strokes that do not adequately address the unique experiences of individuals who contend with multiple and intersecting forms of oppression. As members of at least two cultural groups that have been historically and systemically oppressed in the United States (U.S.), Black women contend with a unique form of *gendered racism*, which "refer[s] to the racial oppression of Black women as structured by racist and ethnicist perceptions of gender roles" (Essed, 1991, p. 31). Defined another way, *sexist racism* and *racist sexism*, refer to the ways "gender colors the way that race is perceived, and vice versa" (Goff & Kahn, 2013, p. 366). Scholars have documented the impact of gendered racism on Black women college students, faculty, and staff, as well as the coping responses they use to endure this specific type of oppression (e.g., see Breeden, 2021; Carter Andrews, 2015; Szymanski & Lewis, 2016). Despite research attesting to negative mental and physical health consequences associated with gendered racism experienced by Black women (e.g., see Jones et al., 2022; Lewis et al., 2017; Thomas et al., 2008), existing campus diversity training approaches have yet to leverage the potential of intersectionality to adequately interrogate and dismantle compounding structures of oppression that maintain Black women's subordination in the academy (Steinfield et al., 2019).

As a critical social theory, *intersectionality* is a historical and contemporary critique of antiracism and feminism, which illuminates and seeks to redress the erasure of Black women and the deprioritization of the unique oppressions they face (Collins, 2000, 2019; Collins & Bilge, 2020; Crenshaw, 1989, 1991; hooks 2015). hooks (2015) noted that:

> no other group in America has so had their identity socialized out of existence as have black women…When black people are talked about the focus tends to be on black men and when women are talked about the focus tends to be on white women. (p. 7)

Ironically, as intersectionality has gained significant transdisciplinary traction, its popularization within mainstream academia has resulted in superficial and reductionist uses of the term, leveraged by some scholars as a type of pseudo-woke social currency; epistemological origination misattributions; and citational politics that continue to silence and dilute contributions of Black women, for whom and by whom the theory was initially advanced (Harris & Patton, 2019). Findings from Harris and Patton's (2019) systematic review of intersectionality in higher education research explicated how these tactics "undermine the capacity of the concept to critique structures of power and domination, produce transformative knowledges, inform praxis, and work toward social justice" (p. 8). Suppressing the scope and sources of intersectionality in scholarship, which is an act of epistemic violence, directly impedes the transformative potential of the theory as critical praxis. Collins and Bilge (2020) noted how popularized conceptualizations of intersectionality tend not to center critical practices that aim to critique, reject, ameliorate, and assist marginalized individuals and groups resist "social problems that complex social inequities engender" (p. 38).

Because Black women are victimized by a unique type of oppression (i.e., gendered racism) that is neither solely racist nor sexist, when higher education administrators implement programs and policies to redress issues of racism or sexism independently (e.g., initiatives geared specifically toward remedying issues impacting Blacks, People of Color, or women in general), the nuanced experiences of Black women enrolled and employed on their campuses are often overlooked or erased. I extend Crenshaw's (1989) metaphor of the exponential harm inflicted on a Black woman caught in the middle of a traffic intersection, who is injured by drivers coming from multiple directions and is refused treatment until one specific at-fault party is identified.

When campus DEIB offices—which ostensibly exist to help make conditions less dangerous for marginalized groups to navigate—do not explicitly use intersectional approaches, it is as if they become dysfunctional traffic lights that have not been programmed to recognize and respond to the unique types of oppression Black women experience. It is as if these traffic lights, which are designed to regulate harm and thus minimize injuries, are only synchronized to address one type of oppression at a time. Unlike Black men and white[1] women who are often the focus and primary beneficiaries of antiracist and feminist movements (McCloud & West, 2023), this leaves Black women students, faculty, and staff—who are trying to navigate their already marginalized position in institutional crosswalks at chaotic and dangerous intersections—highly vulnerable to injury as a result of multiple and compounding forms of sexist and racist oppression.

Notably, these costly albeit faulty traffic lights (i.e., single-axis DEIB approaches), which are not explicitly designed to protect Black women on campus, are also abysmally ineffective at slowing or stopping racism experienced by People of Color, sexism experienced by women, and homophobia experienced by members of the LGBTQ+ community. As Newkirk (2020) noted, despite:

> pledging billions of dollars to commission studies, set up training sessions, and hire consultants and czars to oversee diversity programs....the plodding pace of change a half-century later makes clear the need to reframe the diversity conversation of recent years from a rosy we-are-the-world ideal to one fired by a mission to combat systemic racial injustice and pervasive delusion about where we stand. (p. 14)

In response to this dilemma, a take on Tulshyan's (2022) central question and thesis provides some clues: If we believe implementing DEIB initiatives is both ethical and good business practice, then why are we spending so much money and still failing at it? I believe it is because there is a general reluctance to center Black women and other Women of Color in the fight for DEIB on most college campuses. However, as Keisling et al. (2020) attested, "intersectionality posits that DEI work centering individuals who are the most marginalized results in greater inclusion for everyone" (p. 64). The National Association of Diversity Officers in Higher Education also affirmed that campus diversity leaders:

> have ethical, legal, and practical obligations to frame their work from comprehensive definitions of equity, diversity, and inclusion—definitions that are inclusive with respect to a wide range of identities, differentiated in terms of how they address unique identity issues and complex in terms of intersectionality and context. (Worthington et al., 2020, p. 7)

Among other confounding variables, I surmise that undifferentiated DEIB approaches that do not explicitly target the nuanced issues impeding Black women in higher education may be to blame for the appalling return on investment and "chronically disappointing results" experienced by most colleges with regard to their demographic composition and culture of inclusivity (Newkirk, 2020, p. 14).

The purpose of this chapter is to describe a campus DEIB allyship training program geared towards white women and explicitly developed to enhance the experiences of (i.e., materially benefit) Black women students, faculty, staff, and administrators at Missouri State University (MSU). The following discussion details the development of the Unlikely Allies Conference (UAC) and explicates how intersectionality theory framed the conceptualization and implementation of this program. The chapter closes with recommendations for replication, practice, and research intended to help postsecondary administrators implement and assess DEIB programs that minimize harm to Black women and that are responsive to the current political assault on diversity and inclusion in higher education.

## Unlikely Allies Conference

MSU is a large, public, historically white institution (HWI) in the Midwest region of the U.S. classified by the Carnegie Foundation as a doctoral/professional university. Based on the most current publicly available data, in Fall 2018, MSU enrolled approximately 23,000 undergraduate and graduate students and employed approximately 3,500 faculty and staff. During this same period, Black women comprised 2%, 1%, and 1% of MSU's students, faculty, and staff, respectively (MSU Office of Institutional Research, n.d.). The UAC was piloted at MSU at the end of March 2022 (during the campus' Women's Herstory Month celebration) with self-selected dyads and triads of 45 Black and white women students, faculty, staff, and administrators. The purpose of the UAC was to empower participants with the knowledge, skills, abilities, attitudes, and emotions needed to effectively engage in coalition building, which leads to allyship as a transformative strategy for institutional change.

The three-day conference included a campus-wide lecture with Dr. Karen L. Dace on Friday evening; a modified version of the nationally recognized National Coalition Building Institute (NCBI) prejudice reduction workshop on Saturday; and an interactive "Allyship in Action" workshop I co-developed with a colleague on Sunday. Three separate pre-conference book discussions were also co-facilitated by pairs of Black and white women students, faculty, and staff one week before the UAC.[2] The conference was sponsored by MSU's Faculty Center for Teaching and Learning; the Division of Student Affairs; and the Division for Diversity, Equity, and Inclusion and co-sponsored by several academic colleges and other campus entities.[3]

## Conceptualization

The UAC derived from a Participatory Action Research Counterspace (PARC) I co-facilitated at MSU during the 2020–21 academic year, which was comprised of 11 Black women students, faculty, staff, and administrators. Because PARCs are a type of critical participatory action research (CPAR; West, 2023), as participant co-researchers, we used Wang's (1999) SHOWeD acronym to engage in a photovoice activity to unpack our experiences as Black women at an HWI.[4] The particular focus of our investigation was not only to identify issues facing Black women at HWIs in general but also to select a specific PARC project that could be implemented to enhance the experiences of Black women at our particular HWI. One of the issues we discussed was the strained relationships and need for greater allyship between Black and white women on campus. As a result, the co-researchers developed the UAC for Black and white women on campus. The idea for the conference was primarily inspired by Dr. Karen Dace's (2012) book, *Unlikely Allies in the Academy: Women of Color and White Women in Conversation*, as well as a situation experienced by two members of the PARC a year earlier. One of the PARC co-researchers, who was an assistant professor, had advocated with a white woman faculty colleague, who was a tenured associate professor and who was chairing a campus diversity committee, to use her privilege and focus her diversity work on making a case for the promotion of another PARC co-researchers from an instructor position to a tenure-track position. The following year that Black woman co-researcher was promoted!

The PARC methodological framework, which led to the development of the UAC, was an inherently intersectional approach because it was specifically designed to shine a light on, prioritize, and improve the experiences of marginalized cultural group members who exist at the intersection of multiple forms of oppression (West, 2023). In other words, the PARC framework aims to place:

> explicit emphasis on how multiplicatively minoritized individuals in majority settings (e.g. Black women who are "outsiders within" academia; Collins, 1986) can leverage their perspectives to produce unique approaches with the potential to liberate themselves and others who labor under entrenched oppressive systems. (West, 2023, p. 2)

Further, the co-researchers' success in identifying and implementing a PARC project (i.e., the UAC) that exclusively and unapologetically focused on materially benefitting Black women at our HWI was another way intersectionality theory guided our work.

## Implementation—Conference Goals and Activities

A synthesis of higher education and workplace diversity training and ally-ship literature (e.g., see Brown & Mazza, 2005; Dace, 2012; Dickinson et al., 2022; Erskine & Bilimoria, 2019; Opie & Livingston, 2022) led to the development of the four following conference goals, which were to: (a) facilitate trusting interracial coalitions among Black and white women on campus; (b) provide participants with a brave space to engage in critical self-reflexivity; (c) promote the proliferation of prosocial behavior among Black and white women on campus; and (d) explore the concept of tempered radicalism among Black and white women on campus. These goals were included in participants' invitation and registration materials, referenced throughout the weekend at the beginning of each workshop activity, and were reinforced through promotional materials.

### Goal 1: Building Co-Conspiratorships/Facilitating Trustworthy Coalitions

The first goal of the UAC focused on encouraging white and Black women on campus to develop trustworthy co-conspiratorships. Several DEIB schol-ars have referred to the importance of this type of relationship-building as foundational to the work of eradicating racism, sexism, and particularly gen-dered racism in the workplace (e.g., see Opie & Livingston, 2022; Smith & Nkomo, 2022). Differentiated from the more mainstream (and perhaps more palatable) term "allyship," which we used to name the broader conference, we relied on Smith and Nkomo's (2022) definition of *co-conspirators* to signal the development of authentic and collaborative partnerships between Black and white women who "actively use their decision-making power to advance and sponsor the rise of women who are excluded" (p. 50). Opie and Livingston (2022) built on this definition and created the shared sisterhood philosophy for the express purpose of engaging Black and white women in "collective action toward dismantling racial and gender inequity at work...in the inter-est of eliminating [these] inequities to benefit historically marginalized com-munity members" (pp. 9, 112). A core component of the shared sisterhood model is the establishment of *bridges*. These short- or long-term, personal or professional, authentic, emotional connections are the bedrock of collabora-tive equity work and are characterized by empathy, vulnerability, trust, and risk-taking (Opie & Livingston, 2022).

To begin developing the four characteristics of Opie and Livingston's (2022) authentic emotional connections among UAC participants, a white woman colleague and I (who are both trained NCBI facilitators) modified and facilitated a version of NCBI's Leadership for Diversity Institute. This full-day workshop, which occurred on Saturday, included activities—like Up Downs, Leadership Dyads and Triads, Records, First Thoughts, Caucuses, and Speak Outs[5]—that sought to simultaneously cultivate a brave and safe space for the Black and white women UAC dyads and triads to experiment with emotions and behaviors needed to begin developing healthy and effective co-conspiratorships. The workshop exercises were grounded in the following NCBI principles, which were outlined by Brown and Mazza (2005, pp. ix-x) and are directly aligned with the aforementioned literature:

- One-on-one relationship building is at the heart of effective intergroup coalitions.
- We don't change people's minds; we change their hearts with personal stories of discrimination.
- We all carry records about other groups that prevent us from building effective alliances.
- Risk taking and mistake making are essential for building close relationships across group lines.

## Goal 2: Interrogating Power and Participation/Engaging in Critical Self-Reflexivity

While the first goal of the UAC centered on coalition building among participants, the second goal encouraged participants to critically interrogate in what ways and to what degree they wielded power based on their varying positionalities. This goal (and the remaining two UAC goals) drew from Erskine and Bilimoria's (2019) work on white allyship of Afro-Diasporic women. According to these scholars, *critical self-reflexivity* "entails acknowledging systemic bias and the possibility that one's dominant group may see the status quo as legitimate in order to protect their in-group's advantaged position within the larger social hierarchy" (Erskine & Bilimoria, 2019, p. 325). Although we used this definition to guide the development of the second UAC goal, we believed Opie and Livingston's (2022) concept of *dig* provided a more nuanced and complex approach to transformative allyship in our specific institutional context. From their perspective, dig is a continuous practice of deep contextualized introspection about how one's social identities are imbued with power, which makes bridging across difference possible. While Opie and Livingston's primary focus was on encouraging white women to dig with regard to their membership in a power-dominant group and Black women to dig with regard to racial trauma they have experienced as members of a historically marginalized group, we leveraged their model to ask UAC participants to dig even deeper.

In addition to using workshop activities to prompt white women UAC participants to identify how they routinely benefitted from white privilege, and thus are often viewed as complicit in maintaining the overall system of imperialist white-supremacist capitalist cisheteropatriarchy (hooks, 2004), we also believed it was critical to leverage intersectionality theory to help participants explore the impact of simultaneously holding multiple social identities—some that were marginalized and some that were privileged. Several exercises from the NCBI workshop including Up Downs, Caucuses, and Speak Outs illuminated the wide range of privileged identities occupied by the Black women UAC participants (e.g., able-bodied, heterosexual, cis-gender, Protestant, doctoral degree holders, tenured faculty, from an upper socioeconomic background, etc.) and marginalized identities occupied by the white women UAC participants (e.g., disabled, LGBTQ+, atheist/agnostic, first-generation college students, support staff, from a lower socioeconomic background, etc.). Asking all participants to consider how they consciously or unconsciously benefited from and were harmed by various societal "-isms" (e.g., ableism, classism, ageism, adultism, homophobia, transphobia, xeno-phobia, etc.) raised consciousness about how they may have been unwit-tingly upholding the very systems of oppression they were victimized by. Additionally, engaging in these activities further reinforced the importance of empathy, vulnerability, trust, and risk-taking among the UAC participants and helped the group recognize and resist the tendency to essentialize one another as members of two racial groups who are viciously vilified against one another in the U.S.

Related to Goal #2, we also engaged participants in an activity called "The Circle of My Life." This activity used a variety of colored beads and black and white felt pipe cleaners to help participants reflect on the cultural homo- or heterogeneity they were exposed to in their personal, profes-sional, and/or academic lives. Participants were asked to construct bracelets comprised of beads representing their multiple social identities, as well as the identities of their families and friends, individuals they interacted with socially and professionally, and individuals (positively or favorably) centered in the various types of media they consumed (e.g., music, books, television, movies, social media, etc.). We debriefed this activity in part by asking partic-ipants to contemplate how the particular composition of their circle impacted their capacity and willingness to engage in allyship with one another. We also asked participants to reflect on the part of their bracelets that represented their multiple intersecting identities and to consider the different gradients of marginalization and privilege associated with their individual positionalities.

## Goal 3: Leveraging Privilege/Engaging in Prosocial Behaviors

The third UAC goal specifically helped participants identify ways they could leverage their privilege to benefit others. In the context of white allyship, Erskine and Bilimoria (2019) defined these *prosocial behaviors* as actions that advantage and safeguard Afro-Diasporic women's well-being and success and "have both the intent and impact of creating mutuality, solidarity, and support of [these] women's career development and leadership advancement in organizations" (p. 319). These authors provided several examples of prosocial behaviors, including "providing sponsorship, mentorship, and protection from adverse organizational dynamics," and "engaging in positive deviance and demonstrating courage to interrupt the status quo" (Erskine & Bilimoria, 2019, p. 326). In light of our reliance on intersectionality theory throughout the conference, we remained cognizant that due to their identification with multiple social identities—some of which were more or less marginalized, particularly in the context of a predominantly white higher education institution—Black and white women participants alike had access to both different types of privilege *and* exposure to various kinds of oppression on campus. For example, a disabled white woman administrative assistant who benefitted from white privilege could also experience marginalization due to ableism and institutional elitism. Similarly, while a trans* Black woman professor might have more power as a tenured faculty member, she would also contend with gendered racism and transphobia. The corollary risks associated with engaging in prosocial behaviors as a result of occupying these varying positionalities had to be taken into consideration when discussing this specific UAC goal.

During the "Allyship in Action" workshop, we separated participants into six groups, each consisting of a relatively even mixture of students, faculty, staff, and administrators. We provided each group with one of three different vignettes representing a variety of fairly common microaggressions experienced by Black women on campus and asked them to discuss and brainstorm possible responses.[6] Given the various roles UAC participants occupied on campus (i.e., undergraduate and graduate students, faculty, staff, and administrators), we believed it was important to highlight situations the majority of them could encounter on campus and those in which they might feel most empowered to intervene. We discussed the responses generated by each group with a particular emphasis on how some of the more subtly problematic responses could further harm Black women. We also encouraged participants to think critically about the broader themes reflected in the vignettes and responses and identify other situations where these themes may arise. For example, Vignette #1 highlighted the ways some white women weaponize their tears "to strategically combat racial...uneasiness or distress when faced with discussions about race" (Williams, 2020, p. 9). Another theme we embedded in one of the responses to this vignette (i.e., Try to console the Black woman) was combatting the perception that Black women never need or deserve emotional support because they are always strong and only angry (Ohito, 2022).

## Goal 4: Disrupting the Status Quo/Engaging in Tempered Radicalism

The fourth, and final, UAC goal explored *tempered radicalism*—a concept coined by Meyerson and Scully (1995) to unearth the experiences of individuals who, while laboring in environments that frustrate their longing for social justice and equity, work strategically within these organizations to enact radical, albeit often painstakingly incremental change. More specifically, it has been noted how these individuals challenge the status quo intentionally or just by being themselves, seek moderation by moving adeptly between entrenched norms and alternative epistemologies, have been toughened from being alternately heated up and cooled down, are angered by the misalignment between their values and those of their organization, and are driven by both equanimity and outrage to advance equity (Meyerson & Scully, 1995). Erskine and Bilimoria (2019) further explicated this concept and asserted:

> Tempered radicals serve as quiet catalysts who...are radical because of their desire to change the status quo yet tempered in the way they...work from the inside of organizations, infiltrating them with enough tempering to influence the mainstream, and rock the boat just hard enough to effect change while keeping their professional image, commitments, and capacity to effect further change. (p. 327)

As a scholar who has written about coming to terms with both my deep love for the work I do (and for the Black women on whose behalf I do it) *and* the often-debilitating context of patriarchal white supremacy within which I work (West, 2022), my journey toward becoming an *invested indifferent* is a contemporary example of the Meyerson and Scully's (1995) tempered radical positionality within higher education. I have learned to leverage tempered radicalism to strategically allocate passion and indifference as tools at my disposal to subversively combat oppression against Black women in academia.

While Opie and Livingston (2022) did not explicitly refer to tempered radicals in their shared sisterhood model, they did articulate a similar strategy that is resonant:

> When a critical mass of people have bridged together, they can exert pressure and power within their organization via collective action. This means that no one person will be responsible for the movement, but rather the group of Sisters coordinates efforts, determining who is best positioned to say what, when, and to whom, always circling back to the group as more information is obtained, more power amassed, more goals accomplished. (p. 106)

The first two conference goals focused on intrapersonal exploration, or Opie and Livingston's (2022) notion of dig, and interpersonal relationship building, which was their concept of bridge. The last two UAC goals focused on helping participants learn how to engage in the third and final component of the shared sisterhood philosophy—*collective action*, which is "when historically marginalized and dominant group members work together toward the same equity goals" (Opie & Livingston, 2022, p. 105).

Because engaging in the last two UAC goals would require participants to demonstrate extra-personal adeptness with individuals and in situations beyond the conference setting, we facilitated activities that provided them with knowledge and opportunities to practice specific skills that involved using their privilege (Goal 3) and disrupting the status quo (Goal 4). The primary UAC activity related to Goal 4 was NCBI's Role Plays. In this exercise, we asked participants to brainstorm a list of offensive comments or behaviors they have witnessed or experienced on campus, preferably those targeting Black women. We then selected one comment/behavior and asked for volunteers to role-play how they might respond as an ally to disrupt the comment/behavior and more importantly, shift the attitude of the perpetrator. After a group discussion about the strengths and weaknesses of the ally's response, we provided specific coaching suggestions and asked the ally to try their response again. Our coaching was based on the following NCBI principles (Brown & Mazza, 2005, pp. ix–x):

- When witnessing oppressive behavior, having a chance to vent leads to clearer thinking about what is useful to do next.
- If you wish to move a conflict forward there is no room for two hurts at the same time.
- Underneath every oppressive comment lies some form of injury.
- Listening is not the same as agreeing.

## Implications for Replication and Practice

Here, I offer four recommendations for replication, which should be considered when implementing DEIB or allyship training programs similar to the UAC that are grounded in an intersectional framework. These considerations aim to minimize harm inflicted on Black women by well-intentioned DEIB initiatives that are not culturally responsive and account for the current political assault on diversity and inclusion in higher education.

### 1. Let Black Women Choose Their Allies

We were very intentional about the UAC registration process. We first reached out to Black women on campus (including those who participated in the PARC) and invited them to participate. Once they confirmed their interest, we asked them to identify a white woman in a similar role on campus with whom they would want to partner during the conference. We informed Black women the conference would include difficult dialogue and encouraged them to talk with their potential partner about this before inviting them via email. The purpose of this strategy was to empower Black women to select a white woman partner with whom they already had a relationship and who they believed was ready to engage in this type of work. Due to the severe underrepresentation of Black women on campus, there were more white women interested in participating than Black women, which meant some Black women worked with more than one white woman partner. This resulted in 15 dyads and five triads (see Table 12.1). These conference demographics highlighted how Black women's underrepresentation on campus exacerbated the disproportionality of labor with which they were routinely burdened.

**Table 12.1.** Composition of UAC Dyads and Triads

| Role | # of Dyads | # of Triads | # of Participants |
|------|-----------|-------------|-------------------|
| Undergraduates | 3 | 0 | 6 |
| Graduates | 3 | 1 | 9 |
| Faculty | 2 | 0 | 4 |
| Staff | 3 | 2 | 12 |
| Administrators | 2 | 2 | 10 |
| Mixed Role | 2 | 0 | 4 |
| Total | 15 | 5 | 45 |

## 2. Pay Black Women (and Allies) for Their Labor

There is ample evidence that *cultural* or *identity taxation* in academia, which refers to the invisible and disproportionate ways women and People of Color in academia are saddled with institutional service, continues to be an issue (Reid, 2021; Rideau, 2021). Due to their social location at the intersection of race and gender, this issue is particularly pronounced for Black women in higher education (Hirshfield & Joseph, 2012; Overstreet, 2019; West et al., 2022). To offset conference expenses, participants were encouraged to use their $150 non-credit fee waiver to cover registration but were reimbursed with a $75 gift card after the conference. While a relatively meager amount, we were cognizant that "Black women students, faculty, and staff continue to be recruited to engage in what could be referred to as pro-bono, pro-social diversity work that benefits PWIs, all while depleting themselves with little or no reward or recognition" and offered these stipends as an attempt to disrupt this norm (West et al., 2022, p. 153).

## 3. Move from Allyship to Accompliceship

When we conceptualized the UAC as the Unlikely *Allies* Conference, we wondered whether hosting an Unlikely *Accomplices* Conference would be a better approach. We decided, given our institutional context, that investigating the concept of allyship (which was more widely recognized on campus) was a necessary precursor to exploring accompliceship. However, it is now clear that continuing to advance this work (especially as it relates to the last two conference goals, which move from allyship to accompliceship) will require developing additional training that emphasizes a deeper exploration of how white and Black women in academia can build intentional co-conspiratorships and interrogate their power to effectively engage in collective actions like prosocial behavior and tempered radicalism.

## 4. Preserve the Focus without Broadcasting the Intent

While the intersectional DEIB approach being advanced in this chapter is promising, the current U.S. political climate suggests that programs like the UAC might be difficult to replicate. As of this writing, 76 bills have been authored in 26 states that would severely impede, if not completely obliterate college and university DEIB efforts (Chronicle of Higher Education, 2024). Higher education leaders who understand and are committed to DEIB as both a moral obligation and a sound business practice must act strategically to preserve the focus of DEIB initiatives on campus without broadcasting their intent. The recommendations offered below are presented with this context in mind:

**Be strategic.** Connect DEIB programming objectives to broader institutional missions, student success goals, state priorities, and performance-based funding indices. Make these connections explicit to stakeholders, including students, faculty, and staff.

**Use neutral language.** Avoid naming current hot-button concepts like critical race theory that could be interpreted as divisive or politically charged. Instead use more neutral terms to describe those concepts in order to avoid using words that are closely associated with liberal political movements or ideologies.

**Focus on education.** Frame the diversity, equity, and inclusion training as an educational opportunity for participants. Emphasize the importance of understanding different perspectives and experiences, and the role that diversity plays in creating a successful and inclusive learning environment.

**Highlight research.** Incorporate relevant research and data to support the program's objectives and impact on participants. Highlight studies and findings that demonstrate the benefits of diversity and inclusion in higher education, such as improved academic outcomes, greater student engagement, and postgraduate career success.

**Engage academic affairs.** Decentralize and house these activities in academic colleges (as opposed to DEIB offices) and identify tenured faculty (as opposed to DEIB administrators), whose research expertise lends itself to this work, to facilitate. In states where academic freedom and faculty governance are still intact, this strategy may better protect institutions from legislative interference and position them to assess the efficacy (and return on investment) of these initiatives.

**Foster dialogue.** Encourage open and respectful dialogue among participants during the training program. Emphasize the importance of active listening, empathy, and a willingness to consider different perspectives.

**Offer voluntary participation.** Make participation in the training program voluntary. Encourage participation through positive messaging that highlights the benefits of the program, rather than through mandates or penalties.

**Involve stakeholders.** Engage key stakeholders, including student groups, faculty, and staff, in the development and implementation of the training program. Solicit feedback and incorporate suggestions to ensure the program meets the needs and expectations of the campus community.

**Solicit legal counsel.** Consult with legal counsel to ensure that training programs comply with all relevant laws and regulations. Consider obtaining legal guidance on the specific content and delivery of the program to ensure that it is unlikely to draw unwanted scrutiny from conservative state legislatures.

## *Recommendations for Research*

Findings related to the cognitive, affective/attitudinal, behavioral/skill outcomes of diversity training programs have been mixed (Alhejji et al., 2016;

Bezrukova et al., 2012; Kalinoski et al., 2013). However, two consistent critiques emerged in this literature: limited theoretical grounding and methodological measurement issues. Thus, further exploration of the DEIB allyship training introduced in this chapter, as well as other intersectionally-grounded programs like the UAC, should include the use of culturally responsive theories, approaches, and instruments that center marginalized epistemologies. For example, given the UAC's emphasis on interpersonal relationships and intrapersonal introspection, qualitative studies employing collaborative autoethnography and scholarly personal narrative would add nuance to the existing diversity training outcome literature. Additionally, this research could be supplemented by critical quantitative (i.e., #QuantCrit; Garcia et al., 2018) investigations that merge descriptive, causal-comparative, or quasi-experimental designs with theories like Black feminist thought (BFT; Collins, 2000), critical race feminism (Wing, 1997), and the hip hop feminism model of multiple identities (Payne & West, 2022) to test the impact of DEIB training programs on the experiences of Black women in academia. An analysis of data collected from the Campus Racial Allyship Training (CRAT) survey, which was adapted using BFT and intersectionality theory, is also needed to better understand the impact of the UAC. Opportunities to extend the DEIB training model introduced in this chapter also include replication studies involving other multiplicatively marginalized groups of students, faculty, staff, and administrators in higher education.

## Notes

1 I intentionally capitalize Black but not white when the terms are used to refer to racial groups in the U.S. This practice aligns with several U.S. media organizations as a way to distinguish the collective identity and history shared among Afro-diasporic people in the U.S., including "the experience of being discriminated against because of skin color," and to challenge white supremacist practices of centering and exalting whiteness (Bauder, 2020, para. 2).

2 The pre-conference book club discussions were inspired by one of the University of Missouri-Kansas City's (UMKC) Critical Conversations titled, "A Dialogue among Women of Color and White Women in Higher Education." (https://www.youtube.com/watch?v=rvCOmZNL4Pc). Several UMKC administrators and students participated in the UAC.

3 Five of the university's eight academic colleges and several other campus entities supported the UAC as co-sponsors including McQueary College of Health and Human Services' Diversity, Equity, and Inclusion Council; College of Education's Diversity and Inclusion Task Force; College of Business' Diversity, Equity and Inclusion Committee; College of Natural and Applied Sciences' Diversity, Equity and Inclusion Committee; College of Humanities and Public Affairs' Diversity Council; Diversity

Fund sponsored by Student Affairs; Marketing and Communications; Staff Senate; and Multicultural Programs sponsored by Student Affairs.

4 The following prompt was used to guide the co-researchers: "For this photovoice project, you will be asked to take approximately 30 photographs that provide visual representations of what it means to be a Black woman at a predominately white institution (PWI). You will then select 5 photos to discuss with the other co-researchers during a focus group research meeting. In particular, you will use this project to document issues Black women face as they navigate their daily lives at PWIs as students, faculty, staff, and/or administrators. Issues documented may be related to but are not limited to (1) underrepresentation, (2) isolation, and (3) marginalization." Co-researchers were also asked to complete a SHOWeD narrative for each of the 5 final photographs they selected, which included the following prompts: (1) What do we SEE here?, (2) What is really HAPPENING here?, (3) How does this relate to OUR lives?, (4) WHY does this situation, concern, or strength EXIST?, and (5) What can we DO about it?

5 The NCBI activities included in the full-day, Saturday workshop, which was a modified version of NCBI's Leadership for Diversity Institute, are described in Brown and Mazza's (2005), *Leading Diverse Communities: A How-to Guide for Moving from Healing Into Action.*

6 The vignettes and responses included for discussion during the UAC were included on the Campus Racial Allyship Training (CRAT) pre- and post-test survey I developed based on the work of Chang et al. (2019), Erskine and Billimoria (2019), and Williams and Sharif (2021).

## References

Alhejji, H., Garavan, T., Carbery, R., O'Brien, F., & McGuire, D. (2016). Diversity training programme outcomes: A systematic review. *Human Resource Development Quarterly, 27*(1), 95–149.

Bauder, D. (2020, July 20). *AP says it will capitalize Black but not white.* Associated Press. https://apnews.com/article/entertainment-cultures-race-and-ethnicity-us-news-ap-top-news-7e36c00c5af0436abc09e051261ffff1f

Bezrukova, K., Jehn, K. A., & Spell, C. S. (2012). Reviewing diversity training: Where we have been and where we should go. *Academy of Management Learning & Education, 11*(2), 207–227.

Breeden, R. L. (2021). Our presence is resistance: Stories of Black women in senior-level student affairs positions at predominantly white institutions. *Journal of Women and Gender in Higher Education, 14*(2), 166–186.

Brown, C. R., & Mazza, G. J. (2005). *Leading diverse communities: A how-to guide for moving from healing into action.* Jossey Bass.

Carter Andrews, D. J. (2015). Navigating raced-gendered microaggressions: The experiences of a tenure-track Black female scholar. In F. A. Bonner, A. F. Marbley, F. Tuitt, P. A. Robinson, R. M. Banda, & R. L. Hughes (Eds.), *Black faculty in the academy: Narratives for negotiating identity and achieving career success* (pp. 79–88). Routledge.

Chang, E. H., Milkman, K. L., Gromet, D. M., Rebele, R. W., Massey, C., Duckworth, A. L., & Grant, A. M. (2019). The mixed effects of online diversity training. *Proceedings of the National Academy of Sciences, 116*(16), 7778–7783.

Chronicle of Higher Education. (2024, February 23). *DEI legislation tracker.* https://www.chronicle.com/article/here-are-the-states-where-lawmakers-are-seeking-to-ban-colleges-dei-efforts

Collins, P. H. (1986). Learning from the outsider within: The sociological significance of Black feminist thought. *Social Problems, 33*(6), S14–S32.

Collins, P. H. (2000). *Black feminist thought: Knowledge, consciousness, and the politics of empowerment* (2nd ed.). Routledge.

Collins, P. H. (2019). *Intersectionality as critical social theory.* Duke University Press.

Collins, P. H., & Bilge, S. (2020). *Intersectionality* (2nd ed.). John Wiley & Sons.

Crenshaw, K. (1989). Demarginalizing the intersection of race and sex: A Black feminist critique of antidiscrimination doctrine. *The University of Chicago Legal Forum, 1989*(1), Article 8, 139–167.

Crenshaw, K. (1991). Mapping the margins: Intersectionality, identity politics, and violence against Women of Color. *Stanford Law Review, 43*(6), 1241–1299.

Dace, K. L. (Ed.). (2012). *Unlikely allies in the academy: Women of Color and White women in conversation.* Routledge.

Dickinson, R., Haskins, M., & Saunders, J. A. (2022). The impact of the National Coalition Building Institute (NCBI): Cultivating cultural humility among social work students. *Social Work Education, 41*(8), 1702–1721.

Erskine, S. E., & Bilimoria, D. (2019). White allyship of Afro-Diasporic women in the workplace: A transformative strategy for organizational change. *Journal of Leadership & Organizational Studies, 26*(3), 319–338.

Essed, P. (1991). *Understanding everyday racism: An interdisciplinary theory.* Sage.

Garcia, N. M., López, N., & Vélez, V. N. (2018). QuantCrit: Rectifying quantitative methods through critical race theory. *Race Ethnicity and Education, 21*(2), 149–157.

Goff, P. A., & Kahn, K. B. (2013). How psychological science impedes intersectional thinking. *Du Bois Review: Social Science Research on Race, 10*(2), 365–384.

Harris, J. C., & Patton, L. D. (2019). Un/doing intersectionality through higher education research. *The Journal of Higher Education, 90*(3), 347–372.

Hirshfield, L. E., & Joseph, T. D. (2012). 'We need a woman, we need a Black woman': Gender, race, and identity taxation in the academy. *Gender and Education, 24*(2), 213–227.

hooks, b. (2004). *The will to change: Men, masculinity, and love.* Atria Books.

hooks, b. (2015). *Ain't I a woman: Black women and feminism* (2nd ed.). Routledge.

Jones, M. K., Leath, S., Settles, I. H., Doty, D., & Conner, K. (2022). Gendered racism and depression among Black women: Examining the roles of social support and identity. *Cultural Diversity and Ethnic Minority Psychology, 28*(1), 39.

Kalinoski, Z. T., Steele-Johnson, D., Peyton, E. J., Leas, K. A., Steinke, J., & Bowling, N. A. (2013). A meta-analytic evaluation of diversity training outcomes. *Journal of Organizational Behavior, 34*(8), 1076–1104.

Keisling, B., Bryant, R., Golden, N., Stevens, L., & Alexander, E. (2020). Does our vision of diversity reduce harm and promote justice? *GSA Today, 30*(10), 64–65.

Lewis, J. A., Williams, M. G., Peppers, E. J., & Gadson, C. A. (2017). Applying intersectionality to explore the relations between gendered racism and health among Black women. *Journal of Counseling Psychology, 64*(5), 475.

McCloud, L., & West, N. M. (2023). For ALL my sisters: The impact of cisheteronormativity on scholarship about the gendered and sexualized experiences of Black college women. In N. M. West, & C. J. Porter (Eds.), *The state of Black women in higher education: A critical perspective 20 years later* (New Directions for Student Services No. 182, pp. 69–80). Jossey-Bass.

Meyerson, D. E., & Scully, M. A. (1995). Crossroads tempered radicalism and the politics of ambivalence and change. *Organization Science, 6*(5), 585–600.

Missouri State University Office of Institutional Research. (n.d.). Diversity report 2018–2019. https://www.missouristate.edu/OIR/_Files/DiversityReport_2018-19.pdf

Newkirk, P. (2020). *Diversity, Inc.: The fight for racial equality in the workplace.* Bold Type Books.

Ohito, E. O. (2022). "I'm very hurt": (Un)justly reading the Black female body as text in a racial literacy learning assemblage. *Reading Research Quarterly, 57*(2), 609–627.

Opie, T., & Livingston, B. A. (2022). *Shared sisterhood: How to take collective action for racial and gender equity at work.* Harvard Business Press.

Overstreet, M. (2019). My first year in academia or the mythical Black woman superhero takes on the ivory tower. *Journal of Women and Gender in Higher Education, 12*(1), 18–34.

Payne, A. N., & West, N. M. (2022). The (re)construction of Black womanhood among Black college women at PWIs: A hip hop feminism model of multiple identities. *Journal of College Student Development, 63*(2), 168–184.

Reid, R. A. (2021). Retaining women faculty: The problem of invisible labor. *PS: Political Science & Politics, 54*(3), 504–506.

Rideau, R. (2021). "We're just not acknowledged": An examination of the identity taxation of full-time non-tenure-track Women of Color faculty members. *Journal of Diversity in Higher Education, 14*(2), 161–173.

Smith, E. L. B., & Nkomo, S. M. (2022). Accelerating the path to corporate leadership for all women. *Leader to Leader, 2022*(104), 45–52.

Steinfield, L., Sanghvi, M., Zayer, L. T., Coleman, C. A., Ourahmoune, N., Harrison, R. L., Hein, W., & Brace-Govan, J. (2019). Transformative intersectionality: Moving business towards a critical praxis. *Journal of Business Research, 100*, 366–375.

Szymanski, D. M., & Lewis, J. A. (2016). Gendered racism, coping, identity centrality, and African American college women's psychological distress. *Psychology of Women Quarterly, 40*(2), 229–243.

Thomas, A. J., Witherspoon, K. M., & Speight, S. L. (2008). Gendered racism, psychological distress, and coping styles of African American women. *Cultural Diversity and Ethnic Minority Psychology, 14*(4), 307–314.

Tulshyan, R. (2022). *Inclusion on purpose: An intersectional approach to creating a culture of belonging at work.* MIT Press.

Wang, C. (1999). Photovoice: A participatory action research strategy applied to women's health. *Journal of Women's Health, 8*(2), 185–192.

West, N. M. (2022). Repurposing my status as an outsider within: A Black feminist scholar-pracademic's journey to becoming an invested indifferent. In C. J. Porter, V. T. Sulé, & N. N. Croom (Eds.), *Black feminist epistemology, research, and praxis: Narratives in and through the academy* (pp. 115–131). Routledge.

West, N. M. (2023). Defining the contours of a participatory action research counterspace developed by, for, and about Black women in higher education. *International Journal of Qualitative Studies in Education.* Advance online publication. https://doi.org/10.1080/09518398.2023.2181449

West, N. M., Payne, A. N., Smith, M. D., Bonds, N. T., Alston, A. D., & Akalugwu, W. N. (2022). A collaborative autoethnography of six Black women walking tightropes in higher education. *Negro Educational Review, 72*(1–4), 131–163.

Williams, A. (2020). Black memes matter: #LivingWhileBlack with Becky and Karen. *Social Media+ Society, 6*(4), 1–14.

Williams, M., & Sharif, N. (2021). Racial allyship: Novel measurement and new insights. *New Ideas in Psychology, 62*(100865), 1–10.

Wing, A. K. (Ed.). (1997). *Critical race feminism: A reader.* NYU Press.

Worthington, R. L., Stanley, C. A., & Smith, D. G. (2020). *Standards of professional practice for chief diversity officers in higher education 2.0.* National Association of Diversity Officers in Higher Education.

# 13. *Intersectionality as Praxis for Equity in Medicine: Developing the LMSA Premedical Program*

KATHERINE ARIAS GARCIA AND MARIA ROSARIO G. ARANETA

During the COVID-19 pandemic, health disparities were on display nationwide as the United States (U.S.) witnessed Black, Latinx, Native American and Pacific Islander communities with the highest death tolls during the pandemic (AMA, 2020). Also, many Communities of Color were experiencing access issues to COVID-19 testing, vaccination and healthcare resources. The COVID-19 pandemic emphasized the need for a diverse physician workforce in urban, rural, and Communities of Color. However, the latest *Diversity in Medical Education: Facts & Figures* report (AAMC, 2022) highlights the continued disparity of admissions and shortage of Black, Latinx and Native American medical students and physicians. The number of Latinx student graduates from medical school remains stagnant with only 5.65% of the graduates from medical school with Latinx backgrounds during the 2022-2023 academic year (AAMC, 2022). Latinx students face various structural barriers on the premed pathway, which include unwelcoming and competitive STEM environments, gender bias, and academic redlining through high-stakes testing admissions requirements (Garcia 2020; Grijalva & Coombs, 1997; Nakae & Subica, 2021). Latinx student persistence toward becoming Latinx physicians is critical because Latinx physicians are more likely to practice in underserved communities and provide culturally sensitive and language-concordant care (Komaromy et al., 1996; Moreno et al., 2011).

Hispanic-Serving Institutions (HSIs) are key in Latinx student pathways to STEM and medicine, (Herrera, 2020). HSIs are campuses that have at least 25% Latinx undergraduate student enrollment and HSIs are important because they serve 62% of Latinx undergraduate students (*Excelencia* in Education, 2022). Additionally, there is a growth of emerging Hispanic-Serving Institutions (eHSIs). During the 2020–2021 academic year, thirty-one institutions received the eHSIs designation, which have 20–25% Latinx undergraduate student enrollment (*Excelencia* in Education, 2022). Moreover, HSIs serve a critical role in diversifying the STEM field because HSIs structures include institutional agents in support of Latinx STEM students and HSI campuses have greater community partnerships (Bensimon et al., 2019; Ramirez & Rodriguez-Kiino, 2020). Therefore, HSIs can play a pivotal role in the preparation of Latinx physicians and in addressing the various social identities of Latinx students on HSI campuses.

Furthermore, Latinx undergraduates in premedical studies need institutions of higher education to take on an intersectional approach to address the structural systems of oppression they encounter on their path to medicine that have historically excluded Latinx students from the field of medicine. An intersectional approach provides an understanding of inequity in medicine through a centering of interlocking social identities, such as first-generation status, gender, race, disability, socioeconomic status and immigration status, and how their intersections lead to unique forms of marginalization in higher education (Dill & Zambrana, 2020). Thus, through an intersectional approach, the focus is on intersectional oppression, such as the intersection of racism and sexism and goes beyond focusing on one social category, such as Latinx students only. However, over the past 30 years, much attention has gone into the lack of diversity in STEM and medical fields and the subgroup of Latinx students pursuing premedical studies has been minimally addressed within higher education literature concerning their unique intersectional needs to secure their retention and persistence in premedical studies. This chapter provides an overview of the development of the Latinx Medical Student Association (LMSA) Premedical Program at University of California, San Diego School of Medicine, a research-intensive, emerging HSI.

## Intersectionality and Latinx Students Pursuing Medicine

An intersectional approach is needed to address systems of oppression for Latinx students pursuing medicine to address their various identities, such as, racial/ethnic, gender, first-generation college status, socio-economic class, disability status, sexual orientation, immigration status, including students with individual or family documentation concerns. Kimberlé Crenshaw's intersectionality framework (1991) explains the ways that gender, race/ethnicity, class and sexuality interact with Black women's reality to understand oppression in society. An intersectionality framework examines oppression beyond one single issue, such as Latinx students (i.e., focusing on just ethnicity), and instead incorporates various intersectional identities, such as Latinx first-generation college students and Latinas in STEM and the collision of power dynamics and oppression (Crenshaw, 1991). In STEM, the critical work of Malcom et al. (1976) focused on the *double bind*, which are the experiences of Women of Color in STEM with racism and sexism. Subsequent intersectionality research has continued to center on Black women's lives to understand how marginalized identities and power interact in the lives of Black women. Additionally, an intersectionality approach has been extended to other marginalized groups such as Latinx students in higher education (Núñez, 2014).

In STEM, Latinx students and Latinas in STEM marginalization have also been examined with an intersectionality framework revealing the importance of recognition of intersectional Latinx identities in STEM (e.g., the impact of gendered and socio-economic differences of Latinx students; Herrera et al., 2022; Rincón & Lane, 2017; Rodriguez, Cunningham & Jordan, 2019). Thus, the application of an intersectionality framework on the group of premedical students addresses the structures that have historically excluded Latinx students from medicine, such as the historical legacy of the field of medicine using Black community members as test subjects (e.g., the Tuskegee Study and Henrietta Lacks), an admissions process that focuses on competitive science course requirements, and high-stakes standardized testing, such as the Medical College Admissions Tests (MCAT). Through an intersectionality framework, the various systems of oppression in medicine that impact medical outcomes and a diverse physician workforce can reveal a greater understanding of how converging oppressions contribute to marginalization and inequity in medicine. Thus, this chapter aims to center on how an intersectional approach can be used to develop a program to begin to address the in(opportunities) structures that are a result of the oppression and marginalization of Latinx students in higher education.

## Intersectionality in STEM and Medicine

In this section, we present STEM and medicine literature that examine intersectionality in two areas: (1) oppression related to the intersection of race and first-generation college status and (2) oppression related to the intersection of gender and race. Research on Latinx STEM/premed students has traditionally used deficit framing and focused on Latinx STEM students leaving the sciences (Seymour & Hewitt, 1997). However, through intersectionality and asset-based frameworks, researchers have countered the deficit framing of Latinx STEM students and expanded to include multiple social identities of Latinx students to reveal a nuanced understanding of the marginalization of Latinx students in STEM and medicine. For instance, Jackson et al. (2016) reveals the importance of examining Latinx students' intersectional identities because of the complexity of intersecting identities of being a Latinx student, a racialized experience and a first-generation college student in the sciences. Jackson et al. (2016) reveals the unique aspirations of the Latinx and Latinx first-generation college students in seeking a degree in the sciences that is grounded in their community. Additionally, researchers have shown that Latinx first-generation students experience a lack of sense of belonging, disengagement, and imposter syndrome in STEM learning environment because it is a dominant White field (Rincón et al., 2020; Rincón & Rodriguez, 2021). Also, in medicine, the field is dominated by many physicians that come from a family of physicians, thus being first-generation and Latinx, causes experience of othering and isolation in the pathway to medicine (Romero et al., 2020). Thus, oppression related to the intersection of race and first-generation college status requires an intersectional approach in STEM and medicine research to reveal the intersecting oppressions of Latinx first-generation students in STEM and medicine.

Additionally, oppression related to the intersection of gender and race in STEM and medicine is another area of analysis to address inequities in medicine. For instance, Latinas experienced a combination of sexism and racism in STEM by being assigned less interesting STEM work and/or having to complete extra work to prove themselves to their male peers (Rodriguez et al., 2020). Also, Banda and Flowers (2018) describe the double bind of sexism and racism experienced by Latinas in STEM when the Latinas have difficulties in expressing themselves, asking questions and feeling silenced because of their identity as Latinas in a dominant male-STEM field. Additionally, previous research on Latinas pursuing medicine has focused on the tremendous obstacles they encounter in pursuit of a medical degree, such as competitive, unwelcoming STEM environments and gender bias (Garcia, 2020; Grijalva & Coombs, 1997; McGee, 2016) and once in the profession, encounters with questions of authority through gendered racism (Flores & Bañuelos 2021). Thus, an analysis of the oppression related to the intersection of gender and race reveals the intersection of sexism and racism in the pathways to medicine.

## Program Development to Address Intersectionality

As medical school leaders, Women of Color, and immigrants, we work in the medical school committed to diversifying the medical field and striving towards health equity. We work in an office of diversity and community partnerships, created in 1969, which supports creating pathways to medicine for underrepresented students in medicine. KAG is a first-generation college graduate, an immigrant from Peru with a research background in education and pathways to medicine. MRA is the associate dean of the Diversity & Community Partnerships Office, a professor of epidemiology, an immigrant from the Philippines, with a research background in HIV/AIDS and diabetes disparities. We often discussed the challenges of first-generation college students and students from disadvantaged backgrounds that are trying to enter medical school. We attend recruitment conferences to recruit diverse students to medical school. Through our various years working in the medical school, we understand the structural barriers in higher education and the admissions process that exclude bright underrepresented students, such as the hidden premed curriculum, entry-level exam MCAT and competitive GPAs. Students attending resource-limited high schools with few advanced STEM courses may be disadvantaged in obtaining competitive grades and sustaining high GPAs once they start college, compared to students from resource-rich high schools. Similarly, disadvantaged college students with limited resources to enroll in MCAT preparatory courses compared to classmates with fiscal resources exacerbates education inequity.

To tackle the exclusion and in(opportunities) of Latinx students in medicine, the authors developed the LMSA Premedical Program at the University of California, San Diego School of Medicine (UCSD SOM) in 2020 to address the complexity of oppression and inequity in medicine through an intersectionality approach that recognizes various social identities, such as disadvantaged and underrepresented backgrounds, first-generation college students, and lower socioeconomic college students that have been historically excluded from pursuing medicine. First, we decided to do an in-depth analysis of the admissions data to analyze the barriers in the admissions cycle. We analyzed the data of UCSD undergraduate applicants to examine the trajectories and the points of exclusion of the subgroup of Latinx students, by gender, first-generation college status, and socio-economic background. For instance, we enumerated and compared the number of Latinx applicants, interviewees, and admitted students by California college institution, in addition to mean science GPAs and MCAT scores. This information provided us with an understanding of the structural barriers within the admissions process. Concurrently, the undergraduate campus, an emerging HSI, was making efforts to address the academic needs of Latinx students to become a Hispanic-Serving Institution. Thus, after our analysis, and through a grant from the Equity, Diversity & Inclusion Office, we decided to create a program that will target an underrepresented growing group and address the structural barriers in the medical school admissions process. The goals of the LMSA Premedical Program are (1) to expand the UCSD underrepresented premed pool of applicants to UCSD School of Medicine, and (2) to increase the number of UCSD underrepresented students admitted to UCSD School of Medicine.

## Intersectionality as Praxis

Leading with an intersectionality framework to understand the interlocking of oppression and persistence of Latinx students in the premed pathway, we identified three areas to address inequity in medicine. This approach centers the intersectionality experienced by underrepresented premedical students pursuing medicine. The three areas are: (1) a focus on disadvantaged pre-medical student groups, (2) diverse stakeholders in the development of the LMSA Premedical Program and student selection, and (3) culturally-relevant curriculum and programming to address the hidden curriculum of being a premed student.

### Focus on Disadvantaged Premedical Student Groups

When students apply to medical school, they have the option to self-report their disadvantaged background based on socioeconomic status, parent education background, and community setting. The disadvantaged category allows for a greater understanding of multiple social realities of students and their lived experiences that have impacted their access to medical school. For instance, a first-generation college student from a rural, low-income background may have limited access to honors and Advance Placement Courses. In the LMSA Premedical Program, we aim to support students from the disadvantaged category that have historically been underrepresented in medicine (e.g., Latinx, Black and Native American backgrounds).

Also, the LMSA Premedical Program was intentional in focusing on Latinx students as Latinx students make up only 6% of physicians in the United States. The geographical location of the campus is in Southern California, next to the U.S./Mexico border with a large Latinx community. Additionally, the main campus was engaging in efforts to become a HSI and there was an opportunity to leverage campus efforts to focus on an underrepresented group in medicine. As an emerging-HSI, through disaggregated data, we have found that the Latinx student population has been increasing for the past ten years and is the largest underrepresented group in the Biology

Department. Disaggregating student data is important because many premedical students major in biology. Through disaggregation of student data by gender, first-generation college status and other social identities, then educational inequity can begin to be understood for the differential social groups.

## Diverse Stakeholders

Development of the LMSA Premedical Program began with two faculty and a staff/graduate student that are all involved in the Diversity & Community Partnerships Office. Collectively, all three have vast experience advocating for Students of Color in medicine through the admissions committee, overseeing a Student-Run Free Clinic that serves the majority of undocumented Latinx, providing structure mentorship through post-baccalaureate programs, and research expertise on pathways in medicine. Through our diverse experiences, we were able to initiate critical conversations with the admissions office on diversifying faculty participating in the Multiple Mini Interviews (MMI) and on the admissions executive committee, to address structural changes in admissions. The intersectional approach is the inclusion of diverse stakeholders to address racism and bias in the medical school admissions student selection process (Capers et al., 2017; Talamantes et al., 2019). By expanding interviewers to include a diverse group through gender, sexual orientation, and first-generation college status, the interviewers have a different understanding based on their lived experiences. Thus, we actively recruited the participation of diverse faculty to serve on the MMI and Recruitment and Admissions Committee and recruited Latinx medical students for the LMSA Premedical Program to provide mentorship to premedical student participants.

## Curriculum

We created a curriculum for the LMSA Premedical Program to address inequity in medicine and provide medical school information that is often not accessible by underrepresented, disadvantaged and first-generation college students. The curriculum focuses on bridging the cultural values of Latinx students to the premed pathway to counter the dominant white culture embedded in medicine. The curriculum included four components: (1) strengthening interview skills, (2) an application portfolio, (3) cultural engagement and mentoring, and (4) MCAT enhancement. Each component was developed to address the various intersectional Latinx identities and to embrace Latinx culture in a dominant white field of medicine. For instance, for interviewing skills, the facilitator identifies as Latinx and focuses on embracing the Spanish language and bringing the whole self, including culture, during the interview process. Through an intersectionality approach, the curriculum went beyond addressing one dimension of oppression and instead included topics in medicine that traditionally marginalized underrepresented students. For instance, the language Spanish is marginalized in the U.S., which centers on the English language and further excludes Spanish-heritage speakers in education (Valenzuela, 1999). The application portfolio was essential for the many first-generation Latinx student participants to demystify the application process, address imposter syndrome, and uncover the hidden curriculum of being a premed. The cultural engagement component included participation in the Latino Medical Student Association Conference, which exposed the premeds to Latinx physicians addressing health disparities and networking with other Latinx premeds/physicians. The MCAT enhancement included an instructor that specialized in teaching first-generation college students. Lastly, a financial stipend was provided to the Latinx student participants as the application process is a costly endeavor for many low-income students. Collectively, the curriculum, stipend and program structure are important components for low-income, first-generation college students and native Spanish-speaking Latinx students because they are the most marginalized group in medicine.

Participants in the LMSA Premedical Program complete a pre-survey, post-survey and keep the program updated with their postgraduate activities. From the first three cohorts of 30 Latinx premedical students, 20% have been admitted to medical school or osteopathic school. Twenty-three percent (23%) applied to medical school during the fourth cohort. While writing this chapter, forty-three percent (43%) are completing a gap year and are involved in activities such as employment or research and thirteen percent (13%) were enrolled in master's programs, including master in public health and master in public administration programs. Survey results reveal high satisfaction with the program and improved understanding of applying to medical school.

The following are post-survey comments from the participants. A student majoring in neurobiology shared, "I feel prepared in the sense I know what to expect and the steps to take to become a competitive applicant...I appreciate the helpful and kind staff of this program who made the environment feel welcoming." This student highlights the welcoming environment created by the faculty and staff, all who come from diverse backgrounds and applied a student-centered pedagogy, such as sharing of family narratives that inspire premed trajectory. This welcoming environment contrasts with the competitive STEM undergraduate environment on campus. Another student, double majoring in public health and biology, shared, "I have a much more clear understanding of the process that I did going into the program. I was able to gain a network of support that I am very grateful for." This student revealed the knowledge gained during the program. Also, the faculty and staff emphasized the collective student experience and helping each other to counter the individualism of applying to medical school. Another student, majoring in human biology and minoring in global health, shared:

> I saw peers like myself that have now turned into mentors. I saw physicians that look like me that I want to one day be. I saw myself doing it all and doing it well. My mindset is now ready to continue down this journey whereas before I was nervous, scared, and uneasy.

The program was intentional in having all the facilitators from a Latinx background or diverse background to provide role models and representation of medical students and physicians from diverse backgrounds.

Another component of the program was financial support through a stipend to cover the financial expenses of preparation for medical school. Most of the participants worked two jobs to support their schooling and family financial needs. One student shared the impact of the financial stipend:

> The financial stipend lessened the financial burden to enroll in an MCAT prep course and apply to medical school. With my mother and I undergoing surgery this past year, our family's finances took a toll with us being unable to work. The financial stipend provided me an opportunity I would have otherwise not been able to partake in.

## Conclusion

In conclusion, this chapter presented a program using an intersectional approach at a medical school to begin to address the marginalization and exclusion of Latinx students in the premedical pathway to medicine. To advance toward health and educational equity, an intersectional approach must be taken to transform structures in institutions of higher education and medical schools to reveal structures that uphold racism within the premed pathway.

## References

American Association of Medical Colleges. (2022). *Diversity in medicine, facts & figures 2022*. https://www.aamc.org/data-reports/students-residents/data/2022-facts-app licants-and-matriculants-data

American Medical Association. (2020). *Latinx COVID-19 health inequities report: Insights for the health care field.* https://newsletter.ama-assn.org/downloads/20-473689-CHE-Latinx-COVID-19-report.pdf

Banda, R. M., & Flowers, A. M. (2018). Critical qualitative research as a means to advocate for Latinas in STEM. *International Journal of Qualitative Studies in Education, 31*(8), 769–783.

Bensimon, E. M., Dowd, A. C., Stanton-Salazar, R., & Dávila, B. A. (2019). The role of institutional agents in providing institutional support to Latinx students in STEM. *The Review of Higher Education, 42*(4), 1689–1721.

Capers IV, Q., Clinchot, D., McDougle, L., & Greenwald, A. G. (2017). Implicit racial bias in medical school admissions. *Academic Medicine, 92*(3), 365–369.

Crenshaw, K. (1991). Mapping the margins: Intersectionality, identity politics, and violence against Women of Color. *Stanford Law Review 43*(6), 1241–1299.

Dill, B. T., & Zambrana, R. E. (2020). Critical thinking about inequality: An emerging lens. In C. McCann, S.-K., Kim, & E. Ergun (Eds.), *Feminist theory reader* (pp. 108–116). Routledge.

*Excelencia* in Education. (2022). *Hispanic-Serving Institutions (HSIs) Fact Sheet: 2021–2022.* https://www.edexcelencia.org/research/publications/hispanic-serving-institutions-hsis-fact-sheet-2021-22#:~:text=The%20number%20of%20HSIs%20has,of%20Columbia%2C%20and%20PuPuer%20Rico.

Flores, G. M., & Bañuelos, M. (2021). Gendered deference: Perceptions of authority and competence among Latina/o physicians in medical institutions. *Gender & Society, 35*(1), 110–135.

Garcia, K. A. (2020). A Latina pursuing her medical dream (MD). *InterActions: UCLA Journal of Education and Information Studies, 16*(2). https://escholarship.org/uc/item/6v03r1f7

Grijalva, C., & Coombs, R. H. (1997). Latinas in medicine: Stressors, survival skills and strengths. *Aztlán: A Journal of Chicano Studies, 22*(2), 67–89.

Herrera, F. A. (2020). A national portrait of STEM trajectories through two-and four-year Hispanic Serving Institutions. *HETS Online Journal, 11*(1).

Herrera, F. A., Rodriguez-Operana, V. C., Kovats Sánchez, G., Cerrillos, A., & Marquez, B. (2022). "It was hard, and it still is...": Women of Color navigating HSI STEM transfer pathways. *AERA Open, 8.* https://journals.sagepub.com/doi/full/10.1177/23328584221126480

Jackson, M. C., Galvez, G., Landa, I., Buonora, P., & Thoman, D. B. (2016). Science that matters: The importance of a cultural connection in underrepresented students' science pursuit. *CBE—Life Sciences Education, 15*(3). https://www.ncbi.nlm.nih.gov/pmc/articles/PMC5008889/

Komaromy, M., Grumbach, K., Drake, M., Vranizan, K., Lurie, N., Keane, D., & Bindman, A. B. (1996). The role of Black and Hispanic physicians in providing health care for underserved populations. *New England Journal of Medicine, 334*(20), 1305–1310.

Malcom, S. M., Hall, P. Q., & Brown, J. W. (1976). The double bind: The price of being a minority woman in science. *Proceedings of American Association for the Advancement of Science Minority Women Scientists Conference.*

McGee, E. O. (2016). Devalued Black and Latino racial identities: A by-product of STEM college culture?. *American Educational Research Journal, 53*(6), 1626–1662.

Moreno, G., Walker, K. O., Morales, L. S., & Grumbach, K. (2011). Do physicians with self-reported non-English fluency practice in linguistically disadvantaged communities?. *Journal of General Internal Medicine, 26,* 512–517.

Nakae, S., & Subica, A. M. (2021). Academic redlining in medicine. *Journal of the National Medical Association, 113*(5), 587–594.

Núñez, A-M. (2014). Advancing an intersectionality framework in higher education: Power and Latino postsecondary opportunity. *Higher Education: Handbook of Theory and Research* (Vol. 29), 33–92.

Ramirez, L., & Rodriguez-Kiino, D. (2020). Creating community engaged partnerships to foster trust with STEM & Hispanic Serving Institutions. In G. A. Garcia (Ed.), *Hispanic Serving Institutions (HSIs) in practice: Defining "servingness" at HSIs* (pp. 135–150). Information Age.

Rincón, B. E., Fernández, É., & Dueñas, M. C. (2020). Anchoring comunidad: How first-and continuing-generation Latinx students in STEM engage community cultural wealth. *International Journal of Qualitative Studies in Education, 33*(8), 840–854.

Rincón, B. E., & Lane, T. B. (2017). Latin@ s in science, technology, engineering, and mathematics (STEM) at the intersections. *Equity & Excellence in Education, 50*(2), 182–195.

Rincón, B. E., & Rodriguez, S. (2021). Latinx students charting their own STEM pathways: How community cultural wealth informs their STEM identities. *Journal of Hispanic Higher Education, 20*(2), 149–163.

Rodriguez, S., Cunningham, K., & Jordan, A. (2019). STEM identity development for Latinas: The role of self-and outside recognition. *Journal of Hispanic Higher Education, 18*(3), 254–272.

Rodriguez, S. L., Bukoski, B. E., Cunningham, K. J., & Jones, A. (2020). Critiquing oppression and desiring social justice: How undergraduate Latina students in STEM engage in acts of resistance. *Journal of Women and Gender in Higher Education, 13*(3), 251–267.

Romero, R., Miotto, K., Casillas, A., & Sanford, J. (2020). Understanding the experiences of first-generation medical students: Implications for a diverse physician workforce. *Academic Psychiatry, 44,* 467–470.

Seymour, E., & Hewitt, N. M. (1997). *Talking about leaving* (Vol. 34). Westview Press.

Talamantes, E., Henderson, M. C., Fancher, T. L., & Mullan, F. (2019). Closing the gap—making medical school admissions more equitable. *New England Journal of Medicine, 380*(9), 803–805.

## 14. From Kitchen Tables to Black Spaces: Where Black Women Graduate Students Work Against Intersectionality Crisis

MARQUITA D. FOSTER, BELINDA COLEMAN, INDIA COOLEY, AMANI FRANCIS, JACQUELINE STEVENS, JANA BROWN, ANDREA PICKENS, ALYSIA HUNT WILLIAMS, AND SHANNIKA BACCHUS

Academic blackness in higher education is routinely measured and (re)defined by standards of acceptability and respectability, as the very nature of the academy demands that only certain types of intellectual expression and conduct should represent it. As far back as the nineteenth century in the United States, educational and socioeconomic philosophies dictated the extent to which Black folks should and would engage in advanced learning, and upheld by sexist and racist attitudes of Black men, White women and White men, bound Black women's education *primarily* to racial uplift and improvement into the next century (Perkins, 1983, 1993). Despite the increased presence and advances of Black women in higher education during the late twentieth century (Bonner & Thomas, 2001), there is an ongoing curious expectation of how (much) Blackness can fit in the literal rooms of higher learning—where it is noticeable (i.e., hypervisible) but does not upset norms or cause discomfort (i.e., invisibilized). The relationship between ivory towers and ebony women (Henry, 1994/2017) has always been lopsided and transactional. For contemporary Black women who pursue terminal degrees at a predominantly White institution (PWI), engaging in the academic world of behaving, learning, talking and writing still requires negotiation (Davis, 2019; Scott, 2000, 2017) in which they feel that they must continually defend their character and validate their belonging through their ability to produce commendable intellectual work and scholarship. What requires further study is how Black women engage in negotiation in virtual or online environments.

As a university-based research team who studies the factors that are critical to the success of Black women students in online programs at higher education settings, we continue to seek to learn about the various ways Black women are able to form relationships (i.e., Black spaces) and engage in negotiating their multiple, intersecting identities. Because of our own experiences, we understand the unique challenges of bonding and negotiating in a online, wall-less place. Therefore, in the chapter, we explore the experiences of eight Black women graduate students in a competitive, online doctoral program who took negotiation from an individual act to collective activism (Collins, 1986). These eight students engaged in talks with us over a period of months in 2022. While we share our research findings in this chapter, we are framing our work as practice. In the first section, because negotiation involves accessing one's identity, we feel it is important to reflect on the expanding concept of intersectionality that encapsulates a new wave of contemporary Black women's identities. In the second section, we discuss the eight Black women graduate students' encounters with invisibility and belonging that prompted their resistance to treating their negotiating as an isolated act. In the third section, we briefly explain our methodology in order to show how we collected the data around practice. In the fourth section, we share how the graduate students' collected narratives informed the outcomes of their collective resistance to support their multiple, intersecting identities. We conclude by addressing the significance of student-initiated practices that disrupt factors that contribute to intersecting oppressions in virtual higher education settings.

## *Intersectionality at the Borderlands of the Academy*

This chapter draws upon Black feminist thought (BFT) and intersectionality, which maintains that Black women engage in resistance against systems of oppression by utilizing their lived experiences at the intersections of race, gender and class and rejecting the notion of willing or passive victimhood (Collins, 2009; Crenshaw, 1990). While Crenshaw emphasized that intersectionality serves as a theoretical tool that situates critical analyses in investigating social location and power, the word intersectionality is now more ubiquitous (Jackson, 2019). According to Bilge (2013), intersectionality continues to undergo rethinking and reimagining, in the examination of oppression and social justice, in ways that are both expected (a natural evolution) and problematic (i.e., whitening and depoliticization).

## Intersectionality Crisis

Because of the sociohistorical vivisection of Black women's bodies and their expressions of gender, race and class, they contend with identity constructs such as caricatures, prototypes, stereotypes and even monsters (Calafell, 2012; Corbin et al., 2018; Overstreet, 2019) that do not fall away just because they have entered the ivory tower. These constructs, rooted in colonial oppression, initiated Black women's struggle to control their own images and identities and dispute their sole usefulness to social systems as objects (Collins, 2009; Corbin et al., 2018; Leath & Mims, 2023). Limited research from the 1980s on Black women, specifically focused on how their intersectional identities impacted their experiences in higher education, reiterated (and foretold) a familiar reality: institutions are microcosms of society at large and, unless Black women work against (i.e., resist) intersectional discrimination and (mis)labeling, their identities would remain shaped and defined by others (Howard-Vital, 1989). In this respect, the nuanced and complex lived experiences of Black women warrant examination not only in relation to enduring an identity crisis (struggle to secure an identity; Erikson, 1968), but also, more accurately, a postcolonial identity crisis (struggle to reclaim an identity separated from whiteness; Dizayi, 2019; Fanon, 1952/2008). We argue that in the context of higher education, these compounded crises manifest themselves as an *intersectionality crisis* where highly accomplished and educated Black women have to negotiate which combination of identities must be surrendered or utilized in order to ensure the likelihood of their surviving the academy.

Though it is still very necessary to explore Black women's experiences at intersections of race, gender and class, in our chapter, we look deeply into the subsets of these social constructs that can reveal the depth of oppression that Black women encounter and must navigate in their daily personal and professional lives. In our research on Black women graduate students, we believe including language (e.g., linguistic expressions, discourse markers and Black body speech) as an intersecting identity because it encounters marginalization and silencing in formal higher education settings (Delpit, 1998). Morgan (2021) noted, "Black women in particular actively insist on language and discourse that both represent and create their world through words, expressions and verbal routines within and outside of the African American community to confront injustice" (p. 290). However, in rigid academic spaces, Black women's altered dialects and linguistic detours may signal the internalization of White ways of communicating that stand as evidence of becoming educated. They may abandon their cultural ways of being and knowing to secure visibility, credibility and belonging (Love, 2019). Ironically, research has grown around linguistic justice for Black children in K-12 education with aims to disrupt anti-Black linguistic racism in the language arts classroom (Baker-Bell, 2020; Boutte et al., 2021; McMurtry, 2021). We assert that the most radical linguistic revolution was Black literacy as resistance during and after enslavement, which aimed to create and sustain a postcolonial identity for Black people. However, linguistic justice in higher education seems to be a foreign and backward notion, because for anyone to be accepted into the prestige of the academy means, in some fashion, that they agree to the prescribed demonstrations of learning and intelligence and the hegemonic standards and protocols of western presentation and conduct—in exchange for membership and educational investment.

In our research on Black women graduate students, we find that linguistic authority (Morgan, 2020) serves as a portal from which other identities emerge (see Figure 14.1): Black women's language choices routinely inform their expressions of Blackness (i.e., race and culture), gender (e.g., identity and expressions), and social class (e.g., educational attainment). Also, the ways in which Black women have historically used language worked as a counter-language (Morgan, 2020) to signal safety and empowerment. Washington (2020) noted that African American Language (AAL) functions through:

> shared speech norms and cultural understandings among members of enslaved populations and their descendants, facilitating intragroup communication and fostering solidarity and survival by effectively sealing AAL users from persons outside the speech community who are unfamiliar with the culturally based norms and values undergirding Black language use. (p. 360)

It is important to note that Black women's choice of dialects or language choices do not always serve these purposes, nor do they tell insiders everything, "there is no monolithic Black women's culture" (Collins, 1986, p. 522) or universal way of being (Black), but Black women do recognize each other by discourse markers and Black body speech.

In sum, when Black women speak, their words become corporal manifestations, coordinated expressions affected by their hands, faces, mouths, and eyes. Black women's use of language not only underscores their identities but also sustains their relationship with other Black women within spaces of struggle and oppression. The ways Black women communicate in the world and the rich meaning in their linguistic choices are often predicated on crossing multiple cultural and physical borders (Scott, 2000). Thus, we assert that Black women are not divested from their linguistic repertoire and authority when they enter institutions of higher education.

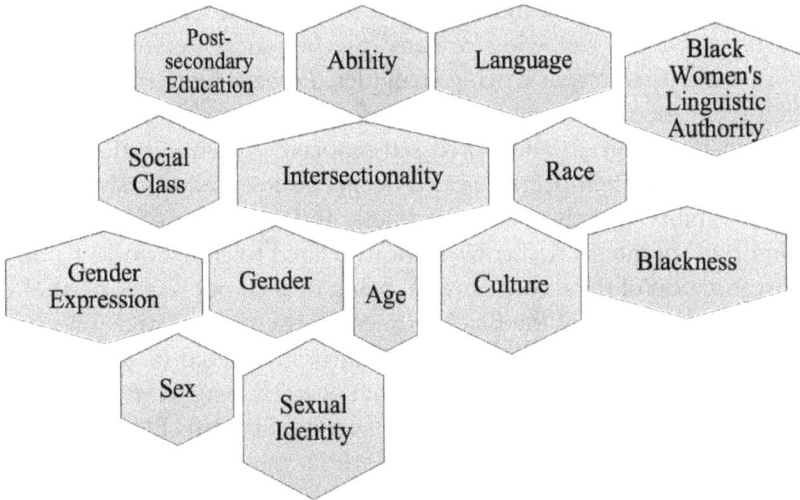

**Figure 14.1.** Intersecting Identities with an Emphasis on Black Women's Linguistic Authority

Note. Authors' image.

## *From Isolation to Collective Activism*

As stated previously, our research team studies factors that promote Black women's successful completion of doctoral programs. In Spring 2022, we focused our research on an online doctoral program at a PWI in southwestern United States, a program brought to our attention by one of our research team members with collegial connections to that PWI. Even though the program's student retention data reflected several concerns about Black women and Women of Color, the research team member noted that the program had made minimal efforts to address these students' sometimes unique, diverse academic needs. In fact, the most noticeable effort to recognize and affirm diversity came from outside the department that housed the program. Per university-generated reports published on its website, endeavors to promote inclusivity and sense of belonging primarily stem from university-level diversity, equity and inclusion (DEI) online, self-paced activities. Faculty, students and staff are mandated to engage in these DEI activities. However, there are no mandated evaluations to measure whether the application of the DEI lessons are making any difference in on-the-ground and online undergraduate or graduate courses.

After we reviewed the DEI reports, we analyzed specific, masked information provided by program leadership and learned that, based on student success data (i.e., retention rates) and exit surveys for the online doctoral program, Black women specifically take a leave of absence or withdraw from their studies for the following reasons: psychological isolation, feelings of inferiority and dissertation writing struggles. Perhaps more meaningful, our research team member had conducted informal talks with 16 Black women students in the program and noted self-reported communications between these students and their peers revealed deeper issues: academic shaming, feelings of invisibility, perceived anti-Blackness, and suspicions of "being pushed out/shut out" of intellectual conversations related to coursework. Upon further investigation of the informal talks, being pushed out was associated with being silenced, especially for Black women whose dialects and ways of verbally or nonverbally communicating are culturally rooted in Blackness. The women reported that these ways were often deemed as aggressive and unprofessional, which reflected the type of intersectionality crisis Black women students experience in higher education. With language choices and dialectal expression being so much a part of how some Black women communicate, to become "unsilenced" meant negotiating and abandoning a combination of their identities.

## Student-Initiated Affinity Group

Because these incidents were overt and troubling, an initial group of six Black women graduate students communicated to a Black woman faculty member about the need for the creation of a support group. While six appears to be a small number, it reflects the reality of how few Black students, of any gender identity, are accepted into doctoral programs. Before the group had its first meeting, the number of interested students grew to almost a dozen. The students believed that such a group would address not only the academic concerns and the unique needs of Black women and Women of Color in their doctoral program but also attend to their emotional support, sense of belonging, and satisfaction. After meeting to discuss these factors, the faculty member and the students collaborated to draft a proposal to be shared with program leadership. The following items highlighted the importance of their initiative:

- The first semester in the doctoral program can be psychologically isolating. Some students have reported that they experience imposter syndrome as well as stereotype threat.
- Students and different-race faculty often encounter communicating issues that may cause students to feel as though they are not being understood.

- While program-designed student groups (based on a cohort model) are a great safety net, they are formed later in the program. Earlier opportunities to connect as a group and with culturally sensitive faculty would be helpful and would impact satisfaction with the program.
- The program's cohort model mimics the cultural practice of other-mothering and communities of care that many Black students and Students of Color find supportive and beneficial.

Program leadership agreed that an *affinity group* could be created to address the intersecting identities of Black women and Women of Color in the program. Soon after, the faculty member began piloting the affinity group, meeting with 10 Black women graduate students in early spring 2022 to establish their meeting schedule, purpose and goals. It is important to note that while the faculty member was involved in the meetings, the students developed the agenda.

## *Method*

After learning about the affinity group, our research team contacted the faculty member with the interest of interviewing the affinity group about their experiences. Upon agreeing to serve as a consultant (we purposefully chose not to use the problematic word *gatekeeper*), our team submitted an Institutional Review Board (IRB) application in fall 2022, receiving an exempt determination. Our lead research team member began conducting and recording semi-structured interviews or talks via Zoom with the affinity group in the fall to learn about their experiences with belonging, the marginalizing of their identities and how they felt the group was a way to counter intersectionality crisis. We believe framing the interviews as talks honors Black culture but also establishes a safe space for Black women to get real. As Few et al. (2003) noted, "Sister-to-sister talk is Afrocentric slang to describe congenial conversations or positive relating on which life lessons might be shared between Black women" (p. 205). Because our ways of speaking often honor our race, class and expressions of gender, we utilized Black feminist-womanist storytelling to capture the narratives of Black women graduate students in the online doctoral program.

## *Kitchen Tables and Black Spaces*

Over the past thirty years, studies on Black women's linguistic repertoire have increased, situating its necessity in female friendships at kitchen tables

(Baker-Bell, 2017; Davis, 2019; Goins, 2011; Hughes & Heuman, 2006; Scott, 2000). Moreover, research also shows that it is not uncommon for Black people to authentically and organically find or design Black space or Black informal networks inside and outside the academy (Allen, 1997; Davis 2019). Thus, talks about creating Black spaces to address the students' needs as Black women, working professionals and graduate students took place at virtual kitchen tables. The next two subsections explain how the Black women graduate students took the initiative to resist oppressive academic expectations as well as to empower each other to create spaces for themselves and their multiple identities in online live sessions.

## Working Against Intersectionality Crisis at Kitchen Tables

The participants in the affinity group met once a month on a Saturday morning via Zoom. Each meeting lasted approximately 1 hour to 1.5 hours for nine months. Even though the participants wished that they could have met sooner in the program and for a longer time on Saturdays, they overwhelming agreed that the time was sufficient in providing them the navigational capital to help them progress through the program and understand academic expectations. Prior to the meetings, the faculty member contacted the affinity group to create an informal agenda that remained flexible and open-ended so that they could add additional concerns or topics as needed. Dissertation-related topics included:

- Understanding the expectations and structure of dissertation
- The research designs best supported by program resources and advisor experience (requested by affinity member)
- Developing appropriate research questions (requested by affinity member)
- Deciding on the best theoretical framework (requested by affinity member)
- Understanding qualitative research software (requested by affinity member)

It is important to note that over those nine months, the affinity group enrolled in and successfully completed six doctoral-level online courses (two courses per semester). Per program data, while the majority of students across various racial or ethnic demographics pass these six prerequisite courses, Black women and Women of Color tend to be less prepared for the dissertation course that follows, and this "lack of preparation" was reflected in their low retention rates. Therefore, the faculty member saw the need to frontload information, provide resources and answer questions about dissertation coursework even though the affinity members were not at this stage in the program.

More importantly, many Black women, as a result of their experiences with the interlocking forms of oppression, find ways to empower subjugated others and model for them how to navigate spaces that come with barriers (Collins, 2009). Because the trusted faculty member was also a Black woman, the participants reported that the greatest benefit of their kitchen table meetings was being able to learn from the faculty member's experiences. For example, because the program lacked resources that were attractive to emerging Black scholars and researchers, the participants stated that getting help finding theoretical frameworks or methodologies that centered their race, culture, gender cleared a major obstacle in their making progress in the prerequisite courses. As part of instilling the affinity group with navigational capital, the participants shared that the trusted faculty member demonstrated how to engage and inform their future advisors about the valid and appropriate ways of researching the Black lived experience.

Finally, though most of the virtual kitchen table meetings focused on academic concerns, the affinity group members occasionally sought advice and suggestions to address personal and professional conflicts with their peers and instructors. The participants reported that the open-ended agenda was an empowering tool to ask questions not only about the doctoral program but also about how Black women should and could accomplish program requirements without having to surrender themselves. It is important to note that while instructor-student relationships were overwhelmingly positive, the few fractured relationships seemed irreparable and warranted intervention from program leadership. Social-relational topics included:

- Communicating concerns to instructors (requested by affinity member)
- Seeking a new advisor when irreconcilable differences occur (requested by affinity member)
- Establishing a supportive Black space within the cohort model (requested by affinity member)
- Practicing self-care

Of the four social-relational topics, communicating with instructors was where an intersectionality crisis often started and was sustained. Four of the eight participants in the affinity group shared that they wanted to ask their instructors clarifying questions during the online live sessions or seek assistance from their instructors during their office hours; however, the participants already felt silenced and did not want to appear to be incapable or incompetent in front of their peers or instructors.

## Using AAL to Make Sense of the Academy

While our research team structured each talk primarily around learning about participants' academic experiences, we were expressly curious about how the participants utilized their linguistic authority during online sessions and/or in Black spaces to make sense of the academy. It is important to note three of the eight participants only had one Black instructor during the first year in the program, and they found learning from different-race faculty did not always produce desired results. Thus, differences in communication styles, supported by cultural, linguistic and gender differences, warranted their seeking help from other Black women to make sense of coursework, class discussions and even written feedback from non-Black instructors.

The participants all noted that they never openly or consciously used Black discourse markers or Black body speech during the live sessions; however, they did so purposefully in private through text messages or off camera (i.e., hiding their communications from persons outside the speech community). The participants reported that the inability to be themselves made them feel socially and emotionally disconnected during the live sessions. Not surprisingly, the participants reported being in the affinity group meetings allowed them to feel free and talk the way that they wanted to. They could share without having to consider formalities and choosing their words "safely" because they knew everyone at the table would understand them. They could explain things to one another in culturally rooted words and expressions. As part of the preliminary analysis of the talks, our research team reviewed the Zoom recordings and was able to categorize the three ways the participants freely expressed themselves with us (see Table 14.1).

We assert the simple action of talking "the way they wanted to" was the most liberating part of being present at kitchen tables and Black spaces because negotiating or abandoning any of their intersecting identities was not a concern or expected. It is also important to note that the participants believed talking the way they wanted to was not about being able to use AAL or AAVE in Black spaces. It was about having the freedom to do so without feeling inferior or silenced or negotiating their linguistic authority, including any identity that emerged from this portal.

**Table 14.1.** Observed Participants' Linguistic Repertoire

| Characteristics | Linguistic Repertoire | Examples |
|---|---|---|
| Tone of voice | Verbal Language | *High or low to punctuate both positive and negative experiences; voice becomes softer when leaning in (as if sharing a secret), denotes comfort and trust with researcher* |
| Diction | Verbal Language | *Doctoral vocabulary but often paired with AAL; sentences rich in both Standard American English (SAE) and African American Vernacular English (AAVE); topic-chaining* |
| Gesturing | Body Language | *Hand gestures follow tone of voice; gestures almost serve as a form of sign language, aligned with diction. Body posture goes from alert to relaxed depending on the topic.* |

## Conclusion

Much has been written about the psychology of colonial identities, particularly around the phenomenon that the oppressed internalize their oppressors' assessment of their worth. Fanon (1952/2008), most notably, investigated the fragility of identity under colonialism, insisting that upon internalizing a colonial identity, the colonized assumes an inferiority complex. Furthermore, Fanon (1963/2005) predicted that generations of Black people would have to contend with wounds that colonialism brought against them, and we argue that these wounds remain ever present in our academic experiences. To be clear, the complicatedness of educating the Black individual still stems from deep-rooted social, cultural and political contexts that require control over Black intellect and intellectual expression. Most importantly, we sense that the lingering fear that a liberating education could promote courageous thinking, being and doing have strong attachments to historical insurrections or rebellions against official authority. Thus, for Black women in particular, we assert that these factors continue to cause their post-colonial identities harder to forge and sustain in educational places still bound by colonialism and beholden to hegemony.

In our research of a student-initiated affinity group in an online doctoral program, we found efforts to create Black spaces to resist the feelings of intellectual inferiority and form free identities through discourse markers and collective activism. Furthermore, their creating Black spaces and virtual kitchen tables is reminiscent of being (re)educated in Black ways and addressing the double consciousness that seemed to plague them. As Du Bois (1903/2005) noted, Black people long to merge our double identities into one true self, one that values and affirms all our multiple, intersecting identities. We argue that the significance of their efforts to address intersectionality crisis arose and was maintained by student-initiated actions and practices. While we commend the program leadership for agreeing to the development of the affinity group, we would like to point out that the additional support did not happen without the Black women graduate students advocating for themselves.

Finally, this study of Black women's linguistic authority in higher education settings lays the groundwork for recognizing intersectionality crises in higher education settings. We recommend a larger empirical study that explores the influence of kitchen tables and Black spaces on Black women's language use in other educational realms. We argue that revealing the complexities of intersectionality in an educational system framed in Western, middle-class Whiteness, demonstrate the need for practices that support and affirm the intersecting identities of Black women graduate students in online doctoral programs.

## References

Allen, P. (1997). Black students in 'ivory towers.' *Studies in the Education of Adults, 29*(2), 179–190.

Baker-Bell, A. (2017). For Loretta: A Black woman literacy scholar's journey to prioritizing self-preservation and Black feminist–womanist storytelling. *Journal of Literacy Research, 49*(4), 526–543.

Baker-Bell, A. (2020). Dismantling anti-Black linguistic racism in English language arts classrooms: Toward an anti-racist Black language pedagogy. *Theory Into Practice, 59*(1), 8–21.

Bilge, S. (2013). Intersectionality undone: Saving intersectionality from feminist intersectionality studies. *Du Bois Review, 10*(2), 405–424.

Bonner, F. B., & Thomas, V. G. (2001). Introduction and overview: New and continuing challenged and opportunities for Black women in the academy. *The Journal of Negro Education, 70*(3), 121–123.

Boutte, G. S., Earick, M. E., & Jackson, T. O. (2021). Linguistic policies for African American language speakers: Moving from anti-blackness to pro-blackness. *Theory Into Practice, 60*(3), 231–241.

Calafell, B. M. (2012). Monstrous femininity: Constructions of Women of Color in the academy. *Journal of Communication Inquiry, 36*(2), 111–130.

Collins, P. H. (1986). Learning from the outsider within: The sociological significance of Black feminist thought. *Social Problems, 33*(6), 514–532.

Collins, P. H. (2009). *Black feminist thought: Knowledge, consciousness, and the politics of empowerment.* Unwin Hyman.

Corbin, N. A., Smith, W. A., & Garcia, J. R. (2018). Trapped between justified anger and being the strong Black woman: Black college women coping with racial battle fatigue at historically and predominantly White institutions. *International Journal of Qualitative Studies in Education, 31*(7), 626–643.

Crenshaw, K. (1990). Mapping the margins: Intersectionality, identity politics, and violence against Women of Color. *Stanford Law Review, 43*(6), 1241–1299.

Davis, S. M. (2019). When sistahs support sistahs: A process of supportive communication about racial microaggressions among Black women. *Communication Monographs, 86*(2), 133–157.

Delpit, L. (1988). The silenced dialogue: Power and pedagogy in educating other people's children. *Harvard Educational Review, 58*(3), 280–299.

Dizayi, S. A. (2019). Locating identity crisis in postcolonial theory: Fanon and Said. *Journal of Advanced Research in Social Sciences, 2*(1), 79–86.

Du Bois, W. E. B. (1903/2005). *The souls of Black folks.* Routledge.

Erikson, E. (1968). *Youth: Identity and crisis.* W.W. Norton.

Few, A. L., Stephens, D. P., & Rouse-Arnett, M. (2003). Sister-to-sister talk: Transcending boundaries and challenges in qualitative research with Black women. *Family Relations, 52*(3).

Fanon, F. (1952/2008). *Black skin, White masks.* Grove Press.

Fanon, F. (1963/2005). *The wretched of the earth.* Grove Press.

Goins, M. N. (2011). Playing with dialectics: Black female friendship groups as a homeplace. *Communication Studies, 62*(5), 531–546.

Henry, M. (1994/2017). Ivory towers and ebony women: The experiences of Black women in higher education. In *Changing the subject* (pp. 42–57). Taylor & Francis.

Howard-Vital, M. R. (1989). African-American women in higher education: Struggling to gain identity. *Journal of Black Studies, 20*(2), 181–190.

Hughes, P. C., & Heuman, A. N. (2006). The communication of solidarity in friendships among African American women. *Qualitative Research Reports in Communication, 7*(1), 33–41.

Jackson, J. M. (2019). Breaking out of the ivory tower: (re)thinking inclusion of women and Scholars of Color in the academy. *Journal of Women, Politics & Policy, 40*(1), 195–203.

Leath, S., & Mims, L. (2023). A qualitative exploration of Black women's familial socialization on controlling images of Black women and the internalization of respectability politics. *Journal of Family Studies, 29*(2), 774–791.

Love, B. L. (2019). *We want to do more than survive: Abolitionist teaching and the pursuit of educational freedom*. Beacon.

McMurtry, T. (2021). With liberty and Black linguistic justice for all: Pledging allegiance to anti-racist language pedagogy. *Journal of Adolescent & Adult Literacy, 65*(2), 175–178. https://doi.org/10.1002/jaal.1187

Morgan, M. H. (2020). "We don't play": Black women's linguistic authority across race, class and gender. In H. Samy Alim, A. Reyes, and P. V. Kroskrity (Eds.), *The Oxford handbook of language and race* (pp. 261–290).

Morgan, M. H. (2021). Counterlanguage powermoves in African American women's language practice. *Gender and Language, 15*(2), 289–299.

Overstreet, M. (2019). My first year in academia or the mythical Black woman takes on the ivory tower. *Journal of Women and Gender in Higher Education, 12*(1), 18–34.

Perkins, L. M. (1983). The impact of "culture of true womanhood" on education of Black Woman. *Journal of Social Issues, 39*(3), 17–28.

Perkins, L. M. (1993). The role of education in the development of Black feminist thought, 1860–1920. *History of Education, 22*(3), 265–275.

Scott, K. D. (2000). Crossing cultural borders: 'girl' and 'look' as markers of identity in Black women's language use. *Discourse & Society, 11*(2), 237–248.

Scott, K. D. (2017). Young, shifting and Black: Leaving the language of home and back again-a cautionary tale of crossing race and gender borders. *Qualitative Inquiry, 23*(2), 119–129.

Washington, A. R. (2020). 'Reclaiming my time': Signifying, reclamation and the activist strategies of Black women's language. *Gender and Language, 14*(4), 358–385.

## 15. No Longer Cast Aside: A Critical Approach to Serving Queer and Trans Students of Color in Higher Education

MEG E. EVANS AND JASON K. WALLACE

Even in our best efforts, higher education professionals overlook and neglect the intersectional needs of Queer and Trans Students of Color (QTSOC) on college campuses. Failing to acknowledge and honor all students' identities lies in direct conflict to the goals of professionals who seek to meet the needs of students from admission through graduation. In this chapter, we discuss the experiences of QTSOC on college campuses by providing practical tips to better serve QTSOC underlining the importance of centering this population in philosophy and praxis.

### Our Philosophy and Positionality

Addressing affirming praxis for serving QTSOC necessitates a discussion of our philosophy when approaching this work. We believe "a diverse student body creates positive learning environments, promotes cross-racial interactions, and is positively associated with student learning outcomes" (Karkouti, 2016, p. 59). The existence of QTSOC on college campuses affords all students the opportunity to engage in ways that not only enrich their learning but texturizes their campus experience. We believe that centering QTSOC in praxis provides permission for all students to live their truth and explore their social identities beyond the context of White, hegemonic environments that higher education promotes. If professionals can engage in praxis that holistically meets the needs of a queer-trans-femme Woman of Color, then this praxis inherently liberates people of all gender identities, sexual orientations, gender expressions, and varying racial and ethnic identities.

MEE's positionality: I identify as a queer, non-binary white person who is deeply engaged with self-reflection and self-work around racial justice. I recognize I am on a journey to continue to unlearn my socialized patterns of white dominance and fragility. I have worked in higher education for over a decade and deeply believe that we have failed when trying to serve our students who hold multiple minoritized identities.

JKW's positionality: As a queer, cisgender, Christian Black man with over a decade of experience in higher education, theory and lived experience inform my lens for praxis. Though I hold salient minoritized identities, which drive my passion for this work, my numerous dominant identities call for me to do my own work to unlearn harmful, cisnormative and patriarchal practices, and leverage my privileges for our collective liberation.

## Our Theoretical Framework

White institutional presence (WIP; Gusa, 2010), queer theory (Turner, 2000), critical race theory (CRT; Bell, 1987), and intersectionality (Crenshaw, 1991) provide the theoretical framework for our praxis. Embedded ideologies of Whiteness negatively impact campus climate, explicitly for Students of Color (Gusa, 2010). Gusa (2010) posits detailed attributes of what she coins as White institutional presence to explain how Whiteness dominates college campuses. Queer theory "critically analyzes the meaning of identity, focusing on intersections of identities and resisting oppressive social constructions of sexual orientation and gender" (Abes & Kasch, 2007, p. 620). Queer theory resists inherent ideas of heteronormativity and postulates that society, particularly people who identify in dominant groups, socially construct both gender and sexual orientation. We also engage concepts from Queer Scholars of Color using notions of quare theory (Johnson, 2001) to further inform our philosophy. CRT notes that race permeates everything (Bell, 1987). "CRT offers conceptual tools for interrogating how race and racism have been institutionalized and are maintained" (Sleeter, 2017, p. 157). Finally, when discussing intersectionality, Crenshaw (1991) posited that because of Black women's minoritized identities in both race and gender, they experience a unique form of oppression and discrimination. WIP, queer theory, CRT, and intersectionality serve as strategic frameworks to illuminate and validate the necessity for our campuses to engage in this work and help to frame how professionals can learn to work within systems of oppression to meet QTSOC needs.

## QTSOC Experiences in College

QTSOC experience many forms of overt and covert discrimination on college campuses (Brockenbrough, 2015). From racial microaggressions to misgendering, QTSOC find themselves in danger of verbal and physical violence based on their race, ethnicity, sexual orientation, gender identity and/or expression (Balsam et al., 2011; di Bartalo, 2015; Nadal et al., 2011; Nicolazzo, 2015; Sue et al., 2008). This trauma often leads to negative impacts on mental health (Kulick et al., 2017).

QTSOC often experience racism in what some would consider "safe spaces" for queer and trans folks such as gender and sexuality resource centers, women's centers, and student organizations purposed for queer and trans folks (Fox & Ore, 2010). Conversely, QTSOC experience homophobia/biphobia/transphobia in race-alike spaces such as culture houses, multicultural offices, culturally based student organizations, and multicultural Greek-lettered organizations (Negrete & Purcell, 2011). Due to the challenges faced by QTSOC, it is imperative that professionals put forth intentional efforts to make certain that students within this demographic feel supported on campus. It is systems of oppression embedded within campus structures that make college campuses uncomfortable and potentially dangerous for QTSOC (Gusa, 2010).

## 7 Tips for a QTSOC-Affirming Campus

In this section, we offer professionals practical tips to serve QTSOC. By making these intentional efforts, QTSOC will not only feel seen on campus but valued. Though we have witnessed how these recommendations work on a variety of campuses, we also name that each institution is different, and the following recommendations may not prove effective for all campuses. Context matters, and we fully recognize that the tides of change roll slowly.

### 1. White, Straight, and/or Cis Folks: Do Self-work

Society socializes us all to think, act, and react in certain ways, and that socialization is often handed down from generation to generation (Harro, 2000). Socialization impacts ways of knowing and may impact the ways in which people engage with the world. Often, white professionals do not even know the impact, often negative, they have on Students of Color (Gusa, 2010). Before professionals can authentically engage in QTSOC liberation, those with dominant racial, sexual, and/or gender identities must do their own self-work of unlearning racist, sexist, misogynistic, homophobic/bipho-bic/transphobic beliefs (Linder, 2018).

*Note*: Be mindful of engaging in self-work at the expense of People of Color and/or queer and trans people. Instead of demanding free QTSOC labor, engage in workshops, trainings, and webinars where facilitators offer their time and expertise and are adequately compensated for their labor. Also, use available resources such as documentaries, books, blogs, and podcasts for further education. The information is out there—find it and use it.

## 2. *Engage New Accountability & Assessment Practices*

Before professionals can know what issues to address regarding QTSOC inclusion on campus, they must know what the current lived experience is for QTSOC on their campus. Pre-assessments like an office, campus, or commu-nity climate survey can help. The assessments must include contextual fac-tors that are environment specific. Remember, context matters. Professionals must engage in continual assessments to meet the needs of QTSOC and decolonize structural barriers while accounting for the principles of CRT, queer theory, WIP, and intersectionality.

Once professionals know the needs of QTSOC, they can look for accountability partners to help meet those needs. Professionals should have an open relationship with their accountability partners as there is a need for comfort in honest disclosure and feedback. This relationship should include regular check-ins with short-term and long-term goals for specifically serv-ing QTSOC. For those who supervise, set specific expectations for direct reports, and then serve as one of their accountability partners to further cen-ter QTSOC needs and experiences. Scheduling regular time with an account-ability partner is critical to better serving QTSOC (Washington, 2011).

## 3. *Explicitly Name QTSOC Labor*

A straightforward way to serve QTSOC is by naming their labor. CRT dis-cusses the importance of offering counternarratives in dominant spaces (Bell, 1987). Many students, faculty, and staff offer mental, physical, and emo-tional labor by going beyond their role to educate the larger campus com-munity about QTSOC (Abustan, 2017; Aguilar & Johnson, 2017). QTSOC experience both racial battle fatigue (Smith et al., 2007) and queer battle fatigue (Wozolek et al., 2015) which uniquely place them at the intersection of two oppressive systems. Though professionals may not ask for this labor, they often use QTSOC to educate White, cisgender, and/or straight people about their lived experience which is both fatiguing and exploitive (Aguilar &

Johnson, 2017). To ask QTSOC to create the environment they need to succeed without asking other students to do the same upholds White supremacy. Avoid tokenizing QTSOC and give rewards when they serve as educators. Additionally, acknowledge when queer and Trans Professionals of Color are putting forth this labor, especially when it is not in their job description. Recognize when faculty members mentor QTSOC, and take their labor into consideration during the tenure and promotion process.

## 4. Create an Intentional Space Purposed for QTSOC

All students need spaces where they can feel welcomed, accepted in their fullness, and centered in the vision of a space. Creating an intentional space for QTSOC may mean the creation of a student organization, a student lounge, or simply a discussion group. As in most spaces, those dedicated specifically to QTSOC are affected by varying power dynamics. It is important to honor the tenets of CRT and queer theory by naming, addressing, and interrupting toxic masculinity, anti-Blackness, cisnormativity, xenophobia, misogynoir, biphobia, colorism, and other oppressive systems and behaviors that arise. QTSOC spaces are not exempt from White supremacy.

Remember that QTSOC are not a monolith. Like all other students, QTSOC needs vary from student to student; however, unless spaces are created that center QTSOC, those specific needs will likely go unvoiced and unnoticed. It is important to recognize that QTSOC support and affirmation cannot, and often does not, happen in identity-based offices/centers alone. "LGBT campus centers are often critiqued for being White-centric, and multicultural centers are often critiqued for being heteronormative and cisnormative" (Johnson & Javier, 2017, p. 5). If QTSOC are experiencing campuses this way and not finding places where they can engage in their fullness, what can institutions do on both a macro and micro level to more fully embrace QTSOC?

## 5. Develop Purposeful Collaborations & Partnerships

Professionals seeking to center the experiences of QTSOC must not forget the importance of network building (Kezar & Lester, 2009). Collaborations and partnerships proven effective in serving QTSOC include student affairs practitioners and administrators, faculty from varying academic departments, student organizations, community organizations, and staff from non-profits focused on gender, sexuality, and/or racial justice. In the initial stages of collaboration, it is important to be purposeful when identifying partners (Kezar & Lester, 2009). Not everyone will see the importance of centering their praxis, at least in part, around QTSOC, nevertheless interest convergence may prove effective (Bell, 1995). Who are the other professionals who can place a critical eye to programming, policies, and office norms? It may be best to initially select collaborative partners that already show an interest in partnering or at least demonstrate an interest in serving minoritized students. Selection of these partners may start with those who have already proven a commitment to QTSOC through research, praxis, or engagement. Once professionals identify initial collaborators, a snowball type strategy might be used—gaining subsequent collaborations through current participants and collaborators (Kezar & Lester, 2009).

## 6. Make Strategic Professional Hires

Hiring professionals who not only display certain diversity competencies but can speak to specifically serving QTSOC is imperative (Kayes, 2006). For new hires to be open to this learning and collaboration, there is a need for diversifying search committees to include queer and Trans Professionals of Color and other professionals who recognize the need and simultaneously desire a diverse campus. Many universities publish guidelines for hiring managers to help reduce bias (Kayes, 2006). These guidelines could serve as a model that centers Queer and Trans People of Color more specifically to ensure a more just and equitable search process.

When asked to be on committees, it is of crucial importance to use CRT to be reminded that Whiteness is pervasive (Bell, 1987) and name the *who* and *what* is missing on those committees. Who is being asked to sit on and chair committees? What practices are in place to help remove bias from the selection process? It is critical to be strategic and advertise in places that serve and center Queer and Trans People of Color—like *Diverse Issues in Higher Education* and the Consortium of Higher Education LGBT Resource Professional's job boards, Facebook groups, GroupMe's for Queer and Trans People of Color, X, LinkedIn, etc. Hiring managers can work with human resources to craft QTSOC affirming statements for job postings. Finally, professionals must make sure policies and practices that seek to center and affirm QTSOC are also in place to help retain Queer and Trans Professionals of Color.

## 7. Celebrate, Recognize, and Foster Joy as a Form of Resistance

Celebrating, recognizing, and fostering QTSOC joy is, likely, the most powerful form of resistance that we offer to professionals. The lives of QTSOC are more than just the difficult ways in which QTSOC navigate campuses not created for them. By celebrating a new QTSOC relationship, a birthday, a coming out, a passed exam, or simply their existence, professionals resist the racist and heteronormative idea that only White cisgender straight people deserve happiness. Add a black and brown stripe to the rainbow flag and include gender pronouns on door tags, business cards, and name tags. Highlight Queer and Trans trailblazers like Marsha P. Johnson, Gloria Anzaldúa, Bayard Rustin, Raquel Willis, and countless others. To provide a landscape for discussions about queerness outside White dominant structures, explore the cultural nuances of queer identity such as two-spirit in Indigenous culture or hijras in South Asian culture (Hossain, 2012; Lang, 2016). Queer theory (Turner, 2000) gives the permission to be confident in creating the new normal on our campuses and honor QTSOC.

In addition to the small wins, it is important to celebrate the successful matriculation and graduation of QTSOC. Programs like Lavender Graduation should not only exist but include cultural components that specifically honor QTSOC. Consider what it would mean for Lavender Graduation to include a variety of languages, cultural cuisine, culturally relevant music, and keynote speakers who identity as Queer and Trans People of Color. Additionally, it is vital that professionals nominate QTSOC for university-wide awards as those who hold dominant identities rarely acknowledge QTSOC labor (Gusa, 2010). Centering joy and celebration in QTSOC praxis can transform the ways in which QTSOC engage on campus.

## Conclusion

Queer and Trans Students of Color are not a problem to be solved (Marine, 2010) and it is imperative that professionals work on engaging and centering QTSOC in praxis. By operating outside of a single axis of social identity (Chan et al., 2017) and utilizing ideas from WIP, queer theory, CRT, and intersectionality, QTSOC may be seen, understood, and honored on campuses. Intention influences impact, yet action has a larger influence. Professionals have the responsibility to lead by example (di Bartalo, 2015) and not just ask the questions that need asked to support QTSOC, but also act in ways that center this important population in both philosophy and praxis.

## References

Abes, E. S., & Kasch, D. (2007). Using queer theory to explore lesbian college students' experiences. *Journal of College Student Development, 48*(6), 619–636.

Abustan, P. (2017). Collectively feeling: Honoring the emotional experiences of queer and transgender Student of Color activists. In J. M. Johnson & G. Javier (Eds.), *Queer People of Color in higher education* (pp. 31–56). Information Age.

Aguilar, D., & Johnson, J. M. (2017). Queer Faculty and Staff of Color: Experiences and expectations. In J. M. Johnson & G. Javier (Eds.), *Queer People of Color in higher education* (pp. 57–72). Information Age.

Balsam, K. F., Molina, Y., Beadnell, B., Simoni, J., & Walters, K. (2011). Measuring multiple minority stress: The LGBT People of Color microaggressions scale. *Cultural Diversity and Ethnic Minority Psychology, 17*(2), 163–174.

Bell, D. (1987). *And we will not be saved: The exclusive quest for racial justice.* Basic Books.

Bell, D. (1995). Brown v. Board of Education and the interest convergence dilemma. *Harvard Law Review, 93*, 518–533.

Brockenbrough, E. (2015). Queer of Color agency in educational contexts: Analytic frameworks from a Queer of Color critique. *Educational Studies, 51*(1), 28–44.

Chan, C. D., Erby, A. N., & Ford, D. J. (2017). Intersectionality in practice: Moving a social justice paradigm to action in higher education. In J. M. Johnson & G. Javier (Eds.), *Queer People of Color in higher education* (pp. 9–30). Information Age.

Crenshaw, K. (1991). Mapping the margins: Intersectionality, identity politics, and violence against Women of Color. *Stanford Law Review, 43*(6), 1241–1299.

di Bartolo, A. N. (2015). Rethinking gender equity in higher education. *Diversity & Democracy, 18*(2). https://www.aacu.org/ diversitydemocracy/2015/spring/dibartolo

Fox, C. O., & Ore, T. E. (2010). (Un)covering normalized gender and race subjectivities in LGBT "safe spaces." *Feminist Studies, 36*(6), 629–649.

Gusa, D. L. (2010). White institutional presence: The impact of whiteness on campus climate. *Harvard Educational Review, 80*(4), 464–489.

Harro, B. (2000). The cycle of socialization. In M. Adams, W. Blumenfield, C. R. Castaneda, H. Hackman, M. Peters, & X. Zuniga (Eds.), *Readings for diversity and social justice* (3rd ed., pp. 15–21). Routledge.

Hossain, A. (2012). Beyond emasculation: Being Muslim and becoming Hijra in South Asia. *Asian Studies Review, 36*(4), 495–513.

Johnson, E. P. (2001). "Quare" studies, or (almost) everything I know about queer studies I learned from my grandmother. *Text and Performance Quarterly, 21*(1), 1–25.

Johnson, J. M., & Javier, G. (Eds.). (2017). *Queer People of Color in higher education.* Information Age.

Karkouti, I. M. (2016). Black students' educational experiences in predominantly White universities: A Review of the related literature. *College Student Journal, 50*(1), 59–70.

Kayes, P. E. (2006). New paradigms for diversifying faculty and staff in higher education: Uncovering cultural biases in the search and hiring process. *Multicultural Education, 14*(2), 65–69.

Kezar, A., & Lester, J. (2009). *Organizing higher education for collaboration: A guide for campus leaders.* Jossey-Bass.

Kulick, A., Wenick, L. J., Woodford, M. R., & Renn, K. (2017). Heterosexism, depression, and campus engagement among LGBTQ college students: Intersectional differences and opportunities for healing. *Journal of Homosexuality, 64*(8), 1125–1141.

Lang, S. (2016). Native American men-women, lesbians, two-spirits: Contemporary and historical perspectives. *Journal of Lesbian Studies, 20*(3–4), 299–323.

Linder, C. (2018). *Sexual violence on campus: Power-conscious approaches to awareness, prevention, and response.* Emerald.

Marine, S. B. (2011). "Our college is changing": Women's college student affairs administrators and transgender students. *Journal of Homosexuality, 58*(9), 1165–1186.

Nadal, K., Wong, Y., Issa, M., Meterko, V., Leon, J., & Wideman, M. (2011). Sexual orientation microaggressions: Processes and coping mechanisms for lesbian, gay, and bisexual individuals. *Journal of LGBT Issues in Counseling, 5*(1), 21–46.

Negrete, N. A., & Purcell, C. (2011). Engaging sexual orientation and gender diversity in multicultural student services. In D. L. Stewart (Ed.), *Multicultural student services on campus: Building bridges: Re-visioning community* (pp. 81–93). Stylus.

Nicolazzo, Z. (2015). *"Just go in looking good": The resilience, resistance, and kinship-building of trans\* college students* (Doctoral dissertation). http://www.ohiolink.edu/etd/

Sleeter, C. E. (2017). Critical race theory and the Whiteness of teacher education. *Urban Education, 52*(2), 155–169.

Smith, W. A., Allen, W. R., & Danley, L. L. (2007). Assume the position... You fit the description": Psychosocial experiences and racial battle fatigue among African American male college students. *American Behavioral Scientist, 51*(4), 551–578.

Sue, D. W., Capodilupo, C. M., & Holder, A. M. B. (2008). Racial microaggressions in the life experience of Black Americans. *Professional Psychology: Research and Practice, 39*(3), 329–336.

Turner, W. B. (2000). *A genealogy of queer theory.* Temple University Press.

Washington, J. (2011). Preparing diversity change leaders. In D. L. Stewart (Ed.), *Multicultural student services on campus: Building bridges: Re-visioning community* (pp. 81–93). Stylus.

Wozolek, B., Varndell, R., & Speer, T. (2015). Are we not fatigued?: Queer battle fatigue at the intersection of heteronormative culture. *International Journal of Curriculum and Social Justice, 1*(1), 1–35.

# 16. Hitting the Books: Partnering for Intersectional Leadership Education

S. GAVIN WEISER, TASHAY DENNIE, AND MALLORY JALLAS

This chapter concerns itself with an innovative program rooted in the aim to reconceptualize leadership education as intentionally intersectional and focused on liberation scholarship (Harper & Kezar, 2021b; NCLP, 2016). The initial genesis of this program, the Leadership for Liberation Pop-Up Library (LL-PUL), emerged from a campus collaboration that united leadership learning with academic library resources to engage students in critical exploration and dialogue about intersectional identities and topics.

The program centers on leadership education as a vehicle to motivate students to "grapple with complex, interconnected systems of oppression and domination that prevent the envisioning of a liberated world" (Harper & Kezar, 2021b, p. 1). With a focus on shifting systems, structures, and cultural norms, the framework centers on six values (i.e., liberation, power and oppression acknowledgment, systems challenging, storytelling, support networks, and fellowship) and five cultural commitments (i.e., community, empathy, creativity, inclusion, and love). At its core, the program showcases cultural leadership as a form of creative resilience by centering the margin on leadership and academic library discourse.

Here we focus on the partnership between academic affairs and student affairs at a large, public midwestern institution to craft new articulations of understanding about intersectionality and liberatory leadership education. Conscious of the way intersectionality has become a buzzword "bandied about in conference spaces, academic research, and graduate preparation classrooms" (Stewart, 2019, p. xi), here we focus on the ways our program centers on liberatory education. With a deliberate intention to challenge how historical patterns of oppression influence laws, policies, and social norms of today, this innovative program equips students to reflect on the critical positions from which intersectionality arose to public consciousness (Crenshaw, 1988, 1991). Drawing from the work of Guthrie et al. (2017), this program also aims to "confront the myriad ways that racism, sexism, religious oppression, heterosexism/cisgenderism, and classism advantages and disadvantages individuals' lives" (p. 62).

## *Theoretical Undergirding*

Theory, as often taken up within the profession of student affairs, is often rooted in a developmental model and built out of the work of individuals such as Lewin, Sanford, Erikson, and others (Patton et al., 2016). These frames are oriented in a different world rooted in positivism and awash in deficit perspectives. Over the last decade, higher education scholars have begun to ride the wave of critical approaches to theory (Abes, 2016; Jones, 2019), and one of these third-wave approaches is intersectionality. As theory guides practice within our field, we must be more intentional in our work to "evaluate and challenge how overarching systems of power inform [our] assumptions, knowledge, and disciplines" (Wijeyesinghe, 2019, p. 32).

Further, the socio-historic legacy of *leadership studies* carries with it an origin deeply rooted in exclusivity, influence, status, power, and privilege which ultimately reinforce domination and control (Dugan, 2017). Where dominant leadership theories fail to interrogate these roots, critical leadership studies examine "the patterns of power and domination associated with leadership and relating these patterns to broader ideological and institutional conditions" (Alvesson & Spicer, 2014, p. 45). Emerging generations of students are changing the face of what leadership means, how we design and deliver leadership development, and how students are engaging in leadership experiences. The reality of many of our student leadership development programs is that they are in desperate need of critical examination. This includes creating leadership education models that promote culturally relevant and asset-based pedagogy within a multicultural and multigenerational campus community. The leadership for liberation framework anchors the program in critical leadership learning outcomes that equip students to tackle tough challenges internally, interpersonally, and institutionally.

Oriented within the theoretical landscape of both intersectionality (Crenshaw, 1988, 1991) and the praxis of leadership for liberation (Freire, 2000; Harper & Kezar, 2021b), this program leads with theory to create an experience for the campus community. To do so at the intersection of leadership learning, this program series asks the questions of why, for what, and for whom (Guthrie et al., 2021) to ensure that we are considering how leadership must be rooted in intersectional justice, otherwise it is likely to reify that status quo of leadership's long-history of hegemonic oppressions.

## *The Leadership for Liberation Pop-Up Library Series*

The Leadership for Liberation Pop-Up Library (LL-PUL) series is a collaborative programming initiative focusing on intersectional experiences by bringing these lenses to life–rooted both in the literature but also in the presence of dialogue and conversation to ensure that words absent of context are not mis/dis-interpreted (Call-Cummings & Martinez, 2016). Understanding praxis as the exploration and reflection upon the world to engage in action to transform these spaces (Freire, 2000), this project is engaged with the act of praxis within student leadership development programming. While this program does not intend to fix all the ails of society or even of the institution, we are reminded of the wisdom of James Baldwin (1962), who stated that while "not everything that is faced can be changed, but nothing can be changed until it is faced" (p. 11).

### *History of the Program*

The genesis of the LL-PUL series originated from a series of conversations between two colleagues at Illinois State University. One colleague was serving as a student success librarian and the other was serving as an assistant dean of students for leadership education and development. The connection point for both colleagues centered around exploring potential collaboration initiatives that could effectively engage students in critical librarianship and critical leadership studies. In understanding our campus's challenge of re-engaging students in co-curricular programming after the COVID-19 crisis period, we knew that our programming model needed to be accessible, adaptable, and attractive to students' varying levels of social engagement capacities and time commitments. Ultimately, we embarked on a journey to answer this simple question: If a student only had a few minutes to engage with us, how can we still engage that student in concepts of social justice, intersectionality, and culturally relevant leadership learning in a new and refreshing way?

Centering the leadership for liberation framework (Harper & Kezar, 2021a, 2021b), the program series aims to engage our campus communities in leadership learning from the cultural perspectives of various communities, while providing space for critical dialogue about historical and current social injustices facing historically marginalized communities. The program's objectives include providing participants with an opportunity to explore collections of literature, curated resources, and other cultural archives from historically marginalized communities, engaging participants in critical dialogues that center social injustice from the lens of marginalized communities, and promoting storytelling and fellowship as key components of social justice and leadership education. Intergroup dialogue pedagogy (Hopkins & Domingue, 2015) is also a key element of the program design, which provides participants with intentional space to gain competencies in systems-perspective thinking, critical sensemaking, and collective leadership building.

## Libraries as Contested Spaces

Libraries are powerful spaces in which learning and resistance can occur. This has perhaps never been clearer than with the recent attacks on libraries (Burnett, 2022; Harris & Alter, 2022). This is, however not the first time that libraries and librarians have been central to resisting epistemological critiques. Freedom Libraries, run by librarian activists during Freedom Summer of 1964, also faced backlash for providing librarianship services to their communities (Hunt, 2022). However, not all aspects of libraries are liberatory. Like anything crafted by humans, there is the reality of shortcomings oriented to the onto-epistemologies beyond those known by the initial crafters. In the mid-20th-century, libraries in the Southern United States were a battleground for desegregation, with activists like the Tougaloo Nine in Jackson, Mississippi, and other groups organizing protests and taking direct actions to uphold access to libraries for all citizens (Wiegand & Wiegand, 2018).

Reckoning with the profession's past and future is the cornerstone of *critical librarianship*, which operates at the intersection of critical theory and information science. This theory of librarianship interrogates the conscious and unconscious ways that librarians support systemic oppression through their work (Garcia, 2015). Critical librarianship in practice is the critique and efforts to change subject headings that reflect deficit-oriented language of the oppressor rather than the language of those who are the subjects themselves (Adler, 2013; Berman, 1993; Drabinski, 2013; Weiser et al., 2019). Libraries and information are not neutral, and pushing forward library work that identifies and counters power and privilege in the library landscape is central to critical librarianship. As such, critical librarianship connects with intersectionality to recenter narratives that are often neglected, alongside a critique of power denoting these narratives are the outcome of the "intersections of different social locations, power relations, and experiences" (Hankivsky, 2014, p. 2).

## Pop-Up Libraries as Innovative Spaces

The idea of a *pop-up* space is a global phenomenon. From retail industries to restaurants–the idea of a space that is here albeit briefly appeals to many people who may see these spaces as a *limited-edition* experience, as it may be unknown how long these spaces may last. Here we think of both events such as a traveling carnival or the annual arrival of Spirit Halloween stores. These retail-oriented pop-ups use this innovative form to drive short-term profits, engage a potential new customer base, or move excess stock. These goals differ for pop-up libraries.

Pop-up Libraries are perhaps most alive in the imagination of the general populace with the Little Free Libraries (n.d.) that pop up and take residence in many areas of the country and may operate on a *take-one-leave-one* orientation. Some pop-ups are intentionally oriented toward social justice. For instance, in Sydney, one young woman began a pop-up library specifically for the city's homeless population (Davis et al., 2015). The Occupy Wall Street movement also had a pop-up library that the New York Police Department tried to destroy, but "librarians' resistance prevented this and ensured the library's continuing growth" (Davis et al., 2015, p. 97).

With the continuing rise of attacks on libraries, libraries must continue to innovate to "reimagine libraries' relationships with communities and achieve library goals of being valued and integral parts of users' daily lives" (Nicholson, 2019, p. 333). One type of innovation is to engage with pop-up libraries, bringing the materials into the daily lives of individuals in an easier way to access learning instead of having to go to the brick-and-mortar space of a traditional library. In 2014, the University of Birmingham set up temporary and staffed stalls around their campus to bring the library to the students (Barnett et al., 2016). They found that pop-up libraries are effective in two different ways. First, pop-ups provide an opportunity for learning about libraries and the "multifarious ways an academic library can support learning and research" (Barnett et al., 2016, p. 15). They also understand that being *in* the community allows them to craft a stronger understanding of the needs of the community to better offer services.

The opportunities that pop-up libraries create align with our aims and those of many academic libraries to connect and support the campus community in a more holistic sense. Traditional library endeavors leverage direct academic support for learning and research. The pop-up events present an opportunity to expand the library's reach and forge positive relationships with the community in new ways. Specifically, the small format of pop-ups provides a limited selection of a library's overall collections, which can help counter library anxiety that often originates from being overwhelmed by the seemingly endless resources an academic library offers (Mellon, 1986).

Beyond the format, the themes and topics in this Leadership for Liberation series of pop-up libraries spotlight gaps and growth areas in the library collections. In selecting materials for the pop-up events, the identified gaps create opportunities for critically interrogating the collection. Why are these topics not represented in our collection? Is this a conscious or subconscious exclusion? Are there books available that address these topics? The asking of these questions engages in a practice rooted in critical librarianship that can and has surfaced vital areas for expanding the library collections to further support the intersectional campus community.

## Interdisciplinary Programming

Partnerships between traditional student affairs and academic affairs departments happen on occasion. While these partnerships are less focused on programming and more often focused on academic support services, this partnership blends theoretical practices from both divisions to create something innovative with an intentional focus on intersectional leadership learning. Slightly different from other orientations to interdisciplinary programming, this program by design intentionally focuses on liberatory education, challenges historical patterns of social injustice and oppression, and supports the learning outcomes of critical sensemaking of how such historical patterns materially influence their experiences today.

### Examples of Programming

The program design and structure have evolved since its pilot in 2021. To date, the LL-PUL series has hosted approximately ten in-person sessions. Initially, with no budget and limited departmental resources, the series began as a two-day, self-paced experience in which students, faculty, and staff could explore the pop-up library on their own on day one and elect to participate in a guided community dialogue on the second day. After the first semester, feedback reflected great value in the community dialogue component of the program. This prompted us to invest more promotional efforts and incentives for the community dialogue, which included sharing the digital session guides on social media beforehand and adding the opportunity to share a meal during the community dialogue segment of the program.

In its current state, the series consists of a two-hour experience with each session centering on a justice-based topic and a community dialogue guided by campus and community activists engaged within the given topic. Book and article collections centering Black, Indigenous, and other Authors of Color are featured in a digital program guide, which is shared on various platforms before and after sessions. Library books are available for reservation through the program guide and check-out during the in-person session to encourage further engagement about the topic. Previous LL-PUP series topics include voter restoration and the evolution of voter suppression within racially marginalized communities, gender justice and the intersection of Black Transfeminism, labor justice and the influences of American chattel slavery on today's leadership and productivity culture, and creative justice and storytelling as a powerful leadership tool for social justice. As such, each event focused intentionally on challenging and learning about historical patterns of oppression and its influence on laws, policies, and social norms.

## Conclusions and Recommendations

In this chapter, we highlight an interdisciplinary and intersectional program that aims to engage students in critical librarianship and critical leadership studies in an innovative and attractive way. Critical learning opportunities such as the one outlined herein are one part of an approach to enacting liberatory-engaged educational change. Student affairs educators have long argued for a theory-to-practice approach to our work. With this program, we have engaged long-existing theory with Crenshaw's intersectionality (1991) with emerging theoretical models (Guthrie et al., 2017; Harper & Kezar, 2021a, 2021b) to craft a meaningful educational experience for not just students, but all members of the campus community. As such, we hope that spreading knowledge of the LL-PUL series may inspire other equity-minded student affairs educators to put their theoretical knowledge to practice and craft new collaborative models of programming to enact meaningful intersectional change.

Now more than ever, the need for collaborative partnerships between academic libraries and leadership education departments is critical and vital to supporting students as they make meaning and navigate the sociopolitical issues of today. Notably, in the first half of the 2022–23 academic year, nearly 1,500 books centering narratives focused on Communities of Color and/or LGBTQIA peoples were banned across 85 school districts in 26 states (Meehan et al., 2023). In real-time, we see the systemic censorship of book banning institutionally enforced nationwide. Even within the local context of a neighboring school district, an award-winning teacher was forced to resign based on inclusive texts provided within her classroom (Campoamor, 2023).

This form of institutional oppression removes books from libraries and syllabi and incapacitates equity-centered educators within entire campus communities. Affecting more than two million students and over 800 authors and illustrators, the social injustice of book banning serves as a prescient reminder of the intersectional nature of oppression. Within this context, programs such as the Leadership for Liberation Pop-Up Library series quite literally safeguards the civic duty of education by centering voices, visions, histories, and legacies of oppression and resilience within historically marginalized communities.

## References

Abes, E. S. (Ed.). (2016). Critical perspectives on student development theory: New directions for student services (New Directions for Student Services, No. 154). Jossey-Bass.

Adler, M. (2013). Paraphilias: The perversion of meaning in the Library of Congress. In P. Keilty & R. Dean (Eds.), *Feminist and queer information studies reader* (pp. 309–323). Litwin.

Alvesson, M., & Spicer, A. (2014). Critical perspectives on leadership. In D. V. Day (Ed.), *The Oxford handbook of leadership and organizations* (pp. 40–57). Oxford University Press.

Baldwin, J. (1962, January 14). As much truth as one can bear; to speak out about the world as it is, says James Baldwin, is the writer's job as much of the truth as one can bear. *The New York Times*. https://www.nytimes.com/1962/01/14/archives/as-much-truth-as-one-can-bear-to-speak-out-about-the-world-as-it-is.html

Barnett, J., Bull, S., & Cooper, H. (2016). Pop-up library at the University of Birmingham: Extending the reach of an academic library by taking "the library" to the students. *New Review of Academic Librarianship, 22*(2–3), 112–131.

Berman, S. (1993). *Prejudices and antipathies: A tract on the lc subject heads concerning people*. McFarland & Company.

Burnett, J. (2022, August 31). Local libraries have become a major political and cultural battleground. *NPR*. https://www.npr.org/2022/08/31/1119752817/local-libraries-have-become-a-major-political-and-cultural-battleground

Call-Cummings, M., & Martinez, S. (2016). Consciousness-raising or unintentionally oppressive? Potential negative consequences of photovoice. *The Qualitative Report, 21*(5), 798–810.

Campoamor, D. (2023, May 15). She offered a LGBTQ-themed book to her middle schoolers. Parents filed a police report. *TODAY.com*. https://www.today.com/parents/teens/police-called-illinois-teacher-offering-book-gay-rcna84144

Crenshaw, K. (1988). Race, reform, and retrenchment: Transformation and legitimation in antidiscrimination law. *Harvard Law Review, 101*(7), 1331–1387.

Crenshaw, K. (1991). Mapping the margins: Intersectionality, identity politics, and violence against Women of Color. *Stanford Law Review*, *43*(6), 1241–1299.

Davis, A., Rice, C., Spagnolo, D., Struck, J., & Bull, S. (2015). Exploring pop-up libraries in practice. *The Australian Library Journal*, *64*(2), 94–104.

Drabinski, E. (2013). Queering the catalog: Queer theory and the politics of correction. *The Library Quarterly*, *83*(2), 94–111.

Dugan, J. P. (2017). *Leadership theory: Cultivating critical perspectives*. John Wiley & Sons.

Freire, P. (2000). *Pedagogy of the oppressed, 30th-anniversary edition* (M. B. Ramos, Trans.; 30th Anniversary edition). Bloomsbury Academic.

Garcia, K. (2015, June 19). *Keeping up with... Critical librarianship* [Text]. Association of College & Research Libraries. https://www.ala.org/acrl/publications/keeping_ up_with/critlib

Guthrie, K. L., Jones, T. B., & Osteen, L. (2017). The teaching, learning, and being of leadership: Exploring context and practice of the culturally relevant leadership learning model. *Journal of Leadership Studies*, *11*(3), 61–67.

Guthrie, K. L., Navarro, C., Weng, J., & Priest, K. (2021). Interrogating leadership education: Why? For what? For whom? *New Directions for Student Leadership*, *2021*(172), 45–52.

Hankivsky, O. (2014). *Intersectionality 101*. Institute for Intersectionality Research and Policy. https://docplayer.net/4773103-Intersectionality-101-olena-hankivsky-phd.html

Harper, J., & Kezar, A. (2021a). Leadership development for racially minoritized students: An expansion of the social change model of leadership. *Journal of Leadership Education*, *20*(3), 156–169.

Harper, J., & Kezar, A. (2021b). *Leadership for liberation: A leadership framework and guide for student affairs professionals*. University of Southern California Pullias Center for Higher Education.

Harris, E. A., & Alter, A. (2022, July 6). With rising book bans, librarians have come under attack. *The New York Times*. https://www.nytimes.com/2022/07/06/ books/book-ban-librarians.html

Hopkins, L. E., & Domingue, A. D. (2015). From awareness to action: College students' skill development in intergroup dialogue. *Equity & Excellence in Education*, *48*(3), 392–402.

Hunt, K. (2022, October 9). Libraries feel attacked—But not like the 'freedom libraries' of 1964. *Washington Post*. https://www.washingtonpost.com/history/2022/10/ 02/freedom-libraries-violence-book-bans/

Jones, S. (2019). Waves of change: The evolving history of student development theory. In E. S. Abes, S. R. Jones, & D.-L. Stewart (Eds.), *Rethinking college student development theory using critical frameworks* (pp. 7–17). Stylus.

Little Free Library. (n.d.). *About us*. https://littlefreelibrary.org/about/

Meehan, K., Friedman, J., Magnusson, T., & Baêta, S. (2023). 2023 banned books update: Banned in the USA. *PEN America*. https://pen.org/report/banned-in-the-usa-state-laws-supercharge-book-suppression-in-schools/

Mellon, C. A. (1986). Library anxiety: A grounded theory and its development. *College & Research Libraries, 47*(2), 160–165.

NCLP, Komives, S. R., & Wagner, W. (2016). *Leadership for a better world: Understanding the social change model of leadership development* (2nd ed.). Jossey-Bass.

Nicholson, K. (2019). Collaborative, creative, participative: Trends in public library innovation. *Public Library Quarterly, 38*(3), 331–347.

Patton, L. D., Renn, K. A., Guido, F. M., Quaye, S. J., Forney, D. S., & Evans, N. J. (2016). *Student development in college: Theory, research, and practice* (3rd ed.). Jossey-Bass.

Stewart, D.-L. (2019). Foreword. In D. Mitchell, J. Marie, & T. L. Steele (Eds.), *Intersectionality & higher education: Research, Theory, & Praxis* (2nd ed., pp. xi–xiv). Peter Lang.

Weiser, S. G., Wagner, T., & Lawter, M. (2019). Double jeopardy: (Trans)versing higher ed as queer trans advocates. *Journal of Curriculum and Pedagogy, 15*(3). https://doi.org/10.1080/15505170.2018.1542359

Wiegand, W. A., & Wiegand, S. A. (2018). *The desegregation of public libraries in the Jim Crow South: Civil rights and local activism*. Louisiana State University Press.

Wijeyesinghe, C. L. (2019). Intersectionality and student development: Centering power in the process. In E. S. Abes, S. R. Jones, & D.-L. Stewart (Eds.), *Rethinking college student development using critical frameworks* (pp. 26–34). Stylus.

# 17. *Weaving In and Out of Ourselves: Syllabus Formation and Assignment Development Through the Centering of Intersectionality*

Ruby Osoria

Through the employment of *testimonio*, which is defined later in this chapter, I reflect on my experience as a lecturer for the University of California education system as a starting point to discuss the reliance on the theoretical understanding of intersectionality as a guiding tool for syllabus formation and assignment development for the diversity, equity, and inclusion (DEI) course, "Language, Culture, and Education." The purpose of the testimonio is to challenge deficit perspectives in higher education that centers the professor/lecturer and western knowledge as the only sources of expertise (Delgado Bernal et al., 2012). Through the testimonio, I seek to bring validity to my lived realities that have been shaped and informed by my intersectional identities as a Woman of Color, first-generation Chicana, and from a working-class background in relation to higher education.

It is from this place of recognition that I intentionally designed a course that allowed students to bring forth their full selves and layered identities. In this chapter, I discuss the development of three major course assignments, informed by intersectionality: "The Pictorial Academic Timeline," "Self-reflection: Institutional Impact on the Education Experience," and "Education Counterstory." Each assignment is intended to (1) provide students from diverse backgrounds the opportunities to think through their own intersectional identities, (2) provide an opportunity to reflect on their experiences within the K-12 education pipeline and higher education pipeline, (3) understand the impact of policy on the educational experiences of students from diverse backgrounds, and (4) recognize their intersectional lived experiences as a valid place of theorization. I will illustrate the alignment of intersectional lived experience, theoretical understanding, syllabus development, and pedagogical practices.

## Testimonio

A testimonio is defined as a "verbal journey of a witness who speaks to reveal the racial, class, gender, and nativist injustices they have suffered as a means of healing, empowerment, and advocacy for a more human present and future" (Pérez Huber, 2010, p. 83). In this section, I rely on the use of testimonio through the process of storytelling to provide insight into the power structures that shaped my higher education journey in relation to intersectionality and inform my course and assignment development. Intersectionality is a prism that assists in understanding how marginalized identities (e.g., race and gender) intersect and result in the compounding of disadvantages and inequalities that create obstacles beyond a conventional understanding of discrimination (Crenshaw, 1989, 1991).

### Testimonio: Unraveling

In the spring quarter of my junior year in the UC system in California, I was enrolled in the course, "Language, Culture, and Education." I had pre-assumptions of what this course would entail; the words *language* and *culture* stood out because, to me, this meant that I would be able to connect how my upbringing, my communities, my family knowledge, and a full version of myself would be recognized in this course. In the context of higher education, up to this point, I had always felt as though I had to break myself into pieces to fit neatly into categories and experiences that had been predetermined based on my categorical identities, *first-generation, low-income, female, and Hispanic/Latino*. The feelings of excitement quickly diminished throughout that spring quarter. I was reading the original work of racist theories (e.g., the culture of poverty) and singular and oversimplified explanations of the immigrant experience (e.g., culture-ecology theory). While the purpose of those readings was to critique theoretical perspectives, the analysis was limited, and there were students who defended deficit theories and overgeneralized Communities of Color and the urban context.

There was no conversation around intersectional identities and how those complexities shaped and informed the power structures that Students of Color were forced to combat and the influence that had on their experiences in the education system, and how those power dynamics differed based on significant factors such as race, gender, and sexuality, for example (Nichols & Stahl, 2019). In the course, the education system was framed as a place. As a result, there was a failure to recognize the education system as a broader structure of U.S. society that reproduces social inequalities (Pérez Huber et al., 2015). Growing up in an urban immigrant community in southern California, I understood that my community's social isolation was a result of redlining (González, 2017). How I experienced my schooling was very much shaped by the social constructions of race and the historic xenophobic perspectives held against Latinx communities and social ideologies and meaning given to working-class Communities of Color (Pérez Huber, 2008). How I experienced the world up to this point was a result of complex social structures that predetermined how I would be seen and treated.

While examining the challenges in urban low-income schools, during the lecture, I remember feeling uneasy. When discussing urban communities and schooling, there was a wide generalization, and the framing reproduced perspectives of the *urban underclass*. I raised my hand and made a comment about my own lived experience in a predominantly Latinx-serving high school, and the professor was quick to stop me and made it clear that we needed to focus on what the data and research were saying. On my way to the residence hall, I was walking with one of my classmates, and she made a comment: "I always hate it when people bring their personal experiences into the classroom; personal experience is not generalizable; data is." I remember shrinking inside while I just smiled and nodded.

I understand now that the ways in which I was constantly corrected and dismissed were rooted in the ways I was allowed to navigate higher education, and the power structures wherein placed that I could not be an expert on topics that I fully experienced and lived; those positions where reserved for individuals who went through a formal schooling process and obtain a doctoral degree that confirmed their ability to conduct research on topics around schooling, degrees that have historically been denied to Communities of Color (Pérez Huber et al., 2015).

As an undergraduate, I would not have guessed that I would eventually return to the same institution as a doctoral student. In my third year as a doctoral student, I was the assigned instructor assistant for the class, "Language, Culture, and Education"; once I advanced to candidacy, I was hired as a lecturer and taught the course in the summer. I took advantage of the ways in which my title placed me in a situation where I could leverage my power and create and develop a course intended to bring forth and honor the various experiences of my students and provide a critical lens when analyzing the role of language and culture within the education system. I took on the task of creating a more inclusive space that challenged traditional practices in higher education that leveraged students' lived experiences as significant as scholarly work. The ability to construct a course and assignments that centered on students' voices was shaped an informed through intersectionality. From an intersectional perspective, the goal of the course, pedagogical practices, and assignments was to affirm students lived realities and address the complex relationship between students' layered identities, language, culture, and education.

## The Course: Language, Culture, and Education

My pedagogical practices are a response to how I have felt marginalized by the course content and university culture. Therefore, I am intentional in creating inclusive learning environments for students who identify as first-generation college students, Students of Color, and students from a low-socioeconomic status that account for their layered identities. My pedagogical practices aim to provide students with the skills needed to be successful throughout their higher education journey and center their lived experiences as a valid start for theorization. What proceeds are key components of the course syllabus and the three main course assignments: "The Pictorial Academic Timeline," "Self-Reflection: Institutional Impact on the Education Experience," and "Education Counter Story." I provide examples of the description of each assignment to bring forth insight into the formation of course assignments and language used to frame student expectations that encourage the centering of their lived experiences. The purpose of the second half of this chapter is to illustrate an example of an intersectional approach to course assignments and pedagogical work.

### Example of Course Description

Informed by critical race theory (CRT; see Chapter 2 for an explanation of CRT), this course aims to provide students with the tools to think critically about education as a social institution and structure, with a central focus on notions of culture and language. Throughout the session, we discuss educational settings, social, linguistic, and cultural dimensions. We pay particular attention to the relationship between culture and language and the intersection of race, ethnicity, and other identities (e.g., nationality, immigration, gender, sexuality, etc.). We examine how representations of culture, language, and intersectional identities impact students' experiences, learning, and achievement in school. The centering of race and intersectionality allows for the examination of the combination of multiple entities in relation to power dynamics within the education system and the larger society.

## Course Assignment Example #1: Pictorial Academic Timeline Description

Students create a digital timeline of their educational trajectory from K-12 and include their recent college experience. Students identify significant moments throughout their academic experience. The timeline consists of items like academic achievements (e.g., honors/awards, passing AP test, getting accepted to university, enrolling in college, first-generation students, transfer students, etc.); participating in institutional support programs (e.g., after-school programs, mentorship, Office of Academic Support and Instructional Services, McNair Scholars, etc.); and highlight institutional barriers (e.g., English only, lack of school and home communication, immigration policy, zero-tolerance policies, etc.); making the connection between community and school impact (e.g., local, state, and national policies); and participation in activism (e.g., community organizing, walkouts, in school protest, political engagement) as examples.

Timeline entries align with the course topics and themes (e.g., culture, language, education, institutional inequity, resistance, intersectionality, the voice of color thesis, etc.). Students include a minimum of 10 personal events and include one image per event. These images can be from students' personal collections or the internet. These images provide further context to their timelines; students are expected to be intentional with the image that will be incorporated into the timeline.

Students also include eight key sociopolitical events throughout the timeline and pictures from the internet. Sociopolitical refers to both social and political factors or conditions (Gutiérrez, 2013). Examples of sociopolitical events are immigration policy, educational policies, and environmental issues. While these speak to more extensive policies, practices, and government, they also have a direct social impact that can shape and inform individual lives. Sociopolitical events can be local, state, national, or even international. For this class, students can also focus on school policies and practices as "under sociopolitical events." An example of this would be an increase of police in schools or sanctuary schools. The design of this assignment provides students with the opportunity to reflect on their multiple identities and situate the significance of intersectionality and recognize how the combination of salient identities creates different realities for students throughout the education pipeline, even among peers with whom they share primary demographics (i.e., race, ethnicity, gender, socioeconomic status, etc.).

## Course Assignment Example #2: Self-Reflection: Institutional Impact on the Education Experience

For this assignment, students must reflect on their "Pictorial Academic Timeline." Students identify one key event in their timeline that they can expand on and further reflect on the impact of power dynamics (e.g., racial, cultural, economic, ideological, etc.) embedded in the relationship between schooling, culture, language, and their own lived experience. Some questions they consider are:

- How did the power structures in your school impact your experience as a student?
- In what ways did you or didn't you identify with the culture upheld in your school experience?
- What language abilities and skills were accepted in your school?
- Through what perspective were topics taught in your school?
- What cultures and languages were celebrated or excluded from your educational trajectory?
- How did "outside social context" impact your schooling?

The prompt for this assignment contains clear parameters (e.g., word count, number of citations, format structure, etc.) for students to follow, but the essay description is open-ended, which allows students to determine the focus of their essay within the context of the course themes. Students will think through their intersectional identities and the ways in which they inform their educational experience. The intent of the essay is for students to bring themselves whole again and think through an intersectional dimension instead of picking parts of themselves to discuss (e.g., gender only). Positioning students to reflect on the privileges that can result from the hegemonic practices of the education system and where they fall within that spectrum. Informed by notions of intersectionality, this assignment dismisses the discourse of a singular experience within the education system.

## Course Assignment Example #3: Counterstory

For the course final, students develop their own counterstory rooted in the theoretical understanding of CRT. Solórzano and Yosso (2002) define counterstories as a method of storytelling that highlights narratives that have often been untold, unrecognized, and unheard. A counterstory can be a tool for exposing, analyzing, and challenging the majoritarian stories of racial privilege; it can shatter complacency and challenge the dominant discourse. Chapman (2020) states that counterstories can reframe deficit narratives about Communities of Color and redirect conversations about access and equity in education towards an analysis of institutional and structural racism.

Counterstories differ from personal story narratives, autobiography, or third-person storytelling as it relies on lived experiences, professional experiences, existing scholarly work, data, and research findings (Solórzano & Yosso, 2002). A counterstory is specifically developed to bring forth stories of cultural ways of knowing, racist policies, socially and economically marginalizing societal practices, forms of resistance, and activism. Counterstories are developed and written by authors who understand that these stories are developed and grounded in lived experiences and reputable research findings (Solórzano & Yosso, 2002). Counterstories are not made up, and they are not exaggerated versions of the truth nor meant to sensationalize the experiences of Students of Color. These characters will be grounded in real-life experiences, research, and relevant social situations; this *is not fiction*.

The students' counterstories must focus on a course theme, for example, language, bilingual, multilingual, language framing, culture, assimilation, acculturation, cultural affirmation, community cultural wealth, intersectionality, K-12 education, education policy (local, state, national), class pedagogy, teacher and administrator experiences, parent experiences, tracking, COVID-19, colonization, race, racism, racist nativism, LGBTQ+ identities, gender, sexuality, resistance, student experience, the connection between community and education. Students' counterstories should connect to the education system directly but not necessarily take place in the school setting (e.g., responses to school policy, students' community organizing around state policy that will impact the local community, interactions with school peers or administrators, etc.). It can be written from the perspective of a student, teacher, principal, parent, counselor, etc. Students cite class sources and outside sources (e.g., newspapers, research reports, policy reports, state or national databases, etc.) and rely on their individual reflections written throughout the course.

Informed by an intersectional perspective, this assignment allows students to grapple with the ways that systems of privilege, power, and oppression are present in the education system and extended to the community and home. Through this assignment, students demonstrate how they understand the role of intersectional identities and how they reveal the functioning within systems of oppression through the counter story. Students reveal unheard stories that speak to diverse realities within educational settings. It is important to note that students are expected to write from a place familiar to them, a place of knowing that is an extension of their own lived experiences.

## An Instructor's Reflection

The description of the previous three assignments is intended to provide insight into assignments that can be modified and leveraged for students to bring forth their various layered identities into the ways that they are learning and understanding broader topics in a DEI course. The structure of the course and assignments are intended to recognize the unique lived experiences of students but also complicate their understanding of power structures embedded in institutions and systems that have historically oppressed People of Color and how these interactions look different depending on intersectional identities. During the lecture, students were divided into small groups and shared their educational timeline; students were given a set of guiding questions that were meant to encourage dialogue among diverse experiences.

Throughout the course, students were given opportunities to reflect on the theoretical and research approach of the assigned scholarly articles and were encouraged to make connections between their own personal experiences and those of people in their communities and peers. The scholarly articles selected for this course consisted of theoretical pieces and empirical papers rooted in critical theories and understandings (e.g., intersectionality, CRT, and Women of Color theories). Embedded in the course were also "writing workshop days," where students were given assignment prompts and rubrics. Through the writing workshops, students completed an idea flow chart as a brainstorming tool; this was a guided way to bring forth all of the knowledge that was being developed through various forms, scholarly work, lived experiences, research data, storytelling, among other forms of knowledge development. It is necessary to note that this course consisted of undergraduate students from various racial and ethnic backgrounds. Most of the students consisted of sociology and education studies majors, along with students enrolling in the course to meet DEI requirements. All students were expected to reflect on notions of subordination and privilege within the real social constructs embedded in U.S. society and the education system.

This chapter contributes to further understanding of praxis in higher education using intersectionality as a guiding framework for syllabus structuring and as a pedagogical tool. The central focus of this chapter was to provide one example of how curriculum development in higher education can be used to support the intersectional identities of students while simultaneously challenging marginalized and oppressive practices and ideologies. Through this chapter, I sought to highlight the significant role and responsibility of faculty and instructors to create inclusive spaces that account for students' intersectional identities and reimagine higher education practices by bringing forth and creating space in the lecture hall for historically marginalized communities.

## *References*

Chapman, T. K. (2020). Introduction: When the magic happens. Critical race storytelling. *InterActions: UCLA Journal of Education and Information Studies, 16*(2). https://escholarship.org/uc/item/8v36956m

Crenshaw, K. (1989). Demarginalizing the intersection of race and sex: A Black feminist critique of antidiscrimination doctrine, feminist theory, and antiracist politics. *University of Chicago Legal Forum, 1989*(8), 139–167.

Crenshaw, K. (1991). Mapping the margins: Intersectionality, identity politics, and violence against women of Color. *Stanford Law Review, 43*(6), 1241–1299.

Delgado Bernal, D., Burciaga, R., & Flores Carmona, J. (2012). Chicana/Latina testimonios: Mapping the methodological, pedagogical, and political. *Equity & Excellence in Education, 45*(3), 363–372.

González, E. R. (2017). *Latino City: Urban planning, politics, and the grassroots.* Taylor & Francis.

Gutiérrez, R. (2013). The sociopolitical turn in mathematics education. *Journal for Research in Mathematics Education, 44*(1), 37–68.

Ladson-Billings, G. (1998). Just what is critical race theory and what's it doing in a nice field like education? *International Journal of Qualitative Studies in Education, 11*(1), 7–24.

Nichols, S., & Stahl, G. (2019). Intersectionality in higher education research: A systematic literature review. *Higher Education Research & Development, 38*(6), 1255–1268.

Pérez Huber, L., Lopez, C. B., Malagon, M. C., Velez, V., & Solórzano, D. G. (2008). Getting beyond the 'symptom,' acknowledging the 'disease': Theorizing racist nativism. *Contemporary Justice Review, 11*(1), 39–51.

Pérez Huber, L. (2010). Using Latina/o Critical Race Theory (LatCrit) and racist nativism to explore intersectionality in the educational experiences of undocumented Chicana college students. *Educational Foundations, 24*, 77–96.

Pérez Huber, L., Malagón, M. C., Ramirez, B. R., Gonzalez, L. C., Jimenez, A., & Vélez, V. N. (2015). *Still falling through the cracks: Revisiting the Latina/o education pipeline* (CSRC Research Report. No. 19). UCLA Chicano Studies Research Center.

Reyes, K. B., & Curry Rodríguez, J. E. (2012). Testimonio: Origins, terms, and resources. *Equity & Excellence in Education, 45*(3), 525–538.

Solórzano, D. G., & Yosso, T. J. (2002). Critical race methodology: Counter-storytelling as an analytical framework for education research. *Qualitative Inquiry, 8*(1), 23–44.

# Editor Biographies

## Editor

### Donald "DJ" Mitchell, Jr., Ph.D.

Donald "DJ" Mitchell, Jr., Ph.D., served as editor for the third edition of *Intersectionality & Higher Education: Theory, Research, & Praxis*. His scholarship theoretically and empirically explores race and racism, gender and sexism, and identity intersections and intersectionality in higher education settings. Mitchell has produced over 60 scholarly publications, including serving as lead editor for *Student Involvement and Academic Outcomes: Implications for Diverse College Student Populations*, lead editor for the first edition of *Intersectionality & Higher Education: Theory, Research, & Praxis*, and lead editor for the second edition of *Intersectionality & Higher Education: Theory, Research, & Praxis*, all published by Peter Lang in 2015, 2014, and 2019, respectively.

Mitchell is recipient of the *Diverse: Issues in Higher Education*'s 2020 Emerging Scholar recognition; the Association for Fraternity/Sorority Advisors and Sigma Phi Epsilon's 2018 Dr. Charles Eberly *Oracle* Award; the Ethnographic and Qualitative Research Conference's 2016 McGraw Hill Distinguished Scholar Award; the American College Personnel Association's 2015 Emerging Scholar Award; Grand Valley State University's 2015 Distinguished Early-career Scholar Award; the Multicultural/Multiethnic Education Special Interest Group of the American Educational Research Association's 2014 Dr. Carlos J. Vallejo Memorial Award for Emerging Scholarship; the American College Personnel Association's Standing Committee for Men and Masculinities 2014 Outstanding Research Award; and, the Michigan College Personnel Association's 2013 John Zaugra

Outstanding Research/Publication Award. He was also awarded the Center for the Study of the College Fraternity's 2012 Richard McKaig Outstanding Doctoral Research Award for his dissertation, "Are They Truly Divine?: A Grounded Theory of the Influences of Black Greek-Lettered Organizations on the Persistence of African Americans at Predominantly White Institutions."

Mitchell earned a Bachelor of Science in chemistry from Shaw University, the first Historically Black College or University in the South; a Master of Science in educational leadership from Minnesota State University, Mankato; and a Ph.D. in educational policy and administration with a concentration in higher education from the University of Minnesota–Twin Cities.

## Associate Editors

### Jakia Marie, Ph.D.

Jakia Marie, Ph.D., served as associate editor for the third edition of *Intersectionality & Higher Education: Theory, Research, & Praxis*. Marie also served as associate editor for the second edition of *Intersectionality & Higher Education: Theory, Research, & Praxis* published by Peter Lang in 2019. Marie is currently assistant professor of interdisciplinary studies and program coordinator of African/African American Studies at Grand Valley State University in Allendale, Michigan. Marie's scholarship explores race and ethnicity with an emphasis in cultural identity, immigration, and international education and identity development and experiences of minoritized students in higher education.

A native of Muskegon, Michigan, Marie is a first-generation college student who earned a Bachelor of Arts in liberal studies and Master of Education in higher education with a concentration in college student affairs leadership, both from Grand Valley State University. Marie also holds a Master of Arts in anthropology and a Ph.D. in Pan-African studies, both from the University of Louisville in Kentucky.

### Patricia P. Carver, Ph.D., CPA

Patricia P. Carver, Ph.D., CPA, served as associate editor for the third edition of *Intersectionality & Higher Education: Theory, Research, & Praxis*. Carver is an assistant professor in the Rubel School of Business at Bellarmine University in Louisville, Kentucky. She has brought her professional experience to the classroom, enhancing the learning opportunities in business administration and accounting for students for over 20 years. Prior to teaching, Carver served 25 years in government and private industry. In addition to serving as a professor, Carver serves as the director of the Women of

Color Entrepreneur Certificate program offered through Bellarmine's Rubel School of Business. Carver's scholarship explores Women of Color in university and business settings.

Due to her outstanding research in the area of intersectionality and the social and academic experiences of Black women students attending predominantly White colleges and universities, Carver received the Dissertation of the Year Award from Bellarmine University's School of Education in 2019, the 2020 Outstanding Dissertation Award (honorable mention) from the National Association of Diversity Officers in Higher Education, and the 2020 Outstanding Dissertation Award (honorable mention) from the American Association of *Blacks* in Higher Education. Bellarmine University recognized Carver's philanthropy, diligence, activism, and commitment to her students by naming the Office of Identity and Inclusion in her honor, inaugurating the Dr. Patricia P. Carver Office of Identity and Inclusion in 2020.

A graduate of the University of Louisville, Carver obtained a Bachelor of Science in commerce with a major in accounting and a Master of Business Administration. She earned her Ph.D. in leadership in higher education from Bellarmine University.

# *Author Biographies*

**Allison D. Anders, Ph.D.**

Allison Daniel Anders, Ph.D., is associate professor in the Educational Foundations and Inquiry program and the Qualitative Research Certificate program in the College of Education at the University of South Carolina. She teaches courses in cultural and social foundations of education, critical race theory, sociology of education, narrative, ethnography, and other qualitative methodologies. Her research and scholarship address contexts of education, and issues of access and equity, and include work with children and families with refugee status, LGBTQ+ student athletes and educators, and youth taking college courses in prison.

**Maria Rosario (Happy) G. Araneta, Ph.D.**

Maria Rosario (Happy) G. Araneta, Ph.D., is associate dean of diversity and community partnerships and professor of epidemiology in the Department of Family Medicine at the University of California, San Diego (UCSD) School of Medicine. She received her Bachelor of Arts in biology from UCSD and her Master of Public Health and Ph.D. in epidemiology from Yale University. Her research interests include health disparities in type 2 diabetes and regional fat, longitudinal outcomes of T2D and prediabetes, maternal and pediatric HIV/AIDS, and birth defects. She was appointed to the National Institute of Health (NIH) Advisory Council for the National Institute on Minority Health and Health Disparities and the NIH Council of Councils.

**Shannika L. Bacchus**

Shannika L. Bacchus serves as the director of leadership development in the D.C. Public Charter Schools, dedicated to empowering K–12 executive leaders in the metropolitan Washington, D.C. area to enhance educational opportunities for Black and Brown youth. As an Ed.D. candidate in Baylor University's Learning and Organizational Change program, Bacchus's research centers on understanding the success factors for Black at-promise students within Historically Black Colleges and Universities, explored through the lens of the anti-deficit achievement theory. Bacchus's work exemplifies a commitment deeply rooted in advancing equitable education and fostering positive change for underrepresented communities.

### Renee L. Bowling, Ph.D.

Renee L. Bowling, Ph.D., is an educational administrator with over twenty years of experience in international education and is a researcher affiliated with the College Impact Lab (CoIL) at The Ohio State University. She has conducted and collaborated on national and international research projects related to worldview diversity and campus climate. Bowling's research interests include equity-minded leadership, critical internationalization, worldview diversity, global learning, and international education policy. She serves as chair of the Student Affairs Administrators in Higher Education (NASPA) Spirituality and Religion in Higher Education Knowledge Community and holds degrees in sociology, human development, higher education student affairs, and religion and education.

### Jana Brown

Jana Brown serves as chief human resources officer for eHealth, a leading marketplace for health insurance and Medicare plans. In her current role, Brown is responsible for leading eHealth's Human Capital Strategy and culture transformation, including talent acquisition, leadership development, diversity, equity, and inclusion, learning and development, workforce planning and analytics, and total rewards. Brown also serves on the National Board of Directors of Big Brothers, Big Sisters overseeing executive compensation and chairing the Nomination and Governance Committee. She is an Ed.D. candidate in Baylor University's Learning and Organizational Change program, focusing on the role of human resources executives in preparing organizations for digital transformations associated with Industry 4.0 and Society 5.0.

### Belinda P. Coleman

Belinda P. Coleman is an Ed.D. candidate in Baylor University's School of Education Learning and Organizational program. Coleman's present research on the underrepresentation of Black women in the STEM C-suite stems from her personal experiences, rigorous academic background, and passion for STEM. Coleman navigates the intricate landscape of Black women's history of leadership and the current barriers, sponsorship, and intersectionality systemic inequalities often experienced in attaining senior leadership positions. Utilizing a qualitative lens and andrological theorems, Coleman examines the lived experiences of Black women and the grit exuded in overcoming obstacles during their trajectories to the STEM C-suite. Coleman's fervor for STEM was birthed in her childhood, developed through her educational pursuits, and culminated in her serving as founder and chief executive officer of The Coleman Group, Inc., an innovative information technology solutions provider with a primary core competence in data science.

### Lisa Delacruz Combs

Lisa Delacruz Combs recently defended her dissertation at The Ohio State University in the Higher Education and Student Affairs program. She previously transitioned from her role as program coordinator in the Student Diversity and Multicultural Affairs Office at Loyola University Chicago. Combs's research interests include liminality, identity interconnections, multiraciality in higher education, Filipinx identity development, and poststructural Women of Color feminist perspectives. Combs's also served as the co-chair for the Multiracial Network in American College Personnel Association (ACPA) and has presented about multiracial topics at many conferences including ACPA, the Association for the Study of Higher Education, Critical Mixed Race Studies, and the National Conference on Race and Ethnicity in Higher Education. She received her Bachelor of Arts in political science and English from The Ohio State University and her Master of Science in student affairs in higher education from Miami University in Oxford, Ohio.

### Hilda Cecilia Contreras Aguirre, Ed.D.

Hilda Cecilia Contreras Aguirre, Ed.D., is a STEM education researcher at New Mexico State University. She focuses her research on qualitative studies addressing minority and underrepresented student college performance and persistence through high-impact practices, particularly in STEM disciplines. Her main lines of inquiry examine best practices in mentoring and promotion of undergraduate research in STEM. She also collaborates with the local community colleges to improve graduation and transfer rates. Lastly, she is currently the principal investigator of the Research-Oriented Learning Experiences Engineering program and the Latinidad STEM Mentoring Program, both funded by the National Science Foundation.

## India Cooley

India Cooley is a higher education administrator and scholar-practitioner. India is a Ed.D. candidate in Baylor University's Learning and Organizational Change program. India is an assistant director and a graduate adjunct faculty at Adler University. Through her research, Cooley employs social constructivism to understand how online adjunct faculty create well-rounded educational experiences for their students. Cooley is a co-leader of the National Association of Multicultural Education's Illinois Chapter. Her research interests include diverse learners, online adult learning experiences, Black, Indigenous, People of Color and low-income, first-generation student success, and anti-racist curricula.

## Tashay Dennie

Tashay Dennie is assistant dean of students for Leadership Education and Development at Illinois State University. Interweaving various community, leadership, and student-development theories, the root of Dennie's work lives at the intersection of leadership and equity. As a critical leadership studies scholar and practitioner, Dennie's expertise entail developing high-impact, co-curricular programming that intentionally makes space for critical dialog around the socio-historic implications of leadership and how it intersects with equity, diversity, culture, community, productivity, and power.

## James M. DeVita, Ph.D.

James M. DeVita, Ph.D. is professor of Higher Education at the University of North Carolina at Wilmington (UNCW). DeVita also serves as the director of High Impact Pathways at UNCW and is co-editor of the *Journal of Effective Teaching in Higher Education*. He has presented at numerous international conferences and has published over 20 peer reviewed publications. DeVita currently teaches graduate-level courses that focus on student learning and development, social justice topics in education, and research methods. His research examines the experiences of targeted populations in higher education and scholarship on teaching and learning.

## Antonio Duran, Ph.D.

Antonio Duran, Ph.D., is assistant professor in Higher and Postsecondary Education at Arizona State University. Duran's research agenda involves understanding how historical and contemporary legacies of oppression influence college student development, experiences, and success. In particular, he is passionate about uplifting the experiences of queer and trans individuals with multiple minoritized identities.

## Meg E. Evans, Ph.D.

Meg E. Evans, Ph.D., currently serves as director of education and research for a justice-based national educational non-profit. Before serving in this role, Evans worked in higher education for over a decade, primarily in LGBTQ+ centers and housing and residential life. They have taught at both the University of Georgia (UGA) and the University of West Georgia. Evans holds a Bachelor of Arts from Warren Wilson College, a Master of Science from Duquesne University, and a Ph.D. from UGA. They are an accomplished critical scholar with over a dozen published articles and a co-authored book focused on student activism. Before working in higher education, Evans hailed from the Chicagoland area where they worked as a middle school teacher, emergency medical technician, and a nurses' assistant. Another of Evans's favorite roles is being a parent to their two boys, Zeke and Tru.

## Marquita D. Foster, Ph.D.

Marquita D. Foster, Ph.D., is lecturer in the Department of Curriculum & Instruction at Baylor University's Ed.D. in Learning and Organizational Change program. Foster's primary research interests include Black feminist epistemologies, Black childhood from the antebellum era to the present, the principles of resistance and critical caring within the Black Teaching Tradition, and more recently, Black and Indigenous methodologies that center storytelling, freedom dreams, and narrative (re)mapping. Foster's publications focus on urban elementary education, Blackness as a disruptive pedagogy to affirm Black students' humanity and academic potential, critical caring approaches and othermothering practices in doctoral programs.

## Amani Francis

Amani Francis is a lifelong learner, educator, sustainable forest preservationist, and small business owner. Francis is an Ed.D. candidate in Baylor University's Learning and Organizational Change program and faculty in the Humanities and Communication Department at Embry-Riddle Aeronautical University. Francis's current research focuses on mindfulness through the lens of self-determination theory for Black male college students. Francis's additional research spans a wide range of concentrations to include nature-based mindfulness for marginalized populations, hidden Black indigeneity and cultural intersectionality, the Greek mythical elements of service and aversion in historical and contemporary Black literature, genealogical studies, and ancient autochthonous history.

## Katherine Arias Garcia, Ph.D.

Katherine Arias Garcia, Ph.D., is a Chancellor & National Science Foundation STEM (Science, Technology, Engineering, and Mathematics) Education Postdoctoral Fellow at the University of California, Irvine in the School of Education. Garcia employs critical and asset-based frameworks that center Latinx students' cultural assets and knowledge to examine the persistence of Latinx students in higher education. Garcia's main research agenda is to increase the representation of Latinx individuals in the field of medicine, which are needed to address existing health disparities. Garcia draws from her professional experience working in a medical school with diverse students to address the Latinx physician workforce.

## Beth L. Goldstein, Ph.D.

Beth L. Goldstein, Ph.D., is emerita professor of the University of Kentucky's Department of Educational Policy Studies & Evaluation. Her primary and applied research has focused on how people engage with education in their pursuit of cultural, economic and societal border-crossing, both within the United States and internationally. Other areas of research and teaching have included foci on gender, family and adult literacy, and qualitative research, formative evaluation, and participatory action research. She has extensive work and study experiences in East and Southeast Asia.

## Rose Ann E. Gutierrez, Ph.D.

Rose Ann E. Gutierrez, Ph.D., is assistant professor of equity and diversity in education at the University of Nevada, Reno. Her research is informed by a Pinay epistemology and positionality as a 1.5-generation immigrant, first-generation college student, and only daughter of working-class Pilipino immigrants. Her lens as a race scholar in education undergird her resolve to improve the conditions and opportunities of historically oppressed communities across the lifespan through educational research and practice. Her broader research agenda examines the relationship between knowledge, race, and social transformation in higher education and is anchored by critical theories and critical qualitative methodologies.

## Jessica C. Harris, Ph.D.

Jessica C. Harris, Ph.D., is associate professor of Higher Education & Organizational Change in the Graduate School of Education & Information Studies at the University of California, Los Angeles. Harris centers her research on racial in/equity in post-secondary contexts and often explores issues of race and racism as they concern multiraciality, campus sexual violence, and the mis/use of intersectionality to advance racial equity in higher education. Through her research, Harris aims to analyze and disrupt racism and its intersecting structures of domination, such as sexism and classism, that are embedded throughout the U.S. education system.

### Romeo Jackson

Romeo Jackson is a Black, queer, non-binary femme, feminist dedicated to intersectional justice and cross movement building. Currently, they study Anti-Blackness and settler colonialism within a higher education context with an emphasis on the experiences of Queer and Trans Students of Color. Jackson is committed to uplifting and empowering Queer and Trans People of Color through a Black queer feminist lens.

### Mallory Jallas

Mallory Jallas is assistant professor and student success librarian at Milner Library at Illinois State University in Normal, Illinois. She received her Master of Science in library and information science from the University of Illinois at Urbana-Champaign. Jallas's work centers on connecting students with the library's services and collections to support their academic and personal success. She is the library's liaison to the Dean of Students Office and University College. Her research interests focus on peer learning programs in academic libraries, the impact of affordable textbooks on student success, and campus collaborations for student success.

### Susan R. Jones, Ph.D.

Susan R. Jones, Ph.D., is professor emerita from the Higher Education and Student Affairs program in the Department of Educational Studies at The Ohio State University. Her research interests include psychosocial perspectives on identity, intersectionality and multiple social identities, service-learning, and qualitative methodologies. She has published over 30 journal articles, 33 book chapters, and seven books, including co-author of *Identity Development of College Students* (Jossey-Bass, 2013), *Negotiating the Complexities of Qualitative Research: Fundamental Elements and Issues* (Routledge, 2006; 2nd edition 2014; 3rd edition 2022), and *Rethinking College Student Development Theory Using Critical Frameworks* (Stylus 2019). Jones is one of the co-editors of the 5th and 6th editions of *Student Services: A Handbook for the Profession* (Jossey-Bass, 2011; 2017). She is the recipient of numerous awards including the American College Personnel Association's Contribution to Knowledge Award (2015) and Lifetime Achievement Award (2023).

## Nadeeka Karunaratne, Ph.D.

Nadeeka Karunaratne, Ph.D., is a postdoctoral research associate in the McCluskey Center for Violence Prevention at the University of Utah. She employs intersectionality, both in her teaching as an adjunct faculty member in California Lutheran University's Department of Counselor Education, and in her research on issues of campus sexual and relationship violence. Karunaratne's background in student affairs, specifically her work in campus cultural centers and with university violence prevention efforts, influences her scholarship and teaching. She is also a trauma-informed yoga instructor and leads healing yoga programs on college campuses and in the community.

## Z Nicolazzo, Ph.D.

Z Nicolazzo, Ph.D., is associate professor of Trans* Studies in Education at the University of Arizona. Her scholarly agenda focuses on discourses of gender in education, transmisogyny as a structuring institutional logic in higher education, and grief and loss. She currently serves as the executive editor of *About Campus.*

## Ruby Osoria, Ph.D.

Ruby Osoria, Ph.D., received her Ph.D. in education: transforming education in a diverse society with a specialization in critical gender studies at the University of California, San Diego. Her scholarship explores the role of grassroots community organizing and non-profit work around educational (in)equalities and the formation of community-based social networks, and focuses on intersectional identities, such as race/ethnicity, gender, socioeconomic status, and immigration, as valid measures of analysis. As an adjunct professor in the California State University System, she is committed to expanding pedagogical practices that center the voices of diverse Communities of Color.

## Andrea S. Pickens

Andrea S. Pickens serves as chief consultant at Andrea Pickens and Associates, LLC and founder of ShiftEd, Inc. is an Ed.D. candidate in Baylor University's Learning and Organizational Change program. Pickens's current research centers on exploring how educators consider educational equity when implementing programs such as Response to Intervention and Multi-Tiered Systems of Support to address achievement outcomes for marginalized populations. Pickens is an advocate for equitable learning experiences and outcomes, cultivating educational spaces that embrace students' linguistic and cultural capital, and disrupting systemic barriers that prevent students from reaching their highest potential.

## Christa J. Porter, Ph.D.

Christa J. Porter, Ph.D., is associate dean in the Graduate College and associate professor in Higher Education Administration and Student Affairs at Kent State University. As a leader, teacher, and scholar, she is guided by an equity-minded, collaborative, engaged, and critical praxis. Her areas of expertise include: (1) policies and practices that influence the trajectory of Black women in higher education; (2) student development at the intersections of identities; and (3) theory, research, and praxis in higher education (how and why we do what we do). She has been nationally recognized for her scholarship and teaching, and her work appears in various peer reviewed journals and edited texts.

## Brianna R. Ramirez, Ph.D.

Brianna R. Ramirez, Ph.D., is a postdoctoral scholar with the Research Justice Shop at University of California, Irvine, where she engages in supporting and advancing community-based research training for graduate students working alongside Black, Indigenous, People of Color-led community organizations. She received her Ph.D. in education studies with a specialization in critical gender studies from the University of California, San Diego. Her research draws from critical race feminista methodologies and perspectives to challenge normative forms of knowledge construction in higher education and to explore the intersecting systems and structures of marginality that shape access and transition to college for Chicanx/Latinx students.

## Jacqueline T. Stevens

Jacqueline T. Stevens is an Ed.D. student at Baylor University's School of Education Learning and Organizational program. Stevens's research focuses on the coping and recovery skills of alternative educators due to their work-related trauma. Stevens is a veteran educator with experience working at campuses with historically underserved populations, including alternative education programs.

## Daniel Tillapaugh, Ph.D.

Daniel Tillapaugh, Ph.D., is professor of counselor education and associate dean for equity, outreach, and faculty development in the Graduate School of Education at California Lutheran University. He graduated with a Ph.D. in leadership studies at the University of San Diego and an MEd in Counseling and Personnel Services at the University of Maryland. Tillapaugh's research interests are broadly connected to intersectionality within higher education, particularly the intersections of sexuality and gender on student development.

## Jason K. Wallace, Ph.D.

Jason K. Wallace, Ph.D., is assistant professor of higher education leadership in the Department of Counseling, Higher Education Leadership, Educational Psychology, and Foundations at Mississippi State University. Prior to joining the professoriate, Wallace worked for nearly a decade in student affairs, primarily in multicultural services. His scholarship identifies and addresses issues of equity and inclusion in higher education, with emphasis on Black and first-generation college students. Wallace holds a Ph.D. in education (college student affairs administration) from the University of Georgia, and a master's and bachelor's degree from Texas Christian University. For more information, visit www.drjkwallace.com.

## Yan Wang, Ph.D.

Yan Wang, Ph.D., received her Ph.D. from the University of Kentucky. She has actively advocated for racial justice, devoting herself to diversity, equity and inclusion in higher education. Her research focuses on Students of Color's identity development and college experience. Her book chapter, "Searching for Belonging: How Transnationalism Influences Chinese American College Students' Ethnic Identity Construction," highlighted the precarity of identity construction against the backdrop of cross-national movement. Her research utilizes critical theories, such as critical whiteness studies, critical race theory, disability critical race theory, and intersectionality, to dismantle how power, whiteness and oppression have structured society and impacted the lives of marginalized people.

## S.Gavin Weiser, Ph.D.

S. Gavin Weiser, Ph.D., is associate professor of Higher Education & Student Affairs and coordinates the master's program at Illinois State University (ISU). Weiser is also core faculty in Women, Gender, and Sexuality Studies and affiliate faculty with Latin American/Latino Studies at ISU. Their research interests involve queer and trans subjectivities within educational spaces, and the ethics of community-engaged qualitative research. Weiser works in the intersections of queer theory and education, and how society can continue to challenge the notions of education to create a more radically inclusive space for learning.

## Nicole M. West, Ph.D.

Nicole M. West, Ph.D., is associate professor in the Student Affairs in Higher Education program at Missouri State University (MSU) and also serves as the Special Education, Leadership, and Professional Studies' Assistant School Director in MSU's College of Education. As a Black feminist scholar-pracademic, West's scholarship focuses on enhancing the experiences of Black women enrolled and employed in higher education via the study and development of critical cultural theories, research methods, and praxes. The majority of her articles have been published in top-tier, refereed education journals including the *International Journal of Qualitative Studies in Education*, the *Journal of Diversity in Higher Education*, the *Journal of College Student Development*, and the *Journal of Women and Gender in Higher Education*.

## Charmaine L. Wijeyesinghe, Ed.D.

Charmaine L. Wijeyesinghe, Ed.D., is a consultant and author who explores social identity development, intersectionality, and social justice education in her work and scholarship. She has worked with colleges, universities, and organizations around the United States on issues of inequality and change for almost 40 years. In addition, Wijeyesinghe held numerous positions at the University of Massachusetts at Amherst, served as dean of students at Mount Holyoke College, and was the national trainer for the National Conference of Christians and Jews. Her publications include journal articles on identity development theory and its applications and book chapters on Multiracial identity and intersectionality. Wijeyesinghe was the editor or co-editor of five volumes: two editions of *New Perspectives on Racial Identity Development* (NYU Press), *New Directions for Student Services: Enacting Intersectionality in Student Affairs* (Jossey-Bass), *Multiracial Experiences in Higher Education: Contesting Knowledge, Honoring Voice, and Innovating Practice* (Stylus), and *The Complexities of Race: Identity, Power, and Justice in an Evolving America* (NYU Press). She served on the editorial board of the *Journal Committed Social Change on Race and Ethnicity* and her writing has been recognized by awards given by National Conference on Race and Ethnicity in Higher Education and the American College Personnel Association. Wijeyesinghe's original ecological model of Multiracial identity was adopted by the Anti-Defamation League for its anti-bias curriculum.

**Alysia Hunt Williams**

Alysia Hunt Williams is a positive community change agent with administration and direct service experience helping to empower adults and youth of marginalized statuses. Her professional service backgrounds throughout the United States involve university outreach programming, clinical/human services organizations, and churches. Additionally, she devotes time and insights to community empowerment via local board service and other volunteerism. Williams is earning an Ed.D. in learning and organizational change from Baylor University, where her current research interest explores trauma survivors' civic engagement.

www.ingramcontent.com/pod-product-compliance
Lightning Source LLC
Chambersburg PA
CBHW050634280326
41932CB00015B/2637